SHOOT
OUT
THE
LIGHTS

BOB SPITZ

SHOOT OUT THE LIGHTS

The Amazing,
Improbable,
Exhilarating Saga
of the 1969–70
New York Knicks

HARCOURT BRACE & COMPANY
New York   San Diego   London

Requests for permission to make copies of any part of the work
should be mailed to: Permissions Department, Harcourt Brace & Company,
6277 Sea Harbor Drive, Orlando, Florida 32887-6777.

Epigraph on p. xiii copyright © 1994 by The New York Times Company.
Reprinted by permission.

Library of Congress Cataloging-in-Publication Data
Spitz, Bob.
Shoot out the lights: the amazing, improbable,
exhilarating saga of the 1969–70 New York Knicks/Bob Spitz.
p.   cm.
Includes bibliographical references.
ISBN 0-15-193116-X
1. New York Knickerbockers (Basketball team)—History.   I. Title.
GV885.52.N4S74   1995
796.323'64'097471—dc20   94-19434

The text was set in Fairfield.

Designed by Linda Lockowitz
Printed in the United States of America
First Edition
A B C D E

For Robert Spector

CONTENTS

Photograph insert follows page 146.

AUTHOR'S NOTE

THE WRITING OF this book would have been impossible without the cooperation of the New York Knickerbockers organization, which arranged for me to talk with many of the players, coaches, and basketball officials without ever asking to review the manuscript. Similarly, the National Basketball Association, NBA Entertainment, the NBA Coaches' Association, the NBA Players Association, and the NBA Trainers' Association provided invaluable assistance throughout the research. Other closely guarded doors were opened largely by the gracious efforts of the pubic-relations divisions of the New Jersey Nets, the Atlanta Hawks, the Boston Celtics, the Detroit Pistons, the Philadelphia 76ers, the Golden State Warriors, and especially the Los Angeles Lakers, who showed how easy it is to be stand-up even when you finished second.

I am also indebted to Arthur Krakowski, Beth Fabinsky, Claire Wachtel, Cork Smith, Robert Spector, the Newspaper Annex of the New York Public Library, Sportsbooks in Los

Angeles, the Historical Society of Crystal City, Missouri, the Department of Public Works in Baton Rouge, Louisiana, Jeff and Eddie at the Strand, and most of all to Jenny Canick, for providing everything it takes to write a book (and for everything else).

Of course, this story could never have been told without the personal recollections of the many players, coaches, trainers, basketball personnel, and their respective families and friends, whose time and generosity were ultimately all I had to go on. And, lest I forget, my sincere thanks to the members of the 1969–70 New York Knicks, whom I greatly admire—as players and as men.

—Bob Spitz

TEAM ROSTER
1969–70 New York Knickerbockers

PLAYER	COLLEGE	HEIGHT
Barnett, Dick	Tennessee State	6'4"
Bowman, Nate	Wichita State	6'10"
Bradley, Bill	Princeton	6'5"
DeBusschere, Dave	Detroit	6'6"
Frazier, Walt	Southern Illinois	6'4"
Hosket, Bill	Ohio State	6'7"
May, Don	Dayton	6'4"
Reed, Willis	Grambling	6'9"
Riordan, Mike	Providence	6'4"
Russell, Cazzie	Michigan	6'5"
Stallworth, Dave	Wichita State	6'7"
Warren, John	St. John's	6'3"

COACH

Red Holzman

GENERAL MANAGER

Eddie Donovan

PRESIDENT

Edward S. (Ned) Irish

I N THE FIRST HALF of a Knicks game several weeks ago, John Starks found himself twisted around in the lane and in the air with his back to the basket. He couldn't pass, he couldn't shoot, and he couldn't come down with the ball. He could either remain in that position like a hummingbird, or release the ball. So he shot—flinging the ball over his head without looking at the basket. And the ball went in!

On their halftime television show, the announcer Al Trautwig asked Walt Frazier, the former Knick star guard and now an analyst, "Clyde, did you ever make a shot like that?"

"Never had to," said Frazier. "I was never out of control."

—*New York Times,*
April 13, 1994

1 |THE ARCHITECT

A T FIVE-THIRTY that afternoon, just minutes before the Great Revelation, a chorus of sirens screamed through the streets of midtown Manhattan. Eddie Donovan was scrambling along the sidewalk outside Penn Station as fire engines began to converge from every direction. They came from the east, winding through the congested garment center; down Broadway, past Macy's; up Seventh Avenue, going against traffic on that one-way street; and from the west along Thirty-third Street, cutting around a funky souvlaki stand where pimps, cops, and taxi drivers did their late-day dining in a fragile camaraderie.

Eddie Donovan shook his head sadly as the engines roared past Madison Square Garden, at Thirty-third and Seventh, toward some distant inferno. Sorry bastards, he thought—you got the wrong blaze.

Indeed, Eddie was leaving work with one mother of a fire roaring in his stomach. Again. A five-alarmer, judging from the degree of his discomfort. Chances are he was working on an ulcer

1

the size of . . . well, *a basketball,* and the burning strafed his belly from one side to the other. Unfalteringly, he gulped down heaping breaths of the toxic Manhattan ozone and trained his attention on the cosmos. There, *ah!* Relief came instantly, but Eddie knew it was only temporary, at best.

"Temporary" was the operative word in Eddie Donovan's vocabulary these days. His relief was temporary, his serenity was temporary, and his job—his job was the most temporary condition of them all. He was forty-nine and again was on the verge of being fired. The papers had been predicting it for some time. Come to think of it, they'd probably spearheaded the campaign to dump him. The *New York Post* figured he'd be gone before Christmas. The *Daily News* cited an "unnamed source" who'd interviewed possible replacements. And the *New York Times,* that bible of fact and objectivity, speculated, "KNICKS' DONOVAN HEADED FOR EARLY EXIT???"

Well, the papers had hit the stands a few hours ago and sports fans now had more ammunition to feed the firing frenzy. The New York Knickerbockers had lost again last night. A close one, Eddie reminded himself. But there had been a lot of close ones this month, and none of them—not a one—had notched a victory in the win column.

Not that winning was within his power. Eddie Donovan couldn't win ball games per se. The fact was, he hadn't touched a basketball in years. He didn't shoot, he didn't dribble. He couldn't even stand the smell of a basketball anymore, that noxious stench of processed rubber, which clung to your fingertips like old age. No, Eddie's court skills were exhausted. They were memories, as he liked to tell friends, "of another time and era" when he had coached the game, in college and the pros.

Even so, the heat was on him whenever the Knicks lost. And they lost a lot these days. Eleven games in their last fourteen starts. Thirteen of eighteen for the year. That dropped their record to a dismal five and thirteen—dead last in the gritty Eastern Division's standings. Cellar-dwellers. Like last year, and the year before that—and the year before that. "The Knicks should continue playing when the circus opens here next spring," one of the local writers had proposed. "After all, they are the Garden's resident clowns."

Oh, the torment that jibe had cost him, the humiliation, coming on top of the shit he constantly suffered from the Garden staff. From the ticket takers and ushers, who worked the games for practically nothing in return for a look at the action. From the secretaries, whose husbands and boyfriends got to sit in the green seats (or "nosebleed city," as the rooftop section was known) and gave them advice to take back to their employers. From the maintenance men and technicians, from the hot-dog vendors and beer jerks and peanut guys. And from the fans— he'd taken great gobbing handfuls from the fans.

"When you gonna get us a winner?" they asked. Only they didn't quite ask the way normal people would have. These were New Yorkers, for Chrissake, not *civilized* fans. There was in- sistence in their voices. And menace. "Can't you put a decent team together? Don't you understand the game?"

Understand the game! That was precious, Eddie thought. That was positively un-fucking-believably precious! The game he understood. The game was simple, it was an exact science. Five big, hulking college grads—five pituitary cases—ran the length of a court trying to put a ball through a hoop, while a similar number of opponents attempted to stop them; the team that scored the most points won. There was nothing to the game, as far as understanding it went.

Managing it, however, was a different matter, and that's what Eddie Donovan did for a living. He managed the New York Knicks. He was the team's general manager, to be exact. Their intuitive deal maker. He was supposed to put together the best possible team, a *winning* team. "Eddie Donovan will be the ar- chitect of the great New York Knick teams," declared Ned Irish, the team's no-nonsense owner, when he switched Eddie from coaching to the front office in 1964. And, to some extent, that was true. Eddie's decisions regarding the day-to-day operations of the Knicks would undoubtedly shape the team's destiny, for better or for worse.

Four years later, that destiny was shaping up as an intestinal disaster for Eddie himself. His guts turned somersaults every time he thought about the team he had put on the floor. He felt responsible. The way Eddie saw it, the Knicks had enough talent to win it all. They had height, speed, power, accuracy, aggressiveness, ability, intelligence . . . "The Knicks are loaded with so much intelligence, Albert Einstein couldn't make the team!" fawned a columnist for the *Daily News*. Then he whittled the compliment down to its rhetorical kicker: "If they're so smart, why can't they win a simple ball game?"

It was a damn good question. The general consensus seemed to be that any fool could dribble and shoot, if that was all that was required. But the importance of the intelligence quotient wasn't lost on anyone who followed basketball for more than fifteen minutes. A man had to be smart to play this game. He had to have the ability to go out on a court, to shoot and dribble along with nine other men, but he also needed to have the reflexes, the concentration, the discipline, the coolness, the foresight, and the stamina to weave through the human gridlock and make the one move, the *right* move, that enabled his team to put another two points on the scoreboard. And that skill was beyond just any fool.

To a man, the Knicks could probably boast more intelligence than any other team in basketball. They weren't rocket scientists by any stretch of the imagination, but individually the players had brains and knew how to use them. Eddie was beginning to think that that was the good news *and* the bad news for this team. To paraphrase Marcus Aurelius: What is good for the bee is not necessarily good for the swarm. Or, as Eddie interpreted it: "Are these guys too fucking smart for their own good?"

He glanced at last night's stat sheet, clutched in his savage fist. The starting five, for all their vaunted intellect, hadn't been able to figure out how to get past a dog like Atlanta. They'd been flat and lifeless out there all night. They'd looked like . . . washerwomen. Walt Bellamy, the Knicks' center, was out-muscled by an opponent who was three and a half inches shorter than he was. And Bellamy wasn't any mere center, either—he was a warrior, a dragon slayer. In 1966, Eddie had traded two able-bodied men to get him from Baltimore, and there were times when the deal had seemed like a steal for the Knicks. On good nights, Bellamy could shoot, rebound, and box out any of the league's reigning giants, including Wilt Chamberlain and Bill Russell. On such nights, Bellamy, the team's emotional lightning rod, could be instrumental in squeezing out sparks. But lately he'd played like a slug. He'd looked wooden out there last night, Eddie thought, and Atlanta's pesky guards had feasted on his game like the termites they were.

But Bellamy didn't have to shoulder all the blame. His team-mates had been unable to pick up the slack. Willis Reed, the power forward from Grambling, was hampered by a bum knee. Dick Barnett was getting old—he'd turned thirty-two last month—and his salary dispute with management had proved to be a distraction. Not that money was guaranteed to inspire a player's performance. Hell, Eddie'd learned that the hard way. In 1966 he'd gone all the way to London—had practically crawled there on his knees—to beg Bill Bradley, the Ivy League golden boy, the famous Rhodes scholar, to come home and play for the Knicks. It took a lot of convincing—$500,000 worth, an unheard-of sum—to pry Bradley away from Oxford. On top of all that dough, Eddie sneaked him into the country on an unscheduled flight, called a press conference, and unveiled him—*surprise!*—

like a priceless statue, only to have him play like one. Since joining the team, Bradley couldn't find the basket to save his life, couldn't get into the flow of the game, and Eddie was beginning to wonder if his prize egghead was really a dilettante.

And yet, among the five Knick starters, it was Bill Bradley's light that shone the brightest. Probably the least conspicuous, by this measure, was Walt "Clyde" Frazier. Frazier was a thin, guileless soul, handsome in a self-conscious manner. He was from a ghetto of Atlanta, Georgia. He spoke in a sleepy southern drawl. He was the oldest of nine children—the other eight were seven sisters and a brother, Keith—and had no trace of the sophistication or even of the street sense that was necessary for survival in New York City.

Eddie had recruited Frazier in 1967 out of Southern Illinois University, in Carbondale, a school so far off the basketball map that some of the team's practices had to be held on a playground. *Outside!* Right next to a sandbox and a nursery, if you could believe that, where mothers pushed their kids on swings. It was a low-rent athletic program, all right. But they had this kid, this black flash, whom Eddie had heard about, and when he saw the kid streak across that playground, past the sandbox and the nursery and the kids on swings, he knew he'd found his next point guard.

The trouble was, there was a wide gulf between a playground in Carbondale, Illinois, and the foxholes of Madison Square Garden. In fact, there was a whole ocean of difference, and since joining the Knicks it seemed to Eddie as if Walt Frazier, his errant black flash, was lost at sea. How else could he explain Frazier's performance out there last night? Imagine Tony Curtis being cast in the lead role of *Richard III;* it was that embarrassing. The guy had coughed up six turnovers and dished off to the wrong man. And not just the wrong man, but a man on *the wrong team!* Eddie almost came out of the stands after that play. He could hardly keep from jumping out of his seat behind the an-

nouncer's table, rushing onto the floor and around the refs, grabbing his black flash, and demanding to know if that was some
secretly devised Southern Illinois strategy Eddie had never heard
about. He'd been that tempted.

Mishaps like these stung Eddie Donovan's pride. Just a few
weeks ago, before the season started, it had occurred to him that
these Knicks had the makings of a championship team. They'd
looked great during practice. Really, they had executed plays like
clockwork. It gave him a sense of paternal pride watching them
work the ball around, concentrating, being patient, hitting the
open man. *Bing bing bing!* It was a sight to behold, Eddie recalled.
Willis, Bill, Dick, the two Walts—they were in tune with one
another. No, it was more than being in tune; it was perfect pitch.
They played as if they had a sense of their own greatness, and
it carried them all the way through the stretch of exhibition
games that serve as every season's overture.

When the Knicks rolled over their four preseason opponents,
there was joy once more in the executive quarters of the Garden.
Could it actually be that . . . ? No one wanted to finish the question, or even to ask it out loud. It was bad luck to predict a
winning team. It put the whammy on them. But that didn't stop
people from going around grinning like fools, especially in the
Garden offices, where no one—not even the oldest employee, an
usher—had worked during a winning season.

Everybody had anticipated one four years ago, after the Knicks
selected Jerry Harkness, a scrappy six-foot-two guard from
Chicago-Loyola, in the first round of the National Basketball
Association's annual college draft. Harkness was going to save
the New York Knicks. As a matter of fact, he was only the latest
in a long line of would-be Knicks saviors, but of course this time
it was going to be different. This time, Eddie's foresight and foxy
cunning would pay off, giving the Knicks a foundation in their
perennial effort to rebuild a woebegone team. After all, Eddie
had practically stolen Harkness out from under the noses of the

hated Boston Celtics and the equally revolting Philadelphia Warriors, both of whom had bypassed Harkness for "lesser" players.
Eddie had neatly picked their pockets. He had pulled off a heist
that would have repercussions throughout the Eastern Division
for years to come. How could he be so sure of that? Primarily
because Eddie knew what no other general manager in the NBA
seemed to know: Jerry Harkness was a franchise player. He was
a guy whose presence alone could transform a team, change its
losing attitude, erase all its bad habits, turn a collection of gutless
wonders into superstars. Eddie knew it from the moment he
called out, "The New York Knicks select Jerry Harkness." And
it made him feel like a million bucks.

Two months later, five games into that new season, came an
accident that instantly deflated Eddie's new sense of self-worth.
The Knicks were playing Cincinnati, giving the Royals a real
bruising, when Jerry Harkness went in for a routine lay-up, came
down on his ankle, and snapped it cleanly in half. The team
physician examined the savior after the game and determined
that he'd never play basketball again. His career was over, *just
like that.*

The next year, 1964, the Knicks also had several promising
draft picks—bona fide saviors, to a man. But when their ace in
the hole, the saintly Fred Crawford, developed tuberculosis midway through the season, Eddie's old anxieties flared up again.

He remained optimistic, however, despite the Knicks' foun-
dering in last place. Willis Reed, who had been drafted late in
the second round, was showing signs of developing into a real
player.

Perhaps more fortunately, for the distinction of having finished last in the league the Knicks were awarded not one but
two first-round picks in the 1965 draft, which Eddie used to
select Bill Bradley and Dave Stallworth. They were good names
to have, except that names were about all the Knicks got that
year. Bradley promptly announced he was leaving for England to

fulfill the requirements of his Rhodes scholarship. Then, during an early-season game in San Francisco, Dave Stallworth stumbled over to the bench and began kneading his chest. It was nothing critical, the team physician assured Eddie, *he'd only suffered a mild heart attack!* "And, by the way, you know that kid Willis Reed you're so hot on? I happened to glance at some X rays, and he's got bone spurs."

The way it looked to Eddie Donovan, someone was out to get him. Why else were all his draft choices—his saviors—busy filing disability claims? Now, Eddie was no Pollyanna. He knew the odds that one of them might get hurt were fairly good. You never counted on that happening, but if it did, you could always point to the fact that big kids like these occasionally wear themselves out playing in college. They play that run-and-gun style of ball for four years, without any real supervision, and chances are you might sign a kid who is carrying around injuries that don't show up until he reaches the pros. Bad luck like that wasn't unheard of. When it was two players—when two top draft choices are damaged goods—a general manager starts to look at the big picture to see if anything is out of place. For instance, were your scouting reports accurate? Did you scrutinize the results of each player's physical exam carefully enough? You start to second-guess those kinds of things. Three players are a different story altogether—three players constituted a conspiracy. And *five!* . . . Five players sent Eddie staggering to the street for a stiff highball of that polluted Manhattan air and some rich daydreaming.

By 1966, Eddie began to wonder if the job was taking too much of a toll on his life. Rebuilding the Knicks was his passion—he loved the challenge—but he was coming apart at the seams. His hair was falling out, his weight was up, his stomach, or what was left of his stomach, kept him up nights. The job was consuming him. And when it got down to the nitty-gritty, Eddie had to admit that the results were a lot less than commensurate with his efforts. In fact, the team hadn't made any progress as far as winning was concerned. (And as far as his employers and the fans were concerned, winning was all that mattered.) For all his ingenious trades, roster reshufflings, constant scouting trips, clever draft choices, for all his constant worrying and gastritis, the Knicks had improved not a whit.

There were plenty of new faces on the bench, but the team still didn't have any depth. It lacked a sixth man who could come in off the bench and score. It lacked an enforcer. It lacked another big body to clog the lane. It lacked discipline and experience, and it lacked the right coach. Aside from all that, the team was in perfect shape.

Eddie Donovan clearly needed help. More than that, he needed to decide whether to stick it out, whether to put any more time into this project or to jump ship. If he came right down to it, he might be better off back in college ball, at St. Bonaventure, where the stakes weren't as great. In college, a coach had the time to mold a team to his style of play. The kids grew into their game, and leaders emerged after putting in time on the bench. You could take a hapless team and turn it around in two years' time. The Knicks, on the other hand, might be three, even four years away from a winning season. Would management wait that long for results? Would the fans? The possibility that he might not be around when the Knicks eventually blossomed didn't escape Eddie Donovan's notice. Then again, he refused to panic. Every veteran of the basketball circuit seemed to have experienced these bad strings.

In time, the NBA would compile statistics showing that a career general manager—that is, one who intended to work in the pros for twenty years, as Eddie did—had a 92 percent probability of being fired more than twice. This did not include demotions within the same team, since the organization did not classify a demotion as a job loss. Furthermore, there was a better than even chance, a 53 percent probability, to be exact, that at some point a career basketball executive would elect to resign from a team on his own, before the proverbial ax fell. In an era of intense media coverage of sports, resigning meant calling a press conference and citing failing health or family problems as an excuse for his departure—like a disgraced politician. The act of resignation was itself so unsavory and incriminating that many execs chose to be fired rather than put themselves through that ordeal.

And yet, as the 1967 season loomed, Eddie realized he wasn't ready to throw in the towel. Not by any stretch of the imagination. He had the makings of a magnificent team in New York—he really believed that. Sometimes, when he watched them go through an afternoon of drills, a crush of weight seemed to ease off his shoulders. All at once he would feel relaxed and abundantly confident, as it dawned on him that the Knicks had megatons of untapped potential on the floor. "These boys are stars!" Eddie concluded. "They just don't know it yet."

And then Eddie Donovan would look at the individual players—Bellamy, Reed, Bradley, Frazier, and Barnett, most of them still in their early twenties. He'd imagine them as middle-aged men and see the faces of champions. They had that unmistakable aura about them. There, in the hollow belly of Madison Square Garden—one of the most hellish arenas in the world, a building whose name alone struck fear in the hearts of would-be sports heroes—these players came prepared to do combat. In that alone, they had passed the test—the test of courage.

Thinking back now, Eddie supposed that 1966 and 1967 had been the most agonizing stretch in the Knicks' struggle for respectability. Agonizing because all the components had been in place and they still hadn't served to put the team over the top. Eddie had even been blessed with a promising draft choice in 1966, Cazzie Russell, a fidgety streak shooter with a fall-away jumper who fit neatly into the Knicks' overall scheme.

Russell, too, was heralded as the savior to end all saviors, and this time the prophecy looked to be dependable. He was a surefire superstar. A schoolboy All-American, he had led the heretofore dreadful University of Michigan Wolverines to three consecutive Big Ten titles and been named the outstanding college player of the year by every national poll. In a coin flip with the Detroit Pistons, Eddie had won the right to select first in the college draft, and he had chosen Russell over Syracuse's Dave Bing. For which he almost wound up being lynched by the bloodthirsty New York fans.

"The Knicks choose . . ." *What? Who?*

Eddie, grinning idiotically, could scarcely believe it. Here he'd gotten the number-one pick of the draft, an outstanding player, and yet the fans weren't satisfied. They'd wanted *Bing!* It seemed to be turning into a nightmare for the Knicks and, in particular, for Eddie Donovan, whose turf in the Garden was already dangerously thin.

Dave DeBusschere, representing the Detroit Pistons, wore the same idiotic grin as that 1966 draft meandered through the final rounds. It was DeBusschere, of all people, who'd mistakenly called out tails when the coin was in the air and thereby had ceded Dave Bing to the New York Knicks.

Or so he had thought.

When the Knicks selected Cazzie Russell, DeBusschere was as surprised as anyone else in the room. He was also relieved. As DeBusschere saw it, calling "tails" was just about the stupidest move he'd ever made in his life. Everyone know you *never* call "tails" in a coin flip. *Never!* It's a sucker's gambit; ninety-eight out of one hundred percent of the time you lose. One theory often advanced for the phenomenon is that the "heads" side of a coin has more detail on it and is thus heavier than the "tails." side. Another is that coins are usually flipped from a heads-up position, meaning that it is placed "heads up" on the flipper's forefinger and because of the greater weight usually falls heads

down in the palm before being ceremoniously slapped over—
"heads up"—on the flipper's wrist.

Whatever scientific basis there was for the theory, De-
Busschere was convinced he had blown the call by trying to
psyche out the coin. He had blown the call *and* the first draft
pick, and he was wondering how to explain that to his boss in
Detroit when the Knicks chose . . . Cazzie Russell.

"The Detroit Pistons select *Dave Bing!*" DeBusschere practically screamed.

It was on occasions like this that Dave DeBusschere actually
regretted being the coach of the Detroit Pistons. What the Pistons
needed was a solid front-office man. DeBusschere was a Pistons
player who happened to be moonlighting as their coach, and it
was Detroit's custom to send the coach to the draft. For a while
DeBusschere had been wary about handling official team business.
ness. Sure, he could design plays and work out defensive strategies and tame the younger players. That came with the territory.
And the more complicated deals and contract negotiations were
handled by Detroit's owner, Fred Zollner, and Ed Coil, the general manager. That left DeBusschere free to remain one of the
guys. He didn't do any more of the suit-and-tie chores than he
had to. But the draft seemed like real basketball business, not
some public-relations stunt, and if he had to glad-hand and shoot
the breeze and make small talk with other coaches and general
managers and team owners, then he could do it.

The truth was, DeBusschere was proud of being able to walk
both sides of the line. Few players were ever given the opportunity
to coach in the pros, and fewer yet coached while remaining on
the team's active-player roster. After all, it was damn hard for a
player to be considered anything *but* a player in this business.
Some guys were lucky enough to land a scouting job when they
got too old to play, but everybody knew it was a favor—a way of
easing them into the real world, a bone thrown to an old lame

dog. Ex-players who remained on the payroll were strictly window dressing. For the most part, they were rolled out at old-timers' games, asked to play golf with people important to the team, and on rare occasions sent to check out a college prospect.

But Dave DeBusschere was no ordinary aging jock. He was a mere twenty-four years old. That's right, twenty-four. And in Detroit, where he had lived and played all his life, he was as famous as Henry Ford. He was a local hero of the highest magnitude—which is to say, he was raised right off the assembly line, a boy from the inner city, with a Detroit-based education, no real polish, no pretensions, no sophisticated habits of any sort, who took off the bartender's apron, put on a uniform, and tore up every basketball court he played on.

DeBusschere grew up on Motown's gritty east side, not far from the old Pontiac, Chrysler, Dodge, DeSoto, and Oldsmobile plants. Chances are, he would have followed his father into the bar business had he not developed into one of the deadliest rebounders the game had ever seen. The guy played like he was *unconscious*. He could hit from ten feet out, from fifteen feet out—hell, he could sink them from twenty-five out and still wind up under the basket for the rebound.

DeBusschere perfected this little feat while still in high school, when his Austin High Clippers rolled to the state championship. At the University of Detroit, he developed into the best basketball player the Titans ever had. Besides that, he pitched their baseball team into the national finals. The Pistons signed him right out of college—and so did the Chicago White Sox, for a bonus of $160,000. He was only twenty-two years old then, and playing in two professional sports. He pitched Triple A ball for two seasons with Indianapolis, then the Sox promoted him and he played on the same team as Chicago stars like Luis Aparicio and Nellie Fox. If that wasn't enough on his plate, at the age of twenty-four he accepted the unlikely challenge to coach the Pistons as well.

What else could possibly be expected of Dave DeBusschere? Well, for one thing, the Pistons expected him to win games. That wasn't out of the question, but he needed the help of four other players, and unfortunately the Pistons came up short where talent was concerned. DeBusschere soon discovered he couldn't win games all by himself. The first year of his two-hat tenure, he was named to the starting NBA All-Star team, but his Pistons didn't even make the play-offs. The second year, they finished last in their division. DeBusschere gave up baseball in order to concentrate under the hoops, and he was prepared to relinquish the coaching if things got any worse.

Calling tails at the draft almost made that happen. But suddenly he landed the prize fish—Dave Bing, probably the best college prospect in the country—and Detroit's basketball future looked brighter.

The draft that year had been a regular circus. First there was the coin toss, of all things. It was a scene right out of some Mickey Rooney movie. "C'mon, guys, we'll flip for it!" The NBA had to be off its rocker to run a business like that. Still, Eddie Donovan had seen stranger bits of horse trading. Why, during that same draft, Atlanta, picking fourth, chose a guy named John Morrison from Canisius College. Boston had the fifth selection, and when it was Red Auerbach's turn, he announced, "Boston drafts the *other* guy from Canisius." His eyes scanned the smoky Plaza Hotel suite until he located Atlanta's head scout, Marty Blake. "Hey, Marty—tell them his name."

Blake sniggered humorlessly. "Red, what kind of shit is this?" he asked. "You draft a guy and you don't even know his name?"

The room erupted in a chorus of belly laughter. Any time someone could snooker the Celtics, it was greeted with jubilation.

Richie Guerin, Atlanta's coach, pointed presumptuously at Auerbach. "Tell you what—he'll give you the name for fifty dollars."

"Richie, you're embarrassing me," Auerbach said, with mock humility.

"How can I embarrass *you*? You don't even know the fucking kid's name."

Auerbach waited until the laughter subsided again, then walked quietly over to Marty Blake. Leaning over in a confidential, buddy-buddy manner, he said, "Make it twenty-five dollars."

Blake nodded, and Auerbach handed him two tens and a five, which he immediately slipped into his wallet. Then, swallowing an unrepentant grin, Marty Blake bellowed, "Boston drafts . . . Andy Anderson!"

Ho boy, that draft business took some crazy turns, Eddie Donovan thought. Drafts and deals—you never knew where they were going to take you. Like that poor kid DeBusschere. Who ever heard of calling tails, for Chrissake? Poor dumb schmuck. He should have known better. But, to tell the truth, DeBusschere was carving out a nice little reputation for himself of blowing deals.

Marty Blake claimed the greatest deal he ever made was with DeBusschere, who may not have had the final authority to make deals but was constantly putting them in play. Dave, a notorious beer guzzler, had a few too many one night in San Francisco when he decided to phone Blake, reaching him at two in the morning.

"Do you have any fuckin' idea what time it is?" Blake complained.

"Marty, Marty, I've got to have a guard," DeBusschere moaned. "I've got to have John Miner."

Blake said, "Fine. We'll give you Miner. Now, who you got for me?"

DeBusschere said, "Joe Caldwell."

Blake instantly woke up. *Joe Caldwell!* This was going to be a fuckin' steal. He'd probably be arrested for grand larceny. "You got a deal," he said.

DeBusschere chuckled over the staticky line. "Let's make a big one," he said. "How about Chico Vaughn?"

Blake thought, Whoa! Dave's been drinking—that's the only reason he could possibly want Chico Vaughn. DeBusschere also threw in Rod Thorn and said, "Is John Tresvant available?"

"Yeah," Blake said, "but I don't want any more of your fucking players." So DeBusschere offered him money and a second draft choice to cement the deal.

"Why don't you send me a telegram confirming this conversation in the morning?" Blake said. "Oh, and Dave—you might as well come with the deal, because they're gonna run your ass out of town!"

That didn't happen, but the deal did help to sink De-Busschere's coaching career. The Pistons had had just about enough of his brilliant deals, selling off their players as if they were . . . *slaves.* Eddie Donovan, on the other hand, coveted a big man with DeBusschere's abilities. Before the 1967 draft, he had tried to pry Dave out of the Pistons' vise grip by offering them two players and the rights to Cazzie Russell, but Detroit's front office wouldn't go for it.

Maybe, one of these days . . .

Now, Eddie Donovan rubbed his head reflectively as he thought about all the offers he'd made for DeBusschere. Dave DeBusschere is probably the most thoughtful man playing pro ball this year, Eddie mused. He has my vote for All-Star forward right now. Wincing, Eddie shook his head and gulped in another breath of air.

He looked at last night's stats again, and his depression grew. There was nothing to see but the usual mix of names and numbers—pretty decent numbers, he had to admit, but adding up to another significant loss. It wasn't just Walt Bellamy and Willis Reed; the Knicks had simply been outmanned. There had been a practice earlier yesterday afternoon designed to stifle

Philadelphia's fast-break offense, but early in the first period the 76ers had managed to undo all the extra preparation, and they never let the Knicks get back into the game. A postgame summary put together by coach Dick McGuire offered various excuses for the team's poor showing. The words merely blurred together as Eddie stared at them, like the years blurred, and the sounds out on the street.

What was wrong with these guys, and why couldn't he fix it?

Still deliberating the damn lineup, Eddie disappeared into the bowels of Penn Station and found a seat on his nightly train home to New Jersey. He pulled out a felt-tipped pen and began doodling idly on a tablet. He strung names together in the manner of a crossword puzzle, then inked out one or another and reinserted it at another intersection of the chain. Bellamy—Reed—Bradley—Frazier—Barnett. Eddie was looking for the weak link. He was trying to decide if anyone would benefit from a trade or would bring much in return. He scrawled out Bellamy and wrote in the name of his promising rookie, Phil Jackson, whose long arms and outside shot made him a potential threat near the basket. Jackson was a possibility, but at six-eight he was too short to start at center and too valuable a shooter to sit on the bench. He was also young and inexperienced and, as rumor had it, a *hippie*. Not one of those drug-addict longhairs, but a peacenik, a philosophy freak—worse, a *vegetarian*. Eddie drew a capsule around Jackson's name and doodled in "weirdo?" right below it.

Next he drew a line through Walt Frazier's name and replaced it with Komives. Howard "Butch" Komives was a six-foot-one five-year veteran out of Bowling Green, who served as the Knicks' dependable Sixth Man. He was fast, and he could score despite being bumped or having a hand shoved in his face. He was scrappy. But he had never been satisfied with his role—meaning he wanted more playing time. In that respect, he wasn't a team guy. He threw tantrums and was a bit of a prima donna. Hmmmm, maybe that was the problem, Eddie speculated. Maybe it was a waste of talent to keep Komives on the bench. Frazier was coming along, but his specialty was defense, and perhaps the Knicks should be more concerned with having someone out there who scored from the start. The same went for Cazzie Russell, who was sent in when Bill Bradley needed a rest.

The new chain lacked the right chemistry. Jackson—Reed—Komives—Russell—Barnett. That lineup was top-heavy with shooters; there was no defensive balance. He put Bradley back in for Russell and was about to restore Walt Bellamy's name when an alternative popped into his head. Maybe Willis—hmmmmm. Eddie wondered. Maybe Willis Reed could be turned around to play center again, as he had in college. Not many power forwards could make that adjustment. All their lives they had played crashing toward the boards, and suddenly they were told to turn their backs to the basket and play a different style of basketball. Most big men were unable to get the hang of it, especially this far along in their careers. Oh, they tried and took a few lumps, but it rarely worked out. It took someone willing to make the supreme sacrifice—someone willing to risk his reputation for the good of the team—and, as Eddie knew, Willis Reed was about as unselfish a player as anyone in the game. And he was a *true* center.

It was an intriguing possibility. Driving to the basket would be suicide for an opponent, with Willis clogging up the middle. He was a natural enforcer, he was a leader, but—Eddie could already hear the objections. Walt Bellamy was a Garden favorite. He'd done a decent job as a starter, and he wasn't a huge liability on the court. And, while Reed had some experience at center, he was small. The program listed him at 6'10", Willis insisted he was 6'9½'', but he was probably no more than 6'8". That would force a Bradley-Russell collaboration at forward, and even

Eddie knew that'd never work. But still . . . Eddie moved Willis's name to the front of the chain and began a new game of chess with his human pieces.

With Willis at center, the team's balance of power became more elastic. It became adaptable. Because, as Eddie suddenly realized—and eventually blurted out to his bosses—"Willis was the intractable component." *The intractable component.* He was the type of player who could inspire the other guys, could make them respond, and that was the way you had to build a team— from the inside out. Why hadn't Eddie thought of that before? Furiously he scratched out his original chains and made fresh ones, like DNA molecules, built around Willis Reed.

Instantly the team took on an entirely different complexion. Eddie found himself loaded with options he never knew existed before. Phil Jackson or Nate Bowman could be groomed to back up Willis. Jackson was a project, to be sure; nevertheless, he was smart and stood to benefit as a role player who could come off the bench in difficult situations. And Bowman was a bruiser. Not much of a shooter—in fact, nothing of a shooter—but a bruiser, nonetheless. That'd mean Bill Bradley would gain the freedom to move over and play the corners, where he was comfortable taking those patented set shots of his. Barnett and— who?—most likely Walt Frazier would make sense in the backcourt. They were an odd couple, as the record already proved, but Eddie liked the chemistry between those two, and he was willing to go out on a limb—for a while, at least.

Eddie liked the way things were shaping up here. Reed— Bradley—Barnett— Frazier— In this configuration, the lineup had a foundation of speed and efficiency. And brains! He still needed another big man, a power forward to replace Willis. But who? Phil Jackson was a role player, at best, and damaged goods; he was recuperating from a nasty back injury. Bill Hosket, one of the Knicks' tallest reserve players, had a bum knee and just wasn't healthy enough to start. Cazzie Russell wasn't tall enough, and anyway Cazzie was more interested in scoring, in inflating his personal stats, and this job required a defensive specialist. Or, ideally, someone who could do both—shoot and rebound.

The more Eddie thought about it, the more he knew his answer had to come from the outside. He hated to go shopping this early in the season, but at least he had some trade bait to put on the table. The way Eddie saw it, Walt Bellamy would never accept a substitute role on the Knicks. He would become what coaches called "an unhappy player." Even now, he only got up for tough games. If Willis could make the switch to center, Bellamy was expendable. And he'd bring a good price, too. He was young enough, he had ability, and he had a name (even if it was a better one than he deserved).

That still left the question of who. Who else in the league was of Bellamy's caliber and could fit in with the personality of the team Eddie had just designed? Who could be pried free in a trade? It was a tough spot to fill. And Eddie couldn't appear desperate, or he'd tip his hand and have all the other teams trying to unload their losers on him.

He picked up a copy of the *Daily News* and thumbed through the sports pages. The league standings might give him a clue about what team needed a big man like Bellamy. The season was young, but you already had teams like Baltimore and Philadelphia whose rosters were set in stone—that is, they had winners and wouldn't risk tinkering with a proven formula. By now, Eddie also knew better than to call the Boston Celtics. The Celtics *never* traded with the Knicks. *Never!* The city of Boston suffered from a long-standing inferiority complex of being treated as New York's bastard child. When it came to basketball, however, the tables were turned. In the NBA, Boston was a rich man's paradise, a *dynasty!* Because of that, the Celtics would rather strangle than unintentionally help improve the Knicks.

Then it dawned on Eddie: the Pistons! Detroit was on an embarrassing eight-game slide into last place. They'd gotten off to a horrible start again, and this season looked like it was going to be a repeat performance of last year's mediocre finish. A team like the Pistons usually would listen to trade talk and often could be persuaded to make a deal. And this Pistons team had exactly what Eddie wanted.

It had the missing link:

Dave DeBusschere.

DeBusschere was still Detroit's favorite son, but he was in Uncle Paulie's doghouse. Paul Seymour, the latest in a line of Piston coaches, was less than enchanted with the team's star forward. For one thing, DeBusschere had too much fun at night. He was in tight with a group of locals—buddies from his high-school and college days—and when the team was in town and had a day off the buddies would stay out all night drinking beer and gin. Game days, DeBusschere invariably showed up sluggish and lackluster. That pissed off Seymour, who expected his men to be ready to play.

Another reason he'd grown tired of DeBusschere was the dissension that had begun to creep into the team's psyche. It had a seamy racial undertone that festered when DeBusschere got married and didn't invite a single black player to the wedding. Well, the brothers beat the drums pretty heavily about this lapse in etiquette. You could feel it on the floor. There was a noticeable change in the way the team interacted; there was a bit of unnecessary pushing and shoving—between *teammates*, for Chrissake. Despite a meeting in which the players aired their differences, the damage had been done.

Both of these situations ultimately figured into the Pistons' willingness to move DeBusschere. It was time, they decided. He'd played basketball in Detroit for his entire career. Maybe he'd be better off somewhere else, for a change. Like . . . Baltimore.

As with the Knicks, the Baltimore Bullets had been hot on DeBusschere's tail. They'd been calling Seymour for months, enticing him with various packages, trying to pry DeBusschere free. Some of the offers were pretty interesting, too. Gus Johnson's name had come up, and so had Jack Marin's—two worthy forwards. The Pistons, for their part, exercised a great deal of restraint in not pouncing on any of the deals. They were waiting for the right opportunity. Finally Seymour heard an offer he could live with. The Pistons would send DeBusschere to the Bullets in exchange for LeRoy Ellis and Eddie Miles. Well, Paul Seymour was in hog heaven. This was *it,* he thought, my deal! He and Gene Shue, Baltimore's coach, even shook on it.

One night shortly afterward, however, following a Detroit-Baltimore game, Seymour happened to be walking two steps behind Shue and the Bullets' general manager and overheard them talking about backing out of the deal. He immediately called them on it.

Shue hemmed and hawed, with that beagle face of his. He was clearly embarrassed. Finally he admitted it. "Sorry," he said, "but we've got to renege."

Seymour was livid. "Fuck you!" he shouted. "I'm gonna make that deal with New York. I'll put DeBusschere right in your division, so it'll give you a fucking headache whenever you see the stats. You assholes can pound sand for a couple years!"

The next day, when Eddie Donovan called a-courtin', Seymour knew he had a hot one on the line. Donovan was drooling; he could practically taste the deal—they were that close. For two hours, both men tried out various combinations, using Walt Bellamy as the magic lever. His was the first name they put on the table for DeBusschere. No problem there; the Pistons needed a center. However, they wouldn't go for a straight two-man swap. They wanted some incentive, a sweetener. After all, this was Dave DeBusschere they were parting with, not some termite.

A couple of hours later, Seymour fine-tuned the parameters of the deal, called Donovan back, and insisted that he throw in

Butch Komives as a "gimme." Seymour knew Komives was a head case. He also knew that Komives had been shopped to every team in the league without drawing a sniff. Nobody wanted him. But Seymour and Komives were both from Toledo, Ohio, and, what the hell, Seymour felt like doing the kid a favor by bringing him closer to home. Wasn't that sweet?

"Bellamy and Komives—they could make Detroit an instant contender," Eddie intimated to the Pistons' general manager, Ed Coil, whose ultimate decision it would be to finalize the deal. It was just after four, and he'd reached Coil at the Pistons' offices as the Knicks arrived in Detroit for a timely game. "Think about it. You get two proven starters, both with plenty of years left on their bones. We get the big man we're looking for, and you unload a guy who's on his way down. Gimme a reason we *don't* make this deal."

Coil couldn't, and by the time Eddie hung up the details had been worked out to everyone's satisfaction. Eddie took a deep breath. It was done. He'd been through hell worrying over the details, but it had been worth it. The Knicks had themselves a face-lift and, as far as Eddie could tell, a cast-iron team. A contender. Oh, it was going to be a cat fight on the ol' court tonight!

DeBusschere!

The Knicks had an appointment with destiny.

2 |THE IRON AGE

1968–69

DeBusschere, as the Knicks soon discovered, really could do it all. He could run, block, score, jump, rebound, dribble, screen, dive, drive, stuff, slam, jam, box, spin, snap, crackle, pop, and leap tall buildings in a single bound. But by the end of the 1968–69 season the Boston Celtics had waxed his tail.

The Celtics. Those mothers could fry in hell, as far as the Knicks fans cared. For all of New York's inherent woes, for all the sins wrought by jamming 8 million people onto an island the size of Aruba, nothing stung New Yorkers like the agony of losing to a Boston sports franchise. They took it personally. They hated that two-bit city and its candy-assed teams. The Red Sox and the Celtics—both names brought Bronx cheers from the glottises of surly, spitfire New Yorkers, but only one, the Celtics, stuck in the craw. They were like bad meat. Mighty and arrogant, they stank up the air with their shamrock pride—all that loud talk about honor and dominance—and they rubbed the Knicks' noses in it. Year after year after year after . . .

The Knicks looked to settle the score as the 1968–69 season drew to a close. They dispatched the league-leading Baltimore Bullets in the first round of the Eastern Division play-offs, handled them in a neat four-game sweep, and watched with mounting anticipation as the Philadelphia 76ers and the Celtics dueled for the remaining berth in the division finals. Publicly, the Knicks denied rooting for either team. They didn't want to give anyone some choice inspiration by popping off to the press. But in their hearts, to a man, they wanted the Celtics. They could *taste* the Celtics. Indeed, it would be a delicious series: an aging and battered Boston pitted against the younger, hungry Knicks. Snack time: the Knicks intended to serve up those old heroes on sesame-seed buns.

You had to like the odds from New York's side of the bench. The Knicks were on a roll. As expected, their season had started slowly, with a string of losses to prepare the fans for yet another year of dismal basketball. But after DeBusschere's arrival, the Knicks won three of every four games they played. They materialized into a *team*. Suddenly the play-offs didn't seem like such a gloomy prospect. Cazzie Russell bragged to a TV audience that the Knicks could win it all, and for once, nobody laughed.

Following the first play-off round, in fact, nobody even chuckled. Or winked. The Baltimore series had been a walk when the pundits had predicted a battle. The Bullets had the best record in the NBA, not to mention having Earl "The Pearl" Monroe, the rookie sensation Wes Unseld at center, Kevin "Murph" Loughery, and a blinding fast break that made the Metroliner look like a tin trolley. But the Knicks managed to stave off every Baltimore assault with a counterpunch of their own, confusing and rocking the Bullets' offense until it was nothing but empty casings.

If Boston prevailed in its play-off series, the underdog Knicks had something to shoot for. The Celtics were beatable. *They were beatable—yes!* They'd finished a flabby fourth in the season's standings, and the Knicks had outscored them in six of their seven regular-season matches—for the first time since 1955. They'd even held the Celtics to a 98.4-point average, which was no mean feat. Boston was a team overloaded with sharpshooters: Bill Russell, perhaps the most savvy ballplayer in either league; Bailey Howell, who was pesky, quick off the boards, and with a deadly touch; Satch Sanders, with his built-in radar; Sam Jones, who popped from anywhere on the court and had perfected the bank shot; and swingman John Havlicek, one of the game's emerging superstars and a consistent scoring threat. The Celtics were also self-proclaimed Masters of the Big D, they loved pressure situations, and they were loaded with confidence. But that was old news. The Knicks felt they were beatable.

Still, Boston was a dynasty. They were basketball royalty. The Celtics had won ten league titles in the last twelve years. And there was the intimidation factor to think about. Boston took great pride in psyching out its impudent opponents. Going into Philly, they were underdogs until general manager Red Auerbach declared, "Psychologically, they're afraid of us."

What the fu . . . afraid? Didn't that stogie-smokin' fool read the stats? The Sixers had finished the season right behind the Bullets, they were a young powerhouse, and the oddsmakers gave them a sizable edge. Psychologically, Auerbach was off his gourd.

"The play-offs are something special to Boston players," Russell reminded everyone, shoveling another insult on the 76ers' open wounds.

And, sure enough, the Sixers folded. Fast. Boston went up a quick three games to one, then ended the 76ers' season in five. It was old news to play-off fans. The hard-liners knew the score. "Don't let the Celtics, or beating them in a season series, ever fool you," coach Red Holzman warned his Knicks. "They have so much play-off experience and so many great players. That Bill Russell during the play-offs just murders you."

"Murders you." That was putting it mildly. Some Knicks

players suspected that Russell had a self-portrait moldering in his attic, the guy's stamina was that uncanny. He was thirty-four—decrepit, by NBA standards—a step or two slower than most of his counterparts, tired, achy, run-down, winded, an old horse ready for grazing. During the regular season, he looked due for a new career in investment banking or TV guest spots or wherever ballplayers go after their prime. But come play-off time and Russell miraculously recaptured his youth. No one knew his secret—which magic serum he drank or how much he promised the Devil. But he showed up for play-off games hale and hearty. He'd cover the court like Tinkerbell—those stalky legs beating wildly to the basket, hands appearing out of nowhere to disrupt the perfect pass. His precision timing was impeccably in sync. And suddenly the Celtics would be right there in the game, *in your face,* making weenies out of a division champ.

"Not this time," Mike Riordan told a friend. "It ain't gonna happen." The Knicks were a solid team, they had momentum, and Riordan believed that Willis Reed, who was stronger than Russell and had an outside jump shot to boot, could take the big guy to the ropes.

Others weren't so sure. Russell had slowed down somewhat, but he was cagey—a trait that wasn't lost on any opponent, least of all Willis Reed. The very first time Willis had met him, Russell had used a favorite maneuver that seemed solicitous and helpful on the surface but was calculated to unnerve young players and pull them out of their rhythm during a game. It was in February 1965, the afternoon of the All-Star game, in St. Louis. Both players were staying at the Chase Hotel, and Reed, who was the Knicks' rookie All-Star, encountered his hero stepping off the elevator in the lobby. The young player's heart skipped a beat. Hell, it practically stopped dead when Russell asked Willis to join him for a pregame meal.

In a remote corner of the dining room, over steaks, Russell talked for two hours, preaching his *philosophy* of basketball. Imagine that! Bill Russell sharing his personal view of the game with a rook, a Knicks rook at that, a mortal rival. He told Willis about the mental book he kept on all the players in the league. How he committed to memory their moves, strengths, weaknesses, the way he matched up against them on the floor, where they finished plays, so that he could anticipate how they would respond in game situations.

One can picture the young Willis Reed, artless and open-faced, gobbling it all up. Scarfing up each scrap of basketball wisdom. Beholden forever to the great center for teaching him the "mental aspects of the game"—which was exactly Russell's objective. Because he knew that the next time they faced off, chances were Reed would flash a kindly eye toward his new mentor. Maybe he wouldn't summon the degree of aggression it took to contain a big man like Russell, or wouldn't play him hard enough or close enough. Whatever the consequences, the strategy usually gave Russell the edge he coveted, and he exacted a punishing price for his advice.

It was a stunt he pulled time and again on Wilt Chamberlain. Whenever the 76ers came to Boston, Russell would invite his nemesis to dinner, would even pick up the check, in an effort to soften him up. Some say it took the poison out of Wilt's lethal sting. In any case, Russell would go to work on Chamberlain on the court, swatting away lay-ups, overplaying him, refusing to block his dunk shot in exchange for position at the opposite end of the floor—which really drove Wilt nuts.

No, the Knicks couldn't lay down for a second with Bill Russell in the game. Despite a pair of hobbled knees, he was having another remarkable, if not typical, year, leading the Celtics in minutes played (forty-three per game) and rebounds (1,484). Being the player-coach made him a double threat. And since this year promised to be his last as an active player, he was courting another, final championship ring.

New York was prepared for war. The Knicks, who entered

the play-off round with more than a week's rest, were throwing five proven commandos against Boston's elite guard. Willis Reed had evolved from a decent big man into an immutable force. He played center like the Hulk, crashing boards and bodies while lobbing bombs from fifteen feet out. Bill Bradley, whose first season had been a letdown, had returned to his old college form. The same for Walt Frazier, who for a time had scared the front office into believing he'd be a project. Frazier not only could score at will but had learned how to mug, steal, and pick pockets more smoothly than some of the gnarlier New York fans. Dick Barnett handled the ball as if it was a Ming vase, and unloaded it as if it was napalm. At thirty-three, he was the oldest Knick, but the only one who had played in every game, and had done so with twenty-four-jewel precision. He defied the laws of evolution; he seemed to gain a few steps each year. Finally, of course, there was DeBusschere. A decade later, Reggie Jackson boasted to his Yankee teammates that he was "the straw that stirred the drink," but that statement more accurately defined DeBusschere's role with the Knicks. He was plunked into a team whose liquid moves had been blended into high-octane energy, and he kept them in every close game.

As the Knicks tuned up for the Celtics at St. John's University in Queens, the Los Angeles Lakers were eliminating the San Francisco Warriors from the Western Division semifinals, taking four of six games in a fairly dull, workmanlike series. Jerry West put on his usual scoring clinic, hitting twenty-two points in the opening half of the final game and reducing Chamberlain to his errand boy. With the Atlanta Hawks slated to be their next victim, the Lakers were favored to meet the winner of the Knicks-Celtics series in what promised to be an incredible showdown.

Penn Plaza was a mob scene as fans forsook their Sunday dinners for a taste of Celtic blood. The new Madison Square Garden, which was hardly more than a year old, played host to a capacity crowd of 19,500 for the opening game of the series.

Impetuous New Yorkers quickly scarfed up the 14,000 tickets that became available before the game, and twice as many fans were turned away or were victimized by wily scalpers, who worked the shadows like fireflies. The fans hoped that the first game was not an indicator of things to come. The Celtics gave the Knicks a brutal thrashing, despite a thirty-four-point career high by Walt Frazier. Much of the outcome was due to the play of Bill Russell, who almost effortlessly moved Willis Reed out of the paint—just flicked him out like a gnat—and directed the flow of action from the center like a manic air-traffic controller, windmilling the ball out to Havlicek, Howell, Jones, Em Bryant, or any other missile launcher in his flight path. *New York Times* columnist Leonard Koppett, who only a year earlier had written, "Bill Russell simply can't be the devastating force he used to be night after night," could be seen munching on his words. Russell was a magnificent old horse. He played with a calculated brilliance, and after the game, as if out of spite, he bypassed Koppett to say to another *Times* writer, grinning, "I feel like a thirty-five-year-old man—in the prime of my life."

The Knicks stumbled into their locker room afterward, stunned and roundly humbled. Bill Hosket, who had spelled Reed for a few awkward minutes during the second quarter, had watched most of the action from the bench—through hands cupped timorously over his eyes—and was asked by Dave De-Busschere to analyze the atrocity.

"They kicked the shit out of us, is what happened," Hosket deadpanned.

DeBusschere already knew that. As a Piston—one of the lowliest creatures in the basketball phylum—he'd been frequent cannon fodder for a Celtics charge. That experience, in fact, lingered all too clearly in his mind. He reviewed for Hosket all the gory details, how for years playing the Celtics had been similar to the carnage on Omaha Beach, when wave after wave of Allied troops fell to the inexhaustible tide of German reserves. The

Pistons would start out by facing Boston's starting battery of Bob Cousy and Bill Sharman, who were in the twilight of their careers. Then, at the quarter, when Detroit brought in their third forward and third guard—a couple of meaningless bodies—the Celtics coughed up the Jones boys, Sam and K. C. Perhaps they'd rest Tom Heinsohn and leave Satch Sanders on the floor with Havlicek. "While we're putting a weaker team on the floor," DeBusschere groaned, "they actually got stronger. Their last man on the bench could play rings around you. So we'd be down, say, eight at the quarter—and twenty-five at the half."

Hosket nodded glumly. He understood, especially now, after the current mess. The game had been a nightmare for him, but also a lesson. The regular season, Hoss had discovered, was a smoke screen; come play-off time, it meant squat. Sure, the Knicks had better stats; they'd finished ahead of Boston in the standings; they had home-court advantage and a team of young stud horses—all the meaty tangibles. But in the end it was the Celtics who came to play. They weren't just great. They knew *how* to be great and *when* to be great. And they knew what Bill Russell was all about.

Reed and Barnett had probably known what to expect; maybe even DeBusschere had. But the younger Knicks in the locker room that night were stunned into silence. They'd been whupped, on national television. They'd been cut to size. And no doubt some of them felt the impending doom.

The next day, April 7, was a day off. Most of the Knicks avoided basketball talk, and none of them read the sports pages or went near TV news, other than to check the progress of the annual NBA draft, which was being conducted quite casually via a fourteen-city telephone link. The pickings were lean that year except at the very top, where the mastodonic Lew Alcindor loomed as the all-time NBA door prize. Alcindor was a big man in the finest sense of the word. He was huge, listed at a league-topping seven-foot-one (but closer to seven-four), with brains, savvy, and coordination. Loaded with talent, he had the potential for altering the face of the game. The Milwaukee Bucks, a hapless expansion team, claimed him, following a coin toss with the Phoenix Suns, and thereby reduced the subsequent choices to chattel. Otherwise, Boston pulled off the draft's only major heist. Selecting ninth, they scooped up Kansas court star JoJo White (who was inexplicably still available), a pick that everyone had expected to go fourth or fifth, at the most. But, sure enough, the Celtics reeled him in. The rich get richer, Eddie Donovan bristled, before selecting six-three guard Johnny Warren as the fifth pick.

Warren was a capable, if somewhat reluctant, St. John's standout whose move to the Knicks would create some local noise. But even bigger news on the nearby Queens campus was the basketball player who slipped smoothly into the St. John's gym that afternoon for some programmed scrimmaging. No one had expected Cazzie Russell to play again that year, much less in the play-offs. Maybe never. Certainly that prospect had flashed through Cazzie's mind following his freak collision in January with Joe Kennedy of the Seattle Supersonics. Everything had been rolling along nicely that night. Cazzie was racking up a slew of points, doing the funky chicken off the baseline, when— *schwaaaamp!*—that big lummox fell on him, cracking Cazzie's right ankle.

It was hard luck, all right. Russell, a streak-shooting forward, had opened a spot for himself in the starting lineup, snatched it right out from under Bill Bradley's Ivy League nose, was averaging a superb seventeen points a game, and now . . . sidelined for months. For half a season, he'd watched the Knicks from the bleachers, had sat there in his studly civvies and simmered while Bradley found his touch and fit his name into the Knicks' big picture. But Cazzie had healed faster than anyone thought possible. The ankle felt pretty strong, and now he was determined to put it to the test.

Coach Red Holzman directed Cazzie to suit up for the next game, in Boston—although, to Red's dismay, uniforms don't score points. The Celtics embarrassed the Knicks again, really crushed their bones, in a comical, if combative, Game Two, and even Cazzie's keen presence—a seven-minute stretch to spell the ragged Bradley—went for naught. On the Boston side, the other Russell, Bill, dominated the boards, pulling down twenty-one rebounds in the first half alone, sinking fourteen points, blocking the Knicks' shots like a flyswatter—*zwit! zwit!* Doing it all.

The Knicks played like a bunch of bozos. Dave DeBusschere missed every shot he attempted. *Every one!* Walt Frazier went four for thirteen, Barnett five for fifteen. And Bradley's four-for-thirteen performance betrayed the miserable time he was having trying to keep a much stronger and stubborn John Havlicek off his back. The Celtics put on a clinic for the Boston fans, and the Knicks flew back to New York suffering a whopping inferiority complex. Team spirit was so pitiful, in fact, that De-Busschere stayed up all night reading Red Auerbach's *Basketball*, presumably picking through the book for tips.

The Knicks took the next game, beating the Celtics at home, 101–91, but it was a shaky win. Even with a fifteen-point lead, the New York front line played as if the game was theirs to lose. "We're right in it," Willis Reed insisted after the game, but even his customary poker face was riddled with doubt. The Knicks were tired, confused. The Celtics were doing it to them again.

Back in Boston, their confidence became downright anemic. New York found themselves trailing early in Game Four, with Bill Russell tightening the screws. The aging center was unstoppable that night, pulling down rebound after rebound, jumping out at the shooters like a mugger in the Hub. The Knicks, for their part, refused to die. At one point, Bradley hit three soft jumpers in a row, bringing the Knicks to within four, but the Boston center put a whammy on him that ultimately took Bradley out of the game. It happened midway through the third quarter.

Both teams lined up on the foul line as Emmette Bryant prepared to shoot a free throw. On one side, Bradley wedged his hulky body in between Havlicek and Satch Sanders, who was guarding him. Bill Russell, across the lane, caught Bradley's eye. He stared hard at him, really scowled, bored in deep, then shouted at Sanders, "C'mon, Satch—stop him!" It wasn't meant as a suggestion; it was an order. There was an edge of disgust in his voice, and as Russell glared at Bradley, the Knicks forward felt something ooze out of him. He felt empty, sapped. Russell had stolen his confidence, and for the rest of the game he was held to a measly four points.

Eventually the Celtics won it, and it put them up three games to one. A quick comeback by the Knicks the next night reduced the damage to three and two, but the outlook remained bleak. Walt Frazier, the Knicks' agile playmaker and scoring machine, suffered a groin injury in the final minute of Game Five that threatened to keep him out of the do-or-die contest. With a three-day layoff before the next game, there was time for the injury to heal; nevertheless, his status was listed as "doubtful."

Frazier's teammates were staggered by the news of the injury. The scrappy guard had practically engineered New York's valiant defensive effort against the Celtic bund. That very day, in fact, he'd been elected to the All-NBA defensive squad by a wider margin than any other player in the league—*including Bill Russell.* They needed him on the floor. And they needed him healthy. Sure, Mike Riordan could step in for him if necessary, but so far Riordan had scored a paltry 24 points in sixty-two minutes of the play-offs, while Frazier led both teams, with 113 points and 39 assists. Riordan was a beast of burden among the stallions.

Frazier spent the intervening three days in the tank as a human lab specimen. He took so many whirlpools the room began to spin, endured massages until there were tread marks on his skin, absorbed enzymes—*enzymes*—poured from little brown bottles with *x*'s and *o*'s on the labels, gobbled handfuls of vitamins and other pills, strapped weights across his ankles, stretched his body this way and that, studied charts and graphs and scientific analyses to determine whether he was physically able in body and mind. And when it was all over, when the last specialists had been consulted, when they'd finished examining the records, scratching their heads, and pulling at their beards, the verdict on whether or not he could play was unanimous. All the experts concurred: "Hey, your guess is as good as mine."

It was that exact. The Knicks' physician, Dr. Kazuo Yana-gisawa—known around the Garden as Dr. Yana—issued a similarly scientific opinion. He said, "We have no way of knowing how he will respond or whether he will be available Friday." Which basically sent a message to the team, as well as to Knick fans, that their only hope was prayer. From courtside up to the cheap seats—*Down on your knees, sinners, and pray!* Ask the Lord for forgiveness, and remind Him to throw in a blessing or two for Brother Clyde.

Boston Garden was jammed for the Friday-night showdown. The House of Russell rocked to the rafters, where those damnable pennants—all eleven of them—hung like talismans to the God of Jump Shots. The Knicks eyed them warily. To a man, they believed they could beat these cocky mothers, but they also were feeling the Celtic curse. Their play-off hopes reeled from it. Especially now, in Game Six. After their hard work all season long, here they were again—the underdogs.

Well, what the hell. Nobody had said it'd be another Tea Party. Red Holzman had given them a lot of sound reasons why they should expect to win this grudge match. They were younger, quicker, smarter, heartier, craftier, sharper—all those virile superlatives meant to pump up the ol' jewels. And, for those who believed in natural selection: it was their time.

Still, those lousy pennants! And the specter of Frazier, doing his best not to limp. Clyde was a trouper, even if he did wobble like a poor imitation of Gran'pappy Amos. He took warm-up, with a lot of crippling pain, but it only gave the rest of the guys an even achier outlook. More than twenty years later, Willis Reed can remember that moment with fine-tuned clarity. "I took one look at Clyde," he said, "and knew we were out of it." The guy was clearly damaged goods, and he wasn't able to play more than thirty minutes in all.

Nor could the other Knicks pull the trigger. They came close, though. With five minutes to go and the team trailing, 94–85, Mike Riordan exploded for six points and helped New York draw to within four. Then suddenly they were even. *Tied!* But Sam Jones hit a foul shot with one second left to close the book at 106–105 and give the greedy Celtics their twelfth Eastern title in thirteen years.

C'est la vie! Still, it hurt like hell as the Knicks limped off that famous parquet floor. They'd come *that* close! And the fans . . . those Boston peckerheads knew how to stick it to 'em, raising fists, hurling beers, pointing fingers, screaming, "We're number one! We're number one!" Two wonderguts in kelly green shirts danced along the first-mezzanine railing taunting the New York players with a banner that proclaimed: "Celtics Rule Once Again."

Okay, fair enough, the Knicks thought as they headed into the locker room. They'd taken it fair and square. And there was some satisfaction to be mined from the loss. Next year— Next year, Bill Russell would be gone, Sam Jones would be gone. Next year, Cazzie would be back, and Phil Jackson, too, they hoped. Next year, in 1969, the Knicks would be a year older and even more of a force to be reckoned with.

Walt Frazier looked up from the trainer's table, where wads of tape were being cut from his gimpy leg. "Next year is ours," he said.

Everyone cracked a smile because, deep down in their hearts, they knew he was right.

3 | WILD HORSES

September 1969

NEXT YEAR . . . next year . . . There was always a "next year" in the back of every basketball player's mind. That was the year everything was going to shine. Next year would be The One, you'd see. Come October, there'd be a clean slate, several new guys who were loaded with promise. The fans would have forgotten (and forgiven) the last garbage year, investing the same eight or maybe nine bums with all the hopes and expectations they'd had dashed only twenty weeks earlier. For once, the team would start fast, play together, and hang tough throughout all eighty-two regular-season games. Never mind the plight of the 143 men on the other teams, for whom the same season would be an extraordinarily grim stretch. The dream of a lifetime would finally take shape . . .

Next year.

Ballplayers, to a man, live for that clean slate. It is everyone's annual chance for redemption, when he can be rescued from the purgatory of being just another bum on a losing team. Another rim shot—*clank!* Otherwise, why go on? Why show up year after year, resigned to the fact that, once again, you are going to be part of a hapless eight-month sideshow? No, out of necessity the pro basketball player is a perennially optimistic fellow. He believes profoundly in spiritual rebirth. Especially in the summer, when he is away from the game, from the constant grind, and has time to reflect on the evolution of his situation. Summer is a time of renewal, of recommitment, and of conviction. It is during those off months that a basketball player reevaluates his team's past performance and comes to the vital conclusion that, with a little work, a few breaks here and there, he is with a strong contender. In his mind, the team—and, most of all, his position on it—seems pretty solid. They are comers. Sure, they had a rotten season last year, but all the components are in place. Next season they will be older, wiser, more experienced, more comfortable with each other, more certain of what to expect, at home on the court and able to function as a pinpoint tactical unit.

By June, most players, including the Knicks, will have dismissed their last season as a write-off, a transition year. A cursory examination of the stats shows that they lost a lot of close ones, and—*hey!*—if the score had gone the other way a few times, who knows how things might have ended up? It's how the chips fell. Their talent is still largely hidden, just blossoming. On paper, they are an emerging powerhouse, and come September they'll be breathing fire. In fact, next year . . . *next year* . . .

That's the way it usually goes. For those few intervening months, each ballplayer picks up the intoxicating whiff of success and sucks it deep into his lungs. Once again, he experiences the rush of those glory years in college, when he functioned at the topmost level of competition that prefigured his ascendancy to the pros—when he was the top horse, the stud. In college, he always got the ball, the girl, and the glory (although not always in that order). And his world there, however one-dimensional, was a perfect place.

But in the pros his bloodline is of more common stock. A college star—even one rated the best player in the nation—may enter the NBA and find himself rudely underequipped. What seemed like a natural transition, from college to the pros, becomes instead a sudden, violent jolt as the former BMOC discovers he is either too small, too slow, too weak, or too impetuous to excel in the pros. Many of those players lack the smarts and the savvy it takes to play a finesse game. Even more of them, as it turns out, are too self-centered; they can't execute the type of unheroic, workmanlike plays it takes to win without serving as the team's center of attention. As a matter of course, the majority of college standouts suffer their first losing experiences as rookies in the pros. And often they spend their entire pro careers on the bench, languishing ignobly as scrubs. Oh, a guy can suffer a swift free-fall from grace in the pros. Which is why the promise of "next year" offers such a seductive measure of redress.

Certainly, in the months that predated the 1969–70 season, many basketball players reenacted the ritual metamorphosis with considerable optimism. Opportunity was knocking—loudly—for the cast of also-rans that had waited like understudies outside the Celtics' first-place stronghold. Without Bill Russell and Sam Jones, Boston's greedy domination was up for grabs, and some wishful players, like the Lakers' Keith Erickson, called their teammates during the summer to reinforce the idea that "this year it could be ours."

That battle cry was echoed in almost every NBA city where winning, up to now, had been a trifle scarce. In frost-rimed Milwaukee, for example, pennant fever ran wild as rookies Lew Alcindor and Bobby Dandridge quickly came to terms with the Bucks' management and vowed to "win it all." They were joining a team whose previous—first—year in the league had rivaled the comic three-ring affair with which it shared space in musty Milwaukee Arena for a few weeks each spring, but Lew and Bobby D. put a new spin on the goal. In Los Angeles, the cohesion of triple-threat Wilt Chamberlain, Elgin Baylor, and Jerry West threatened to burn a few barracks. So it was, too, in Phoenix, Baltimore, Detroit, Atlanta, Cincinnati, Philadelphia, Chicago, San Diego, Seattle, San Francisco, and, yes, even nervy Boston, where diehard Celtics fans maintained that the prospects for their team were still hunky-dory as the 1969–70 season loomed near.

The Knicks, however, kept their mouths shut, their hopes in check. Too many of the guys knew that soaring expectations often proved lethal. Sure, they were in a position to win it all, everybody knew that, but it seemed like tempting fate to shoot their mouths off about it. The Knicks believed that if a basketball player had any whiff of class, he didn't run around claiming his team was unbeatable. He didn't boast they were champs before a single game had been played. It'd only serve to piss off the opposition, give them incentive to play harder against you. What's more, it was bush league. The Knicks didn't operate that way. Showboats—the kind of reckless, vulgar players who called press conferences and blabbered their predictions—weren't tolerated in New York then, by either the Knicks players or the team management. A guy like that, if one had managed to slip by the scouts, might find his ass traded to an expansion team or cut without a word.

No, the Knicks were a class act. Edward S. "Ned" Irish, who had founded the team and ran it like a tightfisted bank president, accepted no loose chatter from anyone connected with his Knickerbockers. Irish was a demanding, formal man, tough as nails, who looked as if he'd stepped out of a George Raft film. He always wore an expensive suit and tie—even to the games— and expected to be addressed as "Mr. Irish." As a rule, he didn't interfere with the team, but if you shot off your mouth, you'd hear about it personally.

If the players feared Mr. Irish, they also respected him. He was the Sol Hurok of arena sports. He had practically invented the practice of promoting college and pro basketball games and had a knack for putting butts in the seats every night of the week. The National Invitational Tournament was also his brainchild. Mr. Irish had seen that if you sponsored a competition by inviting, say, eight or ten college teams to play in your arena—why, your scouts got an early look at potential draft prospects. That's why he invited only the best schools to play at the Garden in the NIT. It gave him a chance to look at the kids and cozy up to them. Maybe soften them up a bit. For twenty-three years, Mr. Irish had systematically developed the Knickerbockers franchise, pumping money into a myriad of lousy teams, until by 1967 they seemed dramatically improved enough to be contenders. The Knicks finished in third place in 1967 and 1968, behind the 76ers and the Celtics. They made some noise, got a taste of life in the win column. Now, with the advent of the 1969 season, New York finally appeared poised for a shot at the title.

By that time, too, Mr. Irish was expecting to see a better rate of return. He wanted more action for his money. Sure, sure, the Knicks were improved, but so was the U.S. ground offensive in Vietnam, and that war was going down the crapper. It was time, he insisted, for the Knicks to shit or get off the pot. He'd certainly done his share. They'd wanted half a mil for Bill Bradley and his fancy Oxford pedigree—okay, so it was a preposterous sum for a ballplayer, but he'd given them the money. He came across. A world-class arena? No problem. He'd built a new Madison Square Garden last year, put in big dressing rooms, separate showers, carpet on the floors, pulled out all the stops. Then they'd wanted this guy DeBusschere, *had* to have him, even if it meant giving Detroit two players for one. He'd told them, "Go make the deal."

But now they had to win. He'd seen and heard enough about the Celtics for one lifetime. Red Auerbach was always in his face with the Fightin' Irish, the Irish this, the Irish that. When you came right down to it, *he* was The Irish, and it was about time the Knicks made that point on the court. Otherwise, for many of them, there'd be no . . .

. . . *next year.*

Training camps are usually held on secluded or suburban college campuses that seem especially bleak to a veteran accustomed to the luxurious splash of major American cities. But to a young rookie only three months removed from his last final exam there is the unmistakable scent of the womb. He is used to stumbling, squint eyed from sleep, out of a painted cinderblock dorm and cutting across a quad with its rows of quaint, ivy-covered buildings, one stacked right behind the next, so that from any window, from any classroom, from any seat, an adoring student can follow his progress with the smug certainty that this giant, graceful, glandular high jumper is preparing to don the school colors and defend its honor on the court. And that gives him godlike status.

No doubt a rook feels snug and secure as he arrives on campus for that first day of training camp. The word alone—*camp*—paints a vision of convivial bliss, a peaceful kingdom cut off from the real world and its grotesqueries, where men of unusual talent and dexterity come together in true brotherhood to play the game of basketball—and nothing else but basketball. To return to campus in a Knicks jersey and play in that old ratty gym with the retractable bleachers and run the court so effortlessly, so fleet of foot, weaving through the stampede like a wild stallion who has complete command of the range—who *has* the range—only this time there are nine other stallions out there with you, each one of whom has the range, too, and senses your every move beforehand, that cool, itinerant radar that guides you across all lines, through screens and zones and unnavigable picks, galloping toward the spot where you will finally read the ball with your fingertips, you read it idiosyncratically the way a blind man reads

Braille, measuring the distance between you and the goal so that when you leap into the air, rearing up like a stallion to bury two points in a jowl of soft netting—well, as any rook knows, there is no feeling like it in the world. He knows the others feel it, too, and will recognize in him great, uncontainable potential. However raw, however unrefined, he is another stallion waiting to be broken in—a *wild* stallion, perhaps. Nevertheless, they'll spot his talent, because here on campus a rook can be *himself.* This is the one place where he still has the edge, it is still his turf. Even the size of the gym, with its cozy corridors and chicken-wire doors, the gleaming trophy case ("Girls Field Hockey Champs, 1956–7–8") and the blinking scoreboard, these touches fit him like a glove. Here is a place just like the one where, only months before, he felt appreciated, beloved . . . godlike.

But, oh, how the mighty do fall! As any draft choice discovers—probably on that very first day, probably upon his arrival on campus—in training camp a rook has the standing of a gnat. Worse than a gnat—a flea on a gnat's ass. Rookies are invisible, as far as the vets are concerned. Like ghosts. With any luck, they'll disappear once camp breaks and the team gets on with the business of basketball. Yet somehow a rook has to make his presence felt. He has to prove himself worthy enough to make the team, without stepping on anyone's toes, and still remain as cool under fire as a veteran. That is a task that proves more daunting than anyone might have imagined.

Johnny Warren, an alumnus of St. John's University and the Long Island Expressway, felt the bubble of pressure expand as the Knicks prepared to see if he was pro material. As usual, training camp opened a month or so before the season started—on September 14, 1969, at the State University of New York campus in Farmingdale, Long Island—and Warren, the Knicks' first-round draft pick and their most eligible young stallion, drove the twenty-mile stretch along the L.I.E. in a virtual fluster.

Warren knew this piece of road almost by heart. His girl-friend, Rhia, lived in Westbury, the next town over from Farm-ingdale, and he'd made the drive from his home in nearby Far Rockaway too many times for it to shake his concentration. It was a direct route, practically a straight line. In a manner of speaking, the car could get there all by itself. Yet, as he steered his '67 lemon-drop yellow Chevelle past the familiar exits—past Jamaica, Manhasset, Great Neck, Roslyn, Mineola, Hempstead, even past lovely Westbury—Warren spun along in a kind of logey dreamlike state. He wasn't even sure where he was. Nothing looked familiar. He might as well have been in Cincinnati.

In fact, to stretch a metaphor, Warren was being driven by guilt. Sure, he was the Knicks' first-round draft pick and had negotiated a decent contract with the team. It was in all the papers. It was reality, man! But all along his feelings had been highly ambivalent, and, if the truth be told, he knew he didn't deserve his good fortune. It was like one of those cosmic mistakes on "The Twilight Zone," where some ordinary Joe minding his own business took an unexpected turn and found himself thrust back in time to Ford's Theatre a few minutes before Lincoln's assassination.

Warren had been flabbergasted to learn that he'd gone in the first round. And to the Knicks—a contender, and his hometown team, no less. He, Johnny Warren, an unflashy swing man who played both ends of the floor but with no superhuman distinction. He was of average height, listed at six-foot-five but actually no more than six-three, give or take a half inch. He'd graduated from St. John's, which had had only a so-so year compared to other basketball schools. And the draft that year had been out-standing, a really first-rate crop of guys. Most of them were magicians compared to him, they did tricks with the ball that made your eyes bug out. Johnny, on the other hand, played a more disciplined game. He was more of a team kind of guy.

Johnny Warren had lived nearly his whole life in Far Rockaway. Back then, it was a wispy little beach town that straddled the border of Queens and the rest of Long Island, and it beat the hell out of Sparta, Georgia, where he'd spent the first few years of his life. Sparta, like most of Hancock County, was dirt-poor. His father, John Warren, Sr., a mostly uneducated man, drove a truck there—stuck in the boonies when his brothers and sisters abandoned the rural life for the land of milk and honey, New York. It shot a hole in the senior Warren's pride, really got in his craw. So he went to night school, got his high-school diploma, and by 1955 had managed to save enough money to move his wife and son, Johnny, north—where Johnny saw his first *white* basketball players. There they were on the playgrounds— black and white kids *at the same time*—bumping into each other, pushing off, actually *touching!* It was something to see.

Basketball, he discovered, was a fixture of every city boy's life. It was a street game up here, and in the summer everybody played ball at one of the public playgrounds that served as the social centers of the neighborhoods. Johnny's turf was the Hammas Projects Park, on Eighty-fourth Street in the Rockaways. He ate his way up the food chain there, devouring kids his own age before taking on older players. One by one he gobbled up the local boys, most of whom were just donkeys with a ball. Oh, they had a touch—they could dribble behind the back, shake-and-bake, or dunk the ball like a doughnut. But it wasn't *the* touch. It wasn't artistry. You could tell, none of the Hammas Projects gang was headed for immortality. There weren't any legends in the making on that court, and in New York, if you weren't a legend you might as well hang up the ol' sweat socks and get on with your life.

Everywhere Johnny played, he heard about the *legends*. There were Connie Hawkins and Roger Brown, from Boys High in Brooklyn; they were the Kangaroo Kids, so named because they could jump right out of the gym. In Jamaica, you had Corky Bell, Moose Tillman, and Tom Hoya to contend with. Larry Robertson, from John Adams High, stormed the courts in Queens. And, of course, Lew Alcindor, who was Power Memorial's all-universe, straddled Brooklyn, Manhattan, and the Bronx. These were the pantheon of playground gods, the immortals. But in the Rockaways, legendry was at an all-time low. Oh, there was Ray Harvey, who went to Westinghouse and had a slim bag of tricks to choose from. But Ray was a minnow in the talent pool. He was what you'd call a standout, but no legend. No, the real ballplayers were in Brooklyn and the City. Everybody knew that. That's where reputations were made.

As a result, Johnny Warren didn't have a whole lot to prove. In Far Rockaway he was a minilegend, a local playground virtuoso with a fleet first step, like Mercury, and that suited him just fine. That was all the reputation he required. He had no compulsion to be a legend, like some of the local high jumpers. He wasn't driven by the desire for celebrity. If anything, he preferred the low-key atmosphere of his own little fiefdom, where he could dominate play without having to face each new Threat of the Day out to prove he was the meanest, the fastest, or the baddest motherfucker with a basketball. That's one reason Johnny didn't visit other courts in Queens or Brooklyn, like most of the up-and-coming players, bolstering their reputations in pickup games. No, he was content to reign over Hammas Projects Park and the After School Night Center, where he played ball two or three nights a week.

High-school ball did little to improve his reputation, either. The Far Rockaway High team was a disaster on the court. They were just pitiful. At six-two, Johnny was the tallest player on the squad, and as a result he filled the hole at center. That suited him fine, except the other schools he faced off against had big men who were actually *big*—six-nine or six-ten. Some of the neighboring schools, like Franklyn K. Lane, had *forwards* who were six-seven. So in the two years that Johnny led his varsity team, Far Rockaway won only four games—all of them against the same school.

But along the way something extraordinary happened. Johnny Warren learned how to play defense, and that made him a valuable commodity on the court. As a rule, defensive specialists were high on most coaches' Endangered-Species List. They were hotly in demand, almost to the same degree that coaches covet a smart seven-footer or a pure shooter. Primarily, that is because every player on every team loves to score and at one time or another undergoes hot shooting streaks. After all, the game of basketball requires that you put the ball in the hole; if you can't shoot, you can't put points on the board, and you don't win. So the guys who inevitably wind up on high school, college, and pro squads are all fairly decent shooters. All of them. They have that part of the game down cold. And that is why most coaches subscribe to the theory that defense is the key to winning games. Shut down the opposition, and your offense will take care of itself. On the other hand, the harder an offense has to work for its baskets, the less it will score. Unfortunately, few players bother to learn that side of the game. They virtually ignore it because, as any fool knows, defense may win games, but scoring creates *legends*. Put the ball in the hole time after time after time, and you're practically guaranteed to hear the crowd roar. That triggers a motivation that overrides all logical tactical considerations: I must become a legend.

Well, Johnny Warren entertained no such illusions. He was a versatile swing man—he could play small forward or big guard—but by no means did he approach legendary status. He wasn't even a superstar, probably never would be. Nevertheless, he had mastered the Art of D—largely as the result of an incident early in his high-school playing career. It was in a game against

Jamaica High, he had shot out the lights, knocking down nineteen or twenty points. That night he heard the crowd roar. *Joh-nee, Joh-nee, Joh . . .* The guy he was guarding also had nineteen or twenty points and heard *his* crowd roar, too, but—never mind that noise. The point was, Johnny glowed, he was positively resplendent. The next day, in school, he didn't walk so much as glide down the halls. Friends were clapping him on the back. "Yo, Johnny—nice game, m'man!" All the girls checked him out, flashed those shy, toothy grins. Which is about when he ran into the swimming coach, a man named Metzger. Johnny slowed down a step, preening for the expected compliment, when Metzger growled, "Warren, that was the worst *defense* I ever saw. You let that guy go baseline on you three times in a row. Don't you know *anything* about the game?"

What the fu . . . ?

"You can't just score out there and think you did your job. Next time, try some defense. Man, they walked all over you!"

There, in the course of a few sentences, went the glow, the glide, the m'mans, and the shy, toothy grins. Pulled right out from under him. Mr. Metzger, that chlorinated guppie! What does he think he knows about . . .

Defense. The word kept noodling around in Johnny Warren's head. *De-fense . . . de-fense . . .* He knew the meaning of the word, but it had never really taken hold before. Slowly, he started making some critical connections. Let's see now, defense meant you could get the ball and kick it out for a fast break. That made sense. It meant your opposite number wouldn't have neutralized your nineteen or twenty points with an equal display, in which case Rockaway might have won that game. So, hmmmm.

In a rush of determination, Johnny Warren spent the rest of the year learning to play defense, and the reward it brought was a scholarship to St. John's. He became a Redman, in the tradition of Kevin Loughery, Hank Kluse, Allen Seiden, and the great Tony Jackson. He might have gone to one of the Ivy League schools, he might have played at Columbia or Harvard, but, if truth be told, he was a mama's boy, an only child, and he didn't want to stray far from the womb. St. John's was just a short drive from his home. The new coach there, Lew Carnesecca, stressed a steady diet of defense. And anyway, his idol was a Redman—Sonny Dove.

How many times had Johnny watched Sonny Dove burn those country boys on the court? Sonny was a flamethrower, one of the quickest forwards ever. He had an unbelievable first step, could drive to the hoop, had an amazing jump shot. My oh my! Johnny could close his eyes and almost beam himself back to a game he'd seen on TV in 1964 in which Sonny and the McIntyre boys took on Cazzie Russell and Michigan in the Holiday Festival at the Garden. It was a night to remember, and probably the single factor that most influenced Johnny's decision to enter St. John's University in 1965.

The biggest hesitation he had was that St. John's was a fairly white place. In fact, Johnny assumed that the whole basketball team was white—Sonny, the McIntyre boys, Bobby Dewer. So it was a comfort to find, when he got there, that Sonny, his idol, was actually black. He was light-skinned and had showed up white on the Warrens' black-and-white TV set, but the man was a brother, he was *ru-uuuuude!* And he preached the Art of D.

Better than that, Sonny took Johnny under his wing at St. John's. Johnny became his main man, his protégé, which had its benefits both on and off the court. "Sonny was crazy!" Johnny says, with righteous affection, and that's probably as big an understatement as he's ever going to make. Crazy—hah! Sonny was wired hotter than a Chevy Camaro with a 427 hemi under the hood, the biggest, baddest superspade ever to streak the streets of St. Alban's in Queens. And Sonny had *style*. The man could dress. He knew the heaviest places to hang in the City, the prettiest chicks, the grooviest music, and when Sonny had a dollar in his pocket, *you* had a dollar in your pocket, too.

Sonny also taught Johnny some tricks with a basketball. Specifically, Sonny showed you how to force your man to go one way on the court while you pirouetted right around him toward the hoop for an easy two. And Sonny had a monster of a head fake that would practically hypnotize the opposition. It had the effect of a stun-gun, and Johnny incorporated it into his own private arsenal. By Johnny's sophomore year, Sonny was insisting to Carnesecca that it might be wise to start his young protégé. "If John doesn't start, something's wrong!" He'd say it to anyone who would listen, even the equipment manager. Traditionally, sophomores didn't start on the varsity at St. John's, but Carnesecca, a flexible coach and one who could spot emerging talent, agreed to give it a try.

Johnny learned Coach Carnesecca's system in a flash. It taught him a whole new approach to basketball and opened up his game. In high school, he had been used to playing a one-on-one run-and-gun offense; maybe the team occasionally ran a few plays, but that was as organized as the game got. Carnesecca actually used strategy. Think about it! The man believed you could treat the on-court chaos, the perpetual motion and spontaneous combustion, as a series of predictable events. What incredible chutzpah! The man also had a defensive plan in his head that would counter any offensive tactic. And tons of options. He was forever mapping out plays. Even if you were out having pizza, Coach C. would be scribbling strategy on a napkin or the lid of the box. (Someone once said it was a good thing pizza crust didn't take ballpoint ink, otherwise you'd lose a slice or two over dinner with Coach.) And his password was *teamwork*.

Teamwork, to Carnesecca, was the holy writ. It was a fluid and seamless interaction—like the five fingers of one hand, as a local basketball writer once described it. Sure, a big man can dominate play some of the time; if you've got a seven-footer, he can make up in height for what the rest of the team lacks in stature, but he can't possibly win games alone. Not even The

Great Alcindor. In high school, Lew could personally steamroll over the low-rent competition, but in college the situation demanded four other guys who blended well with him. That was the only way UCLA won its championships when he played there—as a *team*. So Johnny Warren became one of the fingers of the St. John's hand—but the biggest and best finger remained Sonny Dove.

As Sonny's *pro-té-gé*, Johnny was on the receiving end of several perks, the most expedient of which was protection. Sonny was St. John's enforcer and Johnny Warren's personal patron saint. Everybody knew it—if you messed with Johnny, you messed with Sonny—but the point was accentuated in one game against Fordham. Johnny was guarding Kenny Parker, a bulky ball handler who later played football with the New York Giants. On a routine drive to the basket, Parker whacked Johnny in the chest and knocked him out cold. Things like that occasionally happened, and Parker knew the score. *You pay proper respect!* He immediately ran toward Sonny to apologize—stuck his hand out to shake Sonny's—and was greeted by a fearsome sneer: "Get the fuck outta here!" Another time, against Kansas, Johnny was guarding a big bruiser who kept elbowing him, jabbing him in the ribs, the shoulders, the breadbasket; he even got him in the balls. Youch!—that kind of shit hurt. So during a time-out, Sonny shuffled over and whispered in the culprit's ear, "You messin' with m'man. Next time, I mess with your face." When play resumed, the guy forgot he had elbows.

Oh, life was grand at St. John's. Johnny played team basketball, won big games. Mom was right down the road waiting for him. He slept in his boyhood bed every night. Saw Rhia after school. And then he went and got drafted *by the Knicks!* Talk about luck. Only . . . now he was in bed with Willis Reed, Bill Bradley, Cazzie Russell, Dave DeBusschere, Dick Barnett. With *Clyde!* Sweet Jesus, he was scared.

Maybe this was the wrong move. Maybe he should be playing

with another team, one that was less awesome, less burdened
with talent. After all, Johnny could have signed with the other
league, and saved himself a lot of anxiety. Roy Boe, who owned
the New York Nets in the ABA, had wined and dined him at
the Yale Club (where Johnny had avoided the dinner knives,
which he thought looked like sabers). Boe, he knew, had almost
snagged Lew Alcindor away from the NBA's clutches. In fact,
the Nets' interest alone had forced the Milwaukee Bucks to ante
up a whopping $1.4 million for Lew, much more than he would
have pocketed without the ABA breathing down their necks. Rick
Barry had signed with an ABA team, the Oakland Oaks. So had
Billy Cunningham and Zelmo Beaty. And Spencer Haywood, the
University of Detroit star, had jumped to the ABA's Denver
franchise—while still a sophomore. Haywood was jailbait. To
hear the NBA tell it, the ABA was nothing but a bunch of cradle
robbers. But Boe waved off such nonsense. He reminded Johnny
that, with the Knicks, Frazier, Barnett, and Riordan would start
ahead of him; with the Nets, he'd be assured of instant playing
time. And get this: next year, Lou Carnesecca would take over
as coach.

Boe made it sound mighty tempting. Sitting on the bench
behind three stars—not playing—seemed like such a daunting
prospect. Johnny had never been a bench warmer before. Never.
But the ABA, which was only two years old, was a grab bag of
NBA rejects. Well, okay, there were a lot of old-timers, guys on
their way down who could extend their playing life with an ABA
team, and Connie Hawkins, Doug Moe, and Tony Jackson had
signed on despite the shadow cast over them by the 1961 point-
shaving scandals, which had caused the NBA to ban them (they
were later reinstated). But only a few college rooks had bypassed
the NBA draft for an ABA club. It was a shaky proposition. The
league didn't even have a TV contract. And that red-white-and-
blue ball was . . . *embarrassing!* No, he couldn't do it.

Anyway, he'd been a New Yorker all his adult life, and every

city boy followed the Knicks. Johnny could recall with undis-
guised satisfaction the moment he'd heard about the team's picking him. He was in Hawaii, to play in the Aloha Classic, while
the draft was under way. In fact, he'd almost forgotten it was
under way. In those days, the draft wasn't televised, much less
an event of public record. It was conducted in private, in a suite
at the Plaza Hotel in New York, where the various general managers and coaches sat around a table holding and trading players,
like a game of five-card stud. They could barely see each other
through the fog of cigar smoke. And their rules of commerce
were different from today's lottery system. Back then, teams had
territorial rights to any player from a college within a fifty-mile
radius. That meant they had the exclusive right to draft a local
guy in the first round—or they could pass, in which case another
team could snap him up. The most famous territorial case, of
course, involved Bill Bradley, whose Princeton campus was said
to be *one mile* closer to Philadelphia than to New York (because
some genius figured it was okay to take the measurement from
the tip of Staten Island). Unfortunately, there was no Philadelphia team during Bradley's early college days, and when the
Syracuse Nationals petitioned the NBA to move and become the
Philadelphia 76ers, the Knicks held up approval of the move until
Philly agreed that Princeton was actually closer to New York.

Anyway, that rule made Johnny Warren, once he entered the
draft, potentially a territorial claim of the Knicks. They could
draft him, without any competition, on the first round. *Riiiiiiight!*
Johnny felt he was a pretty good prospect, but a first-round pick?
Not a prayer.

The day of the draft, he'd been hanging around the Honolulu
Hilton catching some rays and woofing with the other players.
Most of the guys who played in the Aloha Classic were destined
to go high, he figured, at least in the first or second round. He
glanced around at his illustrious teammates: Ed Sudek out of
Holy Cross, Villanova's Johnny Jones, Bobby Dandridge from

Norfolk State, Tulsa's Bobby "Bingo" Smith, Michigan's Dennis Stewart, JoJo White from Kansas, Drake's Willie McCarter— the *crème de la crème de la court.* He'd be lucky to be picked at all.

As the session got under way, they retired to someone's room to take the edge off. Then things heated up. Word started coming down the hallway very fast. Alcindor went first, no surprise there. The big guy was going to legitimize the Bucks franchise and make a lot of bread. Someone barged in a few minutes later to report that Neil Walk, a six-ten center from Florida, was grabbed next, by the Phoenix Suns. That meant the teams were going for size; big men usually dominated the first round. Bobby Smith went to San Diego, Lucius Allen to Seattle, and then the Knicks, choosing fifth, went for Johnny Warren. They . . . *whaaaat?* Johnny sat there, stunned by the news. He went *fifth! In the first round!* Someone must have gotten his wires crossed. But, no. "Yo, congratulations, John." "Way to go, m'man!"

Johnny stumbled out into the hall. Air, he needed some air. Had to think. *Fifth!* Now, how had *that* happened? His attorney, Arthur Morse, who also represented Sonny Dove, had predicted a good draft for Johnny, but he'd never said a thing about *fifth!* Or about his being a first-round choice at all. Well, what do you know about that?

Fifth! Not everyone had such good luck. Johnny passed Bobby Dandridge, who was visibly apoplectic in the hallway. Bobby D. was spitting bullets. The explosive six-six guard had been left hanging when the first round ended, and his cyclonic wrath was spinning wildly down the hall. Unapologetically, Bobby D. was comparing himself aloud to guys who had gone before him, until someone grabbed him and told him to be cool.

To Johnny, however, all that mattered now was the Knicks' continuing fortunes. He checked back toward the end of the afternoon and found they had also drafted Bill Bunning from North Carolina, Temple's Eddie Mast, a few guys he'd never heard of, and even Dwight Durante, a guard from Catawba in North Carolina, who listed himself at a puny five-foot-eight but was more like five-five or less. Johnny wondered what they wanted from this midget, but, hey, they must have seen something in his game that was spectacular. Anyway, Durante wasn't the most embarrassing draft choice of the afternoon. The San Francisco Warriors tried to draft a girl—that's right, a *girl*—in the eleventh round, but the NBA commissioner, Walter Kennedy, refused to permit it.

Now, as he pulled off the Long Island Expressway and into the Pickwick Motel, the Knicks' official residence during camp, Johnny Warren knew there was no guarantee he'd make the team. There were eleven veterans returning this year, all of whom had no-cut contracts. Even worse, three guards had earned playing time ahead of him—Barnett, Frazier, and Mike Riordan—not to mention Bradley or Cazzie Russell, either of whom could switch comfortably to the backcourt whenever necessary. The last thing the Knicks needed was another guard. Furthermore, they'd invited a few others to try out for the team as well—guys who could raise a bit of dust, like Milt Williams, the Lincoln University guard, who had looked impressive in camp the year before. Williams could pose some trouble for him. Sure, Johnny had a guaranteed contract, but that meant nothing in the long run. The Knicks hadn't invested a lot in him, there was no bonus money, so they could pay him off and say aloha without losing too much face. All of which meant he was going to have to fight hard for a job. He'd have to work his tail off, impress the front office as well as the coach.

Johnny hung around the Pickwick the first day, watching TV and relaxing. The Pickwick was an agreeable nondescript suburban motel. It had comfortable if sparsely decorated rooms, the essence of eau de Lysol hung in the air, and a cigarette burn mottled the hideous shag carpeting. Johnny had no problem with the accommodations other than being away from Mom and Dad.

On the second day, however, reality kicked in. When he arrived at a meeting called by the coach, Red Holzman, in a conference room on the motel's ground floor, the supporting cast made his eyes pop. Seated around the room were Cazzie Russell, Dick Barnett, Bill Bradley, Dave DeBusschere, Walt Frazier— the Heroes of the Revolution. His head started to spin. Nate "the Snake" Bowman, Donnie May, Mike Riordan, Bill Hosket, Dave "the Rave" Stallworth. Then the door opened and in walked . . . *Willis Reed.* It was as if God Himself had chosen to materialize at the Pickwick. Reed cut an incredible figure, dressed as he was in a tank top that stretched across his hulking chest like so much cheesecloth.

Dick Barnett lifted a sleepy eye at Reed and muttered, "Man, what you been doin' all summer—wrestlin' alligators?"

Johnny was speechless. For him, Reed was up there among the immortals. He was indestructible. In fact, the first pro basketball game Johnny Warren had ever seen in the flesh had featured a physical performance by Reed that was legendary for its list of casualties. It was the opening game of the 1966 season at Madison Square Garden, and the Knicks were entertaining the mighty L.A. Lakers. Reed, who was still masquerading as a forward then, was matched up against the tenacious Rudy LaRusso, a take-no-prisoners type of battler under the boards. All night, Reed and LaRusso went at it as Johnny gaped in open-mouthed admiration from his seat in the nosebleed section of the bleachers. He had never seen such a display of pure *muscle.* Those mastodons threw the kitchen sink at each other, trying to outmaneuver their man for position. It was *fierce!* As the night wore on, as frustration set in, one thing led to another, and inevitably LaRusso threw a punch. Bad move, Rudy. Reed, who had radarlike peripheral vision, saw it coming out of the corner of his eye and ducked. That should have been the end of it; however, the next thing Reed knew, Darrall Imhoff, the Lakers' wiry center, had sneaked up behind him and grabbed him from behind. *Boom!* Imhoff went down for the count. When Willis turned around, LaRusso was squaring off to punch him again. "Where are the officials?" Reed wondered. "Hell, if they aren't gonna take care of it, *I'm* gonna take care of it." And so—*boom!* LaRusso went down next to Imhoff. That should have done the trick, too, but then Reed saw John Block, a rookie no less, get up off the Lakers' bench and rush toward him with windmilling fists. Was this kid out of his mind? Reed wasn't taking any chances. *Boom!* Block was stretched out on the floor with a broken nose. After Block came Mel Counts (*boom!*) and Henry Finkel (*boom boom!*). Methodically, Reed put down each Laker they threw at him.

What a ferocious night that had been! Willis Reed was an animal. But here in camp, Johnny thought, he looked user friendly. He had a wide, bashful smile, a gentle timbre in his voice. The other guys gave him good-natured shit, and Willis actually took it. He seemed to enjoy their woofing. "Hey, man, don't your momma know how to *dress* you?" That kind of remark got shaken off with a smile instead of a fist.

You could tell from the outset that the other guys genuinely loved Willis Reed. They respected him. He was the Cap, the team leader, the one who worked the DMZ between players and management to each side's general satisfaction. If you had a business problem, Willis was the man to go to. If you created problems, Willis came to you. In fact, Willis had arrived in camp aware of a situation that required his immediate attention. Throughout the summer, he'd read a number of articles about players who were voicing disenchantment over their salaries. That didn't sit well with Willis. First of all, what a man got paid seemed to him like a private matter; it was crass and un-Knicklike to air those figures in the press. Why did the fans need to know the numbers written on your paycheck? Also, it distracted guys from the business at hand, which was basketball.

"I just want to talk to you as a group for a minute," he said

after the high jinks calmed down. "To my knowledge, every man
here has a contract. Right?" He scanned the room while they all
bobbed their heads up and down. "Okay. Now, I don't know
what your numbers are, and I don't really care. But as far as I'm
concerned, this is the last time I want to hear the words 'contract'
or 'money' discussed the whole year. You decided on a wage—
now work for that wage. From here on in, we're going to play
ball."

You could feel the chill that blew into the room. Some of the
vets weren't particularly thrilled with their contracts. In fact,
over the last couple of years the word "renegotiation" had become
a fixture in the pro sportsman's everyday vocabulary. You didn't
like your contract? Not to worry, just let management know
you're dissatisfied, that you might not be able to concentrate if
your pride is wounded. The tactic was a subtle if effective form
of blackmail that had somewhat loosened basketball's financial
stranglehold over the players, and while it wasn't the most hon-
orable way to gain a raise, it often was the only way. Now, as
far as the Knicks were concerned, Willis had closed the door on
it. The Cap had spoken.

The balance of the meeting covered procedures. Red Holzman, the inscrutable, fox-faced coach, set out his objectives for
the rest of camp. There wasn't going to be a lot of time for
fundamentals, he said. Union rules allotted only twenty-eight
days to the preseason, and ten of those were already committed
to exhibition games; what with travel and time off, he was left
with a measly eight days to diagram the plays and shape a twelve-
man team. So there was a lot of work to get done. Practices, as
always, were scheduled twice daily—one at eleven in the morning, the second at five, breaking in time for dinner. They con-
sisted basically of drills and scrimmages. Red felt the team needed
work on helping-out and double-teaming, so those aspects of the
game would receive special emphasis in every phase of training.

Johnny Warren felt that he was already in pretty decent

playing shape. He'd worked out throughout the summer, hitting the key playgrounds around Brooklyn and Queens. He was healthy and down to proper weight. Getting used to Holzman's style of ball shouldn't be tough, he thought, inasmuch as it resembled the type of game that Lou Carnesecca taught. What concerned him more were the other players in the room who were competing for the sole position open on the squad. *His* position, the way Johnny figured it. Hell, the vultures were already circling overhead. Guys were showing up out of nowhere. They worked out all summer, took two weeks off from their jobs, came here, and tried to make the team. Besides Milt Williams, who arrived in fantastic shape, there was Kenny Morehead, a capable if undistinguished college hopeful, angling for a look-see with the Knicks. Johnny didn't figure on his being any problem. The same went for Jackie Wilson (no, not *that* Jackie Wilson), another guard, who had a good body but an unsightly hitch in his jump shot. No one was putting any money on a guy like Wilson. An even longer shot, Johnny thought, was Roland Rook. Johnny knew Roland from high school. Rook—what a perfect name—came out of the city school system, from Newton High, and had developed a feisty inside game, but that was all he had; there was no way he'd make the Knicks. Finally, there was Eddie Mast, a center from Temple, who could run and was in great shape, and who had come to camp visibly eager to be part of the Knicks. But, like Rook, the odds were stacked heavily against him.

You'd have to have something special to move one of those veterans off the squad, some secret weapon maybe. Better yet— a gun. The way Johnny read it, there might have been more opportunity a year earlier. Back then, Cazzie Russell's ankle was still a question mark. Phil Jackson, the stalky forward phenom, had languished in pain. He'd suffered a leg injury and then, after partial recuperation, had herniated two disks in his vertebrae and wound up in traction. This year, the lineup seemed to be sewn up. A man like Mast—he might have filled the hole left by Phil Jackson, who intended to sit out the first couple of months of the 1969–70 season. In May, however, Dave Stallworth had announced he was coming back.

Stallworth, who was drafted behind Bill Bradley in 1965, had spent the last two years away from pro basketball, in Wichita, Kansas, working with troubled kids and coaching the Builders, a better-than-amateur local team. But that was about it as far as physical exertion went. That heart-attack business had really burnt the man's wick. For a while there Stallworth tiptoed around thinking the next breath he took was going to be his last. It scared the shit out of him. Doctors had filled his head with plenty to worry about, too, predicting an onslaught of dizzy spells, nausea, anemia, exhaustion, feebleness, even blackouts. Any sudden shock, they said, might bring on the big one. Well, you know, you hear something like that, and the last thing you think about is running up and down a court for forty-eight minutes a night. You forget about banging bodies, hauling down rebounds, and chasing loose balls. Instead, you go home, put the leather slippers on, and think about mastering a sport like fly-fishing. You might even needlepoint a bit, like Rosie Grier. Stalls might have lived like that the rest of his life if he'd ever developed a single one of those symptoms the doctors had talked about. But the guy didn't so much as suffer from bad breath. He felt great.

To everyone around him, though, he was practically a dead man, a time bomb just waiting to explode. He'd lace up at the local gym, and nobody would play with him. Nobody. They'd banish him to solitary shoot-arounds at one end of the court while they played five on five at the other end. During games, he'd run up and down the sidelines with his team as if to say, "See—I can keep up, I'm still standing," but even that didn't convince them. So he took up golf.

Before long, however, Stallworth had benched one of his

Builders and put himself into a game. Now, there was a risky proposition. To anyone with a brain, it seemed like Dave was playing a round of Russian roulette and firing from all chambers, but somehow he survived. He survived the next game, too, and the next, and the next—until word filtered back to Eddie Donovan in New York that his wounded bird was airborne. As anyone could have predicted, Eddie went ballistic. Sure, he'd kept Stalls on the Knicks payroll, but as a scout, purely charity work. No one in the front office expected any playing time for their money, nor did they want it. If Dave dropped dead, and word leaked out that the Knicks had been playing him . . . well, the parties responsible for that would be shipped en masse to a franchise in Kuala Lumpur. You could count on that. So Eddie called Dave and laid into him for taking foolish chances; he forbid him to play at all, but it was too late. Stalls had gotten a taste for the ball again. Better still, he'd broken a decent sweat, and, lo and behold, all ventricles were ticking away like a Timex.

Eventually, the doctors had to reevaluate their diagnosis. Maybe the guy hadn't had a heart attack after all. Hmmmmmm. The specialists went to work wiring him up to their state-of-the-art gizmos, monitoring his chest for signs of telltale symptoms and . . . well, nothing doing. They took him out to Wichita State Stadium and put him through a road test on the track. Stationed a doctor every seventy-five yards or so, just in case. Hooked up the ol' monitor again and—still nothing that resembled anything more than exertion. So they scratched their heads and made some notes and compared results and came to the conclusion that Dave Stallworth probably could stand a little basketball. Okay, okay— he could turn the burners up to *high* and, yes, even return to the Knicks. The Knicks! Well, if that didn't beat all. And finally the Knicks, who wanted no trouble as far as Stallworth was concerned, got on board, too. Ned Irish told Donovan to make room for Stalls, who still happened to be under contract.

"Jesus Christ," Eddie thought. "If this guy drops dead, his

family's going to own the team. No, no, forget about the team—they'll own the NBA."

But Red Holzman told Eddie to relax. He'd work Dave in gradually, put him on the floor for five minutes at a clip and see how he took it. Let him work himself back into shape so he could play behind DeBusschere. With luck, the team would wind up with that flashy speed demon it had originally drafted. At worst, Stalls would shore up the bench. Still, everyone—especially the other players, the mortals—was holding his breath.

Nate Bowman, who had played college ball with Stallworth, took one look at Dave the Rave as he rolled into camp and asked, "Hey, man, you got tape over your heart, or what?"

That broke the ice. The other guys cracked up. And Stalls, with that six-six smile of his showing off a gaudy diamond-studded tooth—he just about split a gut laughing. He just about . . . had a heart attack. Oh, baby, Johnny Warren thought, this was going to be some year.

The Knicks camp, as it turned out, was a ball-buster. Those two-a-day practices—someone should have tipped off the Human Rights Watch. They were that brutal. From Johnny Warren's perspective, the experience was humiliating. In college, he'd been called the Iceman for his impenetrable presence on the court; once he hit Farmingdale, he might more aptly have been called Mountain Dew. The Iceman melted from all that heat on the floor.

Right off, he arrived at the gym a few minutes early hoping to get a head start. When he walked out on the floor, however, there was Bill Bradley taking his laps. Well, if that didn't beat all. Warren watched Bradley barrel that fireplug frame of his around the gym, eyes fastened forward, impervious—dead—obviously somewhere else. The guy was a machine, Warren thought. (If only he had known the half of it!) The automation zoomed even sharper into focus when Bradley started shooting the basketball. *Swish! Swish! Swish! Swish!* Johnny had thought he could put the ball in the hole fairly well, but Bradley *never* missed. Then Cazzie Russell wandered out and began firing line drives. *Swish! Swish! Swish! Swish!*

Warren shook his head in amazement. "Damn—I can't compete with these guys."

They were unbelievable, to a fault. Rhythm, motion, takeoff, timing, velocity, orbit, accuracy, *target*—with precision like that, either Bradley or Russell could have landed a missile on Jupiter. *Swish! Swish! Swish! Swish!* The sound was beginning to get to Warren. What he wouldn't give to hear a sweet metallic *clank* off the rim. Just one sign that these guys were human, but no such luck. Stallworth followed the flow on the floor, another crackerjack shooter, and his jumper hit the mark like automatic rifle fire. *Swish! Swish! Swish! Swish!*

Warren remained unobtrusively on the sidelines, frozen in place by the ferocity of this clinic. These pros had cut him right down to size. Maybe he still had Roy Boe's number in his wallet. Maybe— Wait! Who was that mastodon loping onto the floor, that towering black Gumby, bent at an awkward angle like undercooked pasta? Warren recognized Nate Bowman, the gangly six-foot-ten backup center, who handled the ball like he was eating a slice of pizza. Bowman went up for one of his famous elbows-out jump shots and—*clank!* Now, that was music to Johnny's ears. *Clank!* And again: *Clank! Clank!* And—*airball!* Well, what do you know about that?

Warren felt a warm smile spread across his lips. "Oh, thank you, Lord!" he muttered, before hustling onto the floor.

Holzman's camp resembled a concentrated dose of army basic training. He ran it in the very image of Sergeant Rock, too. There was little tolerance for slackers or for men trying to work themselves into shape. Holzman expected his players to be down to playing weight or be damned. It was that simple.

Even Dave DeBusschere, who routinely reported carrying

twenty extra pounds of baggage on his belly, had gotten the message. DeBusschere had never attended a Knicks training camp before. He'd begun the previous season with Detroit, where practices had usually been loosey-goosey. You scrimmaged, took your shots, ran a few laps if you felt like it and—hey, whaddya know!—after a week or two you started feeling like you could go thirty or forty minutes a night. That suited DeBusschere fine, since he spent his summers guzzling enough beer to sink a battleship. In Detroit, he had usually weighed into camp at a bloated 255 pounds; the girth and the brew slowed him to a crawl. To make matters worse, some practices had featured dribbling and shooting contests, after which the losers had to buy the winners *more* beer. They had a high ol' time in Detroit priming those Pistons. But DeBusschere pulled into the Pickwick Motel at a sleek 238 pounds. The rest of the team gaped like they were in a Ford showroom checking out the newly unveiled T-birds. This '69-model DeBusschere, flaunting a more streamlined chassis, came without the standard spare tire. And the hood ornament was lean and fine boned. DeBusschere had switched from beer to scotch, and the difference was clearly visible in his face. And on the floor.

Holzman wasted no time with amenities. He immediately put the men through a set of torturous drills to gauge the extent of their conditioning. The worst one was a little punishment called "pick up." Red stationed himself at one end of the gym, with the team's scout and former coach, Dick McGuire, at the other end, each accompanied by eight players behind their respective baselines. McGuire started one man running the length of the court. When he was halfway to the basket, Holzman rolled a ball along the floor, and the player, half-crazed about tripping over the damn projectile, had to bend down and scoop it up then drive in for a lay-up. If you think it sounds easy, just try it sometime. There is a second of real discombobulation at the exact instant the man touches the ball and tries to dribble with it, a momentary interval when the friction from the ball's rubber surface and the rhythm of the attempted dribble produce completely incompatible motions, and that's when the fun begins. It made the men feel spastic. First of all, these were very big guys, and bending down alone took considerable effort. And there was always an over-enthusiastic rookie who toppled over on his head when he tried it. But sooner or later they all got the hang of it.

Another drill required a player to backpedal the length of the floor while trying to intercept or deflect a floor-length pass. This was murder on the guys with fragile knees. Bill Hosket, the second-year backup center out of Ohio State, was still recovering from intensive surgery, and, while he'd abandoned his knee brace and the wads of tape that had been holding him together, he wasn't up to snuff. That drill did a number on his knees. Cazzie Russell, too, was coming back from a broken ankle, and, though he said it didn't affect him, it was obvious he was being careful about where he put his foot down. So, naturally, this drill sent a ripple of anxiety across the floor.

The men *hated* these exercises. You could see it in their faces. All of them—except for Bill Bradley, who thrived on them—grumbled on their way to the gym, then lingered on the sidelines until the last possible moment before they were motioned into place by McGuire. But the drills were instrumental to Holzman's overall scheme. They stressed playing *defense*, which he believed was the only way you could win in the NBA. Most basketball coaches subscribed to the theory that the high scorer wins. But Holzman, like other great tacticians, was convinced that the low scorer loses. He demanded that his players control the ball and handle it well, keeping it away from the opposition. "See the ball" and "Hit the open man" were his twin mantras. Knowing where the ball was gave a team great floor presence. But his underlying message was *deny, deny, deny.* If you denied the other team the ball, it remained in your possession.

Holzman had developed this strategy as a player with the Rochester Royals from 1946 to 1953. This was before the twenty-four-second clock, and the Royals were notorious for holding the ball. If you were down ten going into the last quarter, it was impossible to beat them. They'd simply . . . hold the ball. They could stall for an entire quarter if necessary. And the fans knew it, too. If Rochester had a lead with six minutes or so to go, the stands would start to empty. Les Harrison, the Royals' coach, would look down the bench, send Holzman and teammate Fran Curran into the game, and they'd just hold the ball until the final buzzer. It was infuriating to play against them.

The twenty-four-second clock did away with that style of play. But Holzman worked out adaptations in the strategy by applying various defenses that made the outcome virtually the same. "Our defense makes our offense," he insisted, and it made good sense. *See the ball. Hit the open man. Deny, deny, deny.* The object, as he saw it, was to stay between your man and the ball, blocking off the passing routes. Move the play toward the sidelines, into the corners. That way, things got crowded; you forced the man with the ball into making mistakes. Presto—instant turnovers. It was a novel, aggressive approach to basketball, far superior to the standard run-and-gun offense that dominated the game, and more effective, too.

It took brains to play this kind of game, and fortunately Holzman had players with the capacity for understanding the ins and outs of defensive basketball. Bradley, Riordan, Reed, Frazier, Warren, and DeBusschere all came from programs structured around the defense. Hosket had learned it from his Olympics coach, the legendary Henry Iba of Oklahoma State. Russell had mastered it after his arrival in New York, as had Stallworth. One thing it required was a certain amount of unselfishness— a willingness to give the ball up to a teammate in better position, rather than to take the shot. This ran counter to the whole motif of playground ball, in which the goal was to make yourself shine, to put up numbers—to become a legend. For a lot of the players, team play was a tough adjustment to make.

Eddie Mast, the rookie from Temple, got blindsided by the concept. As camp opened, he was trying desperately to make a big bang, was burning up the boards, scrambling and diving for rebounds. He ran the floor well, looked for the ball, and took a shot every chance he got. For a few days, his personal stats read like the fourth-quarter figures for IBM. Willis Reed seemed almost docile by comparison. Reed worked slowly, methodically, concentrating on reacquainting himself with team play, and often that meant taking himself out of the action. By the third day, Eddie thought he had Willis all figured out. "He's not the player I thought he was," Mast remarked to a teammate over lunch. "I can *play* with this guy."

The next day, the Knicks were working on a half-court offense when Ned Irish walked unannounced into practice. It was his first visit to camp, and he cut an impressive figure coming in, as he did, with his coat draped over his arm so that his suspenders and tie made an appropriate noise. Everyone knew the boss had arrived, and when play resumed they turned up the steam a few degrees. Especially Willis Reed. He put on a clinic, making eight-footers, ten-footers, power hooks, the whole dog-and-pony show. He just drilled poor Eddie Mast, scoring sixteen straight points against the bewildered kid.

Afterward Bill Hosket reminded the rookie, "You were right—Willis wasn't anything like you thought he would be."

But it was too late for a lesson in etiquette. By the end of the week, Eddie was history, looking for work in Allentown, Pennsylvania, with a jerkwater Eastern League team.

The rookies in camp were virtually ostracized by the other players. They were the lepers. The Knicks had no tradition of hazing, the way veterans on some other clubs did; there was only a little good-natured woofing. But a rookie was there to snatch a veteran's job; at the same time, a rookie star could strengthen the team and help it win a championship. So the rookies were watched but not helped; they were spoken to but not with. DeBusschere, for one, refused even to learn their names. "Why become attached to somebody," he reasoned, "when you have a good idea he's not going to be around?"

Toward the end of the first week, Kenny Morehead became the next rookie casualty, but the way he bought it was one for the books. Morehead, a smooth young stud, mistakenly tried to pick up a woman at the Pickwick in whom Cazzie Russell had more than a passing interest. Now, hoops were one thing, but when it came to women the veterans rolled out the heavy artillery to protect their God-given interests. Russell wasn't about to be outclassed by a rook, either on the court or off. So he simply flaunted the facts—he reminded the woman that he was a Knick today, tomorrow, and next month, while Morehead would likely be history in a day or two. Survival of the fittest, baby! Naturally, she ended up on Cazzie's arm, while Morehead, the poor dog, was cut the next day.

No, the rookies got no respect from the vets—or from each other, for that matter. It was war out there on the battlefield, and the remaining rookies knew they were all vying for the one job still open. That meant they avoided each other almost all the time. On the court, they rarely passed the ball among themselves, not wanting to give their competition an edge in the stats. They either looked for the vets or held onto the ball until they got open. Away from practice, they kept their game faces intact. Two rooks could pass each other in the motel lobby, and you'd never know they were acquainted. They borrowed the philosophy of the veterans: "If I don't acknowledge you, you don't exist."

Among those left standing, only Johnny Warren and Milt Williams had a good shot at becoming the Knicks' twelfth man, a guard. Roland Rook was a terminal case. Jackie Wilson was on the critical list—he'd be gone any day now. But for Warren and Williams it aimed to be a struggle down to the wire.

As it happened, both guards were having a mediocre camp. They were making amateur mistakes—throwing passes out of bounds, bouncing the ball off feet, missing the open man, blowing lay-ups. Typical rookie stuff. Neither player was as bad as he looked, but that didn't help much. Williams, especially, needed to perform. He'd been in camp the year before and had impressed the coaches, but couldn't, for the life of him, crack the solid twelve-man squad. This year he felt he had a better shot. He'd worked out all summer with a YMCA team in Chicago, mastering a Knicks style of play action; specifically, he'd learned how to penetrate defenses so he could dish off to the open man. As a result, the ABA had put a few interesting offers on the table, but when Eddie Donovan promised him another tryout with the Knicks, Williams turned the offers down.

Still, this camp seemed even more daunting for Williams than last year's. In scrimmages, Holzman matched him up against Walt Frazier, and the contrast between the two guards was painful. Frazier was a dynamo with the ball, he was a human Veg-o-Matic, and he chopped, diced, sliced, and ground Williams into so much sausage during their shimmies around the floor. Milt completely misread Frazier's body language; Clyde would give him a hip and make Williams believe he was going left, when he'd actually go right. He'd use the sturdy head fake to flatten Milt's poise. There were little mistakes like that. And Milt's puny height of six-foot-two prevented him from seeing screens as they developed. That left him eating Clyde's dust. The handwriting was on the wall, and if anyone couldn't read it there, the outcome was plainly visible on Williams's face. He looked like a doomed man.

Johnny Warren was having his own problems, but he was too exhausted to worry about them. The two-a-day practices wore him to the bone. Despite being in tip-top physical shape, he wasn't prepared for the nonstop defensive and offensive play that the pro game demanded of him. And the twenty-four-second clock presented an entirely new set of problems. Once, after he made a lay-up, Johnny hesitated around the basket, thinking, "Hot damn! I just scored two points!"—until Holzman called his number. "The game's not over, Warren. *The game's not over!*" the coach shouted. "Get back on defense." In fact, the other nine players were already at the other end of the court engaged in combat. That was an embarrassing moment. There'd been a lot of them lately—stupid little mistakes that had cost him some residual pride. But the exhaustion was the worst part. After practice, Johnny would drag his weary ass back to his room and hit the sack. He did the same during lunch and dinner breaks. He was almost too tired to eat—and too flustered by the veterans' ability to shake off fatigue. Cazzie Russell actually played a round of golf between the morning and late-afternoon sessions and once even invited him along, but Johnny craved only his bed. He was tired, and edgy about being away from home, so the easiest thing for him to do was to sleep.

As if both rookies weren't haunted enough by their mistakes, there was also the specter of Phil Jackson shooting baskets in a secluded corner of the gym. Jackson had turned up in camp despite being unable to play. To his teammates, he looked pretty good for a man who had gone through the wringer—literally. He'd been in back traction for a couple of months, and a series of injections meant to reduce tension around the disks had destroyed muscle tone in his legs, causing serious mobility problems. But even in the best of health, Jackson was an extraordinary sight. He was built like a condor—tall and bony, with a wingspan that put him in league with the 747s flying out of JFK. His shoulders were enormous walls of sinew, hence his nickname of "Coat Hangers." With his head cocked down, arms stretched from baseline to baseline, Jackson was a scary defensive presence on the court. He had a way of swooping down on a guard or forward, slapping a hand out, and stunning his prey into coughing up the ball. Phil was due to have his back brace removed on October 28—less than a month into the new season—and he'd told Holzman that if all went according to plan he should be able to return in December. That was great news for the team, but it meant someone would have to be cut then to make room for him—probably a rookie.

Warren and Williams continued to calculate and reassess their odds. The way they figured it, three men were vying for the reserve guard positions. Mike Riordan, who had seen only limited action last year, still had to win a job. Riordan, they concluded, was vulnerable. He was a scrappy little player with better-than-average defensive instincts, he had a lot of heart and was immensely popular with the fans, but he wasn't an everyday player. He couldn't be counted on to put points on the board. So, in effect, one of the rookies might be able to displace him. There were other factors, too. Dick Barnett, they reasoned, was getting too old to handle a steady backcourt position. At thirty-three, he was the oldest member of the Knickerbockers—surely he'd lost a step along the way, and there was speculation about whether he could even go forty minutes a night. As far as the younger guys were concerned, that made Barnett a target for early retirement. The guy could keel over at any minute! And there was talk of a trade before the season started involving Cazzie Russell—probably only locker room gossip. Still, rookies cling to all the straws when it comes to determining their fates.

The most serious lineup problem for the Knicks in 1969, however, wasn't picking the twelfth man off the bench. Those rookies could eat each other's children, for all anyone cared. No, the immediate question facing Red Holzman and Eddie Donovan was how to go about unsnarling the gridlock at the small-forward position. With Bill Bradley and Cazzie Russell vying for the job, the team was saddled with two supremely talented stallions who both needed to start. Saddled—well, that was an exaggeration. Most teams would have given their eyeteeth for a player of either Bradley's or Russell's caliber. They were equally premier players, bona fide *legends*. In any other city, either man might have been the franchise, too. But the Knicks, who were loaded with talent, found this wealth a growing liability.

The issue wasn't talent, of course—it was pride and jealousy. Each men felt the job belonged to him, and by rights it did. They were both first-string stars. But only one of them was going to start at the small-forward slot; the other—oh, it was too shameful even to contemplate—the other would watch the opening tip from the bench with the rest of the . . . scrubs. Yes, that's what they called them, The Scrubs—the same term applied to people who get down on their knees and wash floors for a living. During scrimmages (where they were referred to as the second team, to spare tender feelings), the scrubs provided bodies so that the starters could perfect their plays. They functioned as stand-ins. And during pregame introductions, when the starters bounded individually onto the floor to the accompaniment of thunderous applause, the scrubs hugged the bench in virtual obscurity. Was that any way to treat a true sports hero, a legend? The sixth man off the bench—the player who might well become the spark plug that ignited this team to a world championship—would have the status of a lowly mule, while his rival, as one of the elite starting five, a stallion, would belong not just to the emerging Knicks dynasty but to basketball history.

"The Bradley-Russell Thing," as Red Holzman called it, was a time bomb of the Knicks' own creation. They'd drafted Bradley as a guard in 1965 knowing there was a better-than-decent chance that he'd never suit up for the team, not even for a workout. They could have taken Rick Barry instead, hardly a consolation prize by any stretch of the imagination—at least he would have showed up for work. But Bradley . . . Eddie Donovan had licked his lips every time he thought of Bill Bradley in a Knicks uniform.

"The way he plays, it's all business," he told Dick McGuire, the team's coach at the time. So they went ahead and blew a first-round draft choice on the outside shot that one day Bradley might get the itch to play professional basketball and they'd have one righteous superstar.

Not that Bill Bradley didn't already possess a fair amount of lunar heat. By the time he graduated from Princeton, he was one of the hottest commodities the NBA had ever seen. He was smart, handsome, clean living, courteous, charitable, patriotic, God-fearing—he belonged to the Fellowship of Christian Athletes, for Chrissake!—and, most unusual of all, a *white* boy who could handle a basketball like no one else his color. At Princeton, where future presidents, Supreme Court justices, and Nobel Prize winners competed for status, Bradley the basketball player was the BMOC. Students packed Dillon Gym for Princeton's regular-season games, and if you think they came to see Tiger basketball you are seriously deluded. When Bradley played freshman ball, no one stuck around for the varsity games. No, Bill Bradley was the only attraction on a court populated by reasonably tall but only marginally talented eggheads. He was a Princeton living legend. John McPhee had already written a profile about him for *The New Yorker* that was then expanded into a book. He'd won a gold medal in the Olympic Games at Tokyo. As a result of this phenomenal combustion, he was scouted by every pro organization in the country. Then, during his senior year, just before Christmas break, Bradley was notified that he'd been elected a Rhodes scholar, and pro basketball was henceforth obliterated from his memory bank.

The Knicks organization didn't know from Rhodes scholars. Mr. Irish probably wondered why someone with Bradley's God-given talent for putting balls in a hoop would want to study something as dull as highways and . . . *macadam.* Everyone knew the guy operated in some other stratosphere, but this development came out of left field. After the draft, Mr. Irish told a clique of reporters waiting for him outside the Plaza Hotel, "Bradley may or may not play when he returns. But in any case, we had to make sure that if he plays, he plays for us. We couldn't keep our franchise if he decides to play in two years and some other team got him." Irish confirmed that he had tried to appeal to Bradley's financial instincts by offering him a three-year, $200,000 contract to forget about school. But Bradley was adamant: he was going to Oxford for two years, where he would be *in statu pupillari* at Worcester College, and after that—who knew? Probably a career in government service or banking or some other worthwhile Oxfordian pursuit. Maybe he'd become the governor of New Jersey—*har, har, har!* But as far as playing professional basketball? Not in this lifetime.

Without Bradley, the Knicks' backcourt remained an unsightly mess. Oh, they had their fairly competent ball handlers back there, workhorses like Dick Barnett, who could bring the ball up court without choking, but no one who could bludgeon the competition. No magician. So the next year, when the 1966 draft rolled around, the Knicks went shopping again for a talented guard to fill the hole.

That was the year those two outstanding guards were up for grabs—Dave Bing, out of Syracuse University, and Cazzie Russell, who'd starred for Michigan, both of them righteous men. It was also the year of the celebrated coin toss. The Knicks and the Detroit Pistons had both earned the right to the first overall pick by virtue of the fact that they'd stunk equally in 1965— they'd tied for most games lost. Detroit had attempted to claim Russell under the territorial rule (the special rule under which the Knicks got Bradley and Philadelphia got Wilt Chamberlain), but it had been repealed, and a special meeting of the owners denied a Pistons appeal by a vote of six to three. To kick off the draft, therefore, the honor of being the worst team in the NBA would be decided by a coin toss, with Dick McGuire calling it for the Knicks and Coach DeBusschere representing the Pistons.

Commissioner Walter Kennedy's office in New York was jammed for the ceremony, which took place on the afternoon of April 27, 1966. It was supposed to be a high ol' time, but you could see an edginess around the eyes of the principals. There was a lot riding on the coin toss—at best, a championship; at the very least, respectability. The money men were dead serious about the outcome. Mr. Irish turned up to protect his interests, and so did Fred Zollner, the Pistons' owner, and Ed Coil, his general manager. To mark the occasion, Kennedy produced a nifty 1907 twenty-dollar gold piece and rolled it around his soft fingers. Everyone *ooooh*ed and *aaaah*ed and chuckled up Kennedy, who mugged shamelessly for the cameras, but deep down all of them wished he'd cut the crap and get on with it.

The assumption had been that Bing, being from Syracuse, would go to the Knicks and Russell would remain in Michigan. It made good sense all around. The players knew the respective territories, and it served everyone's purpose to keep the fans happy; logic had it that local heroes sold tickets. But it had to be settled by the rules. Finally, after all the baloney was over, Kennedy flipped the nugget into the air.

"Call it, Detroit," he said.

Incongruously, DeBusschere—as we've seen—went for tails and hovered expectantly as the coin buried itself in Kennedy's carpet.

Kennedy grunted as he bent down to retrieve the coin. "It's heads," he said.

That put New York in the catbird seat. Considering that it was a foregone conclusion, Dick McGuire was unusually cagey about announcing the Knicks' choice. From Eddie Donovan, he had heard that the Pistons were hot for Bing, were salivating over the prospect of selecting him first. McGuire and Donovan had already made up their minds to take Cazzie Russell, but Dick stalled for time, trying to make Detroit think it was going to be Bing. That way he might swing a last-minute deal for some extra cash or the entire gate receipts on a few preseason games to change his mind. But the charade didn't work.

With Cazzie Russell, the Knicks had finally landed a big fish. He was a streak shooter, a guy who could come in and just explode, completely changing the tempo of a game. McGuire and Donovan had scouted him often over his college years, marveling at his ability to sizzle with the ball. One night, during a break in the action, Dick had said, "You know, Eddie, you could pay four guys a thousand dollars apiece not to give the ball to Cazzie and the first ball would go to him anyway, because he's always there."

Knick management was overjoyed at the selection of Russell, but there were always second-guessers in the stands. A few days after the draft, Red Holzman, the Knicks' head scout at the time, was eating in a Chinese restaurant near the Garden and was accosted by a cleaver-wielding waiter. "Clazy Knicks take Cazzie Lussell, don't take Bing!" That was so much chop suey.

The Knicks weren't the only ones who struck gold in that draft. Cazzie picked Ned Irish's pocket for an eye-popping $100,000 a year. Today that's considered walking-around money, but back then even Willis Reed, the star of the team, was making a measly $25,000 and was happy to get it. Cazzie was worth every penny, to be sure, but you can bet it caused his teammates a few sleepless nights.

Dick McGuire spent the next year reshaping Russell into a small forward. He was too slow against the wiry guards in the league, who skimmed the lanes like Corvettes. His first season produced only a paltry 11.3 points per game—hardly worth the investment—and for a while it looked like another Knicks misjudgment. In Detroit, Dave Bing was ringing up twenty points a night, which earned him Rookie of the Year honors. As it turned out, Cazzie became more productive at forward, and he flourished there—until the news broke that Bill Bradley had undergone a change of heart.

Bradley, back from England, signed his contract with the Knicks in 1967 and, thanks in no small part to Cazzie Russell, snared an unheard-of $125,000 a year, earning him the moniker of "Dollar Bill." Why, when Cazzie heard that, he must have had a stroke. He and Bradley were archrivals from their college days, when they'd gone head to head in the '65 Holiday Festival. Although Michigan won that game, Bradley outscored Russell and was voted MVP. That one still stuck in Russell's craw. Then all of a sudden Bradley showed up in a Knicks uniform, trailing a press entourage worthy of a papal visit, not to mention a hundred and twenty-five simoleons—well, it made a guy want to explode.

To make matters worse, the next year, when Cazzie broke his ankle, who do you think took his job? That's right! Red Holzman, who had become the Knicks' coach, chose to go with Bradley at small forward even after Cazzie returned to the lineup. You could see the flames rise in Russell's eyes. Sitting on the bench—in *Siberia*—he seethed with envy. He sulked and fumed, fretted and chafed, did everything but stick pins in a voodoo doll. There was some mighty high anxiety coming off that bench.

That's why Cazzie came to training camp in 1969 expecting things to be settled once and for all. Naturally he wanted to start. Why, he had earned it. All you had to do was look at the stats. He was a one-man scoring machine. Bradley? He was nothing when he came back from Oxford, except maybe smarter. And fatter—he'd gained weight sitting on his can and studying that highbrow stuff. A resounding disappointment. He was too slow, he'd lost his scoring touch, he seemed distracted. Who knows, maybe all that money was wearing him down. But while Cazzie was recuperating Bradley had found his range as a small forward. The team immediately benefited; you could almost hear the *click* of someone hitting on the right combination. And the Knicks had started winning. And winning. And . . .

Maybe the Knicks would move Russell, the rookies thought,

ship him elsewhere for the sake of team harmony. It wasn't likely, but it was possible. Otherwise, it was out of their hands. A rook had to shine in training camp—he had to practically jump through the hoops—and hope he had impressed the coach enough to earn himself that last lousy uniform.

4 | A FINAL
TUNE-UP

October 1969

DURING TRAINING CAMP, you can practice until you turn blue, but the only way to assess the team's progress is in exhibition games. It's when you get to see what you really have. The preseason scrimmages serve to weed out the slackers and show which guys measure up to the challenge ahead.

Unlike today, there was nothing glamorous about those exhibition games. They weren't played at wonderful-sounding places like the Garden, the Forum, the Mecca, or the Spectrum. Not when the arena owners could rent those joints for ten grand a night to the circus or the Ice Capades. Most arena owners were the same tightwads who owned the basketball teams, so that'd be like charging themselves ten grand. Hell, they weren't *that* stupid. Instead, they loaded the ballplayers into buses and shipped 'em out to the boonies, where it cost only a couple hundred bucks to rent a rinkydink gym. That's right, they sold the team—their prized stallions—to a local promoter for the night, hawked tickets like door prizes, and ran the thing like a fly-by-night carnival.

Of course, the players hated it. Shipped around the country like some itinerant cattle drive, performing in front of rowdy, shit-faced crowds, stowed in roadside motels—it was humiliating. The black players were especially disgruntled. "This is *booolshit!*" they complained, recasting a popular locker-room pejorative. Sure, it was one step up from slavery and offered only marginally better conditions.

The Knicks' first stop in 1969 was in Salem, Virginia—plantation country—where they took on the pesky Baltimore Bullets. Even though the game was meaningless, it shaped up as a grudge match, inasmuch as the Bullets, who'd had the best regular-season record in the league last year, were still recovering from the shellacking the Knicks had given them in the play-offs. Also, the Knicks wanted an early look at Earl Monroe.

Monroe, who went by the *nom de guérre* "Earl the Pearl," was a frisky little guard from West Philly whose intrepid acrobatics kept pace with the Flying Wallendas. He held a Ph.D. in schoolyard moves, which is where he had mastered the game. On defense, he was always in your face—near your nose, by your ear, in your hair, over your eyes, up your ass—while quietly picking your pocket. You could be dribbling neatly downcourt when suddenly a blur would streak by, and next thing you knew the ball was somewhere else. And when Monroe had the ball in his control—forget about it. He was the premier quick-change artist, strutting out a bag of spin moves, behind-the-back dribbles, jackknifes, loop-the-loops, the whole bag of doughnuts. Hell, he practically invented the shake-and-bake. And his game—it was strictly one-on-one. The disciplined Knicks scoffed at all the flash and trash, but they knew better than to ignore the talented Monroe. No, he had something working for him that intrigued the Knicks, and this preseason game gave them a new opportunity to scope out his game.

The exhibition was played at Salem's Civic Center, a euphemism for the city's humble little hall, but the floor was in good shape and the crowd was fired up. The Knicks knew right away that they could make short shrift of the Bullets. They knew it as soon as Earl Monroe waddled onto the court. The Pearl was a hefty bauble. He weighed in at 194, almost ten pounds over his ideal playing weight, and a pulled stomach muscle left him wheezing like a St. Bernard. Playing against Monroe, Walt Frazier usually dished off to an open man, but during the first quarter Clyde saw he had some freedom. "About three minutes after the game started, he was huffing and puffing," Frazier said. "I told him he needed some oxygen." Earl the Pearl . . . oxygen. That was a hot one! Clyde took advantage of the Pearl's girth and went on a solo shooting spree, going nine for eleven and handcuffing his flamboyant nemesis to the bench.

The rest of the Bullets were in customary form. Except for Wes Unseld, they were a team of individual overachievers—emphasis on *individual*. Unlike the Knicks', the Bullets' plays were drawn to create one-on-one situations. Earl Monroe, Gus Johnson, Jack Marin, Kevin Loughery—these were players who demanded the ball. They liked fat stats. The team joke was that their defense was so tough because four of the five Bullets were always able to rest on offense. It was a good joke, too—except during play-offs, when a well-rounded team could eat their lunch.

Wes Unseld was the exception. He was becoming one of the strongest centers in the league, a bulldozer, heavy machinery. Last year, his first, he'd gotten the MVP, edging out Willis Reed, and with more experience he'd be really dangerous. Before the game in Salem, word leaked out that Unseld had a bad ankle. That may have been so, but he bullied Reed out of the paint all night long. "[Unseld's ankle] didn't look bad to me," Willis said after the game, while nursing his sore muscles.

The Knicks beat the Bullets, 116–101, but it was worse than the score showed. Baltimore was out of shape and looked it. "We're in play-off shape," Kevin Loughery insisted, flashing that shit-eating grin of his. Loughery, always good for a quote, was a scream. The Knicks, who were in tip-top condition, loved to laugh—last.

From Salem, the Knicks flew up to Grand Rapids, Michigan, to tiny Calvin College, where they took on the Detroit Pistons. At last, New York was ready to rock 'n' roll. The Pistons were a shambles. They had their fourth new coach in two seasons and a squad that looked like understudies for one of those *Bad News Bears* movies. Dave Bing, their one true artist, was out for several weeks, recovering from minor knee surgery—but his absence was overshadowed by the announcement that in a year he'd be leaving Detroit for an ABA team, the Washington Caps. In all probability, he wasn't going to bust his hump for a team he'd never see again.

The rest of the Pistons, with whom the Knicks were all too familiar, were a bunch of prima donnas. Walt Bellamy, Howie Komives—the Knicks had closed the book on those turkeys. Bellamy—his teammates called him "Bells" to his face but "Board Hands" behind his back—had reported to training camp severely out of shape. Not that it made any difference. The book on Bells was that he'd get up for games against the likes of Wilt Chamberlain, Willis Reed, or the now-retired Bill Russell, then let the weaker centers take him to the boards. Guys who shouldn't even be in the league handled Bells like he was putty. He was Mr. Inconsistent. Komives was just a pain in the ass—always grumbling, disruptive, fighting with the front office, a whiz at alienating his teammates. The sad thing was, he could play. But he played behind Bing and Detroit's leading head case, Jimmy Walker.

Mike Riordan, the Knicks' utility player, knew Jimmy Walker from college. Both had played for Providence—which is like saying Babe Ruth and Mike Gallego both played for the Yankees. But Providence basketball was a top-notch operation, and Jimmy Walker *was* Providence basketball. As Riordan put it, "Walker just dominated everybody he played with, he was always the best player on the floor. In college he was already a *man*. He was bigger and stronger than everybody, and his self-esteem was well developed. He was a fanatic for practicing. And he had no weaknesses: he could play defense, he could rebound and get a shot whenever he wanted, even with someone hanging all over him. At the time I thought, 'This guy is going to be great.' "

Well, things don't always turn out the way you expect they will—and Riordan must have had his suspicions. Walker's talent on the court was colossal, but he was also a colossal fuck-up. He regularly bagged classes—some he never showed up for—and he spent far too much time over on Benefit Street, in East Providence, hanging out with the brothers. At one point, Riordan went to the coaches, behind Jimmy's back, and pleaded with them to give their all-universe star some tutoring. Somehow Walker became the league's number-one draft choice in 1967— he managed to pry $300,000 out of the Pistons' owner, Fred Zollner—and he rolled into Detroit trailing a lot of fanfare. Literally rolled. He was twenty-five pounds overweight, practically a ton by NBA standards. Why, he was almost as large as . . . his attitude.

The word used frequently to describe Jimmy Walker was "uncooperative." You couldn't tell this guy anything. He wouldn't listen. Dave Bing remembers, "Jimmy came in with a class that had Monroe and Frazier—and Jimmy was without a doubt the most talented. He had uncanny ability. But he was his own man. He was indifferent about playing, always late for practices and games. He racked up more fines than anyone I'd ever played with. And Jimmy liked to run the street." The street—in Detroit, of all places. So much for concentration and discipline.

For two years Walker proved to be a Piston failure. That sparked plenty of trade rumors: Chicago desperately wanted him; even the Knicks expressed interest. But this year he had tuned up before coming into camp. He'd gotten his weight down to 203, and had a positive outlook. In a moment of madness, he told a sportswriter that he was sure Detroit would make the play-offs—they'd finish first or second. (Okay, so it was preseason, and he got carried away.) Dave Bing was sidelined, so Walker figured it was his team to run. And that'd be fine—for now. But everyone knew his enthusiasm was fragile at best.

The Knicks handled the Pistons, 100–90, in Grand Rapids, but it wasn't the walk they'd expected. Detroit actually stayed with them for most of the game. A lean and mean Jimmy Walker displayed a rare bit of discipline in the first half, looking for the open man or feeding one of the "trade twins"—Howie Komives and Walt Bellamy—under the hoop, and it worked for a while, too, the way the coaches always promised it would. But in the end a team like the Pistons just couldn't keep up with the Knicks. New York outmuscled them 31–13 in the final quarter, under an assault led by Walt Frazier, and the Knicks pulled away for the win.

After the game, the Pistons' new coach, Willem Henrik "Butch" Van Breda Kolff, jabbered like a magpie as the players congregated in the painted-brick corridor. The press moved toward him like vultures. He had smelled blood in the first half and wanted the win, badly. This was Detroit's first exhibition game—his first as their coach—and more than anything, Butch said, he wanted to instill a winning spirit in this team. Perennial hangdogs, the Pistons had suffered for so long, mopping up the cellar year after year. It seemed that as long as there had been professional basketball, there were pitiful Pistons. These fellas craved a taste of victory. Matter of fact, Butch said, he could have used a taste himself.

Once upon a time, Van Breda Kolff had been used to a winning team. It took the Knicks, with Bill Bradley on the floor, to remind him of it, too. Butch had coached Bradley at Princeton, and what a sweet run they'd had. The kid produced for him night after night, year after year. It was uncanny. All those brains never got in the way of his game. But the year after Bradley left, it

was no longer the same. Butch learned what he'd always suspected was true: without Bradley on the floor, all you had was
tall smart guys, and that wasn't enough to win collegiate basketball tournaments. The magic had worn off, and Butch, like
Bradley, decided to move on.

At that point, Van Breda Kolff could have written his name
on any scorecard in the country. He was at the top of every GM's
wish list. So what did he do? He did what any other coach in
heat would have done—signed on as the skipper of the Los Angeles Lakers. Sure, why not? They'd been on the verge of greatness for so long, what with Jerry West and Elgin Baylor leading
the charge. Jack Kent Cooke had bought the team and built the
Fabulous Forum in Inglewood; he spent a fortune marketing the
Lakers, put them in purple-and-gold uniforms, hired a P.R. staff,
attempted to catch some Hollywood heat. And who could argue
with the L.A. weather, right?

It sounded like a cushy deal. But the chemistry was wrong
from the start. The players resented Butch. He'd been a college
coach for so long that he'd forgotten the Lakers were grown men,
and he made the error of treating them like students. During
Lakers practices, his approach was more or less: "This is the way
we're going to do things." Now, in college, the kids would respond, "Sure thing, Coach, whatever you say," and they'd follow
his orders. But with Jerry West and Elgin Baylor on the squad,
you had to exercise a bit of judgment. You had to consider their
reputations—and their egos. To make matters worse, there were
bed checks. And Butch's mouth—he couldn't keep it shut. He
said what was on his mind—to anyone, at any time—even if
it meant alienating one of his boys. Fuck 'em if they couldn't
take it!

In other respects Butch ran things nice and loose. Practice
times were rearranged to suit the guys' golf schedules. And if he
encountered one of his players in a bar, Butch always bought.
And bought. And bought. Loose—like that.

He and the team managed to coexist his first year as coach, but in the off season Cooke pulled off a spectacular deal—he grabbed Wilt Chamberlain away from the Philadelphia 76ers. And he did it in typical style, not spending a single dollar to get Wilt. The Big Guy had insisted on a trade to a western team, so the Lakers shipped off Archie Clark, Jerry Chambers, and John Block, in a deal that paralleled the Dutch purchase of Manhattan for a handful of baubles. It seemed perfect from L.A.'s point of view—a dynasty, with Baylor, West, and Chamberlain at its core—until the Lakers realized that they had brought the Atomic Era to Los Angeles. Van Breda Kolff and Chamberlain were the key elements—uranium 235 and plutonium 239, respectively—in a chain reaction that eventually produced fission. Positively and negatively charged egos collided. All that collegiate crap Butch tossed at the players didn't wash with Wilt. The schedule of practices, the loosey-goosey stuff—it wasn't Wilt's thing. From day one, there was no love lost between the two men.

By midseason their feud was out in the open. After a game in Seattle, Butch and Wilt finally squared off in the locker room, like two mad dogs, and Baylor and Tommy Hawkins had struggled like crazy to pull them apart. Then, in the play-offs, Wilt took himself out of a game, for a breather, and Van Breda Kolff refused to put him back in. "We're doing well enough without you," he is supposed to have said. Well, that did it. Jack Kent Cooke would have to make a choice—Van Breda Kolff or Chamberlain, one of them would have to go. Butch obviously saw the handwriting on the wall. The morning of the sixth game of the finals with Boston—with the Lakers still in the thick of it—he met with Ed Coil, Detroit's GM, and negotiated a contract to coach the Pistons in 1969. Imagine that! A coach with a potential championship team, who was still under contract to the Lakers, negotiating a secret deal to coach the Pistons. The man had to be a fabulous poker player—or an idiot—to pull that one off.

Somehow Butch landed on his feet, but his mouth was still a problem. After the exhibition-game loss to the Knicks, he was trashing his players in print. Before the season even started! "It's somewhat the same [situation] as Los Angeles," he told a *New York Times* beat writer. "An awful lot of independent stuff while the others stand around and watch. We've got five or six players who want to work, who want to help each other. But most of the guys who are like that don't have the size." Butch said he hoped the remaining exhibition games went well so that other teams would be willing to talk trades.

Talk about confidence builders! The Pistons were hopping mad. Whatsa matter, doesn't Coach think we can read? Does he think he can slip that one past us? In the *New York Times*, for Chrissake?

Of course, the Knicks saw the story, too, and knew what to expect the next day, when they were scheduled to play the Pistons again, at Delta College in Saginaw. Detroit would have something to prove and they'd be fired up, looking to salvage their reputations on the court. Some observers wondered, however, whether it was the Knicks they wanted to silence—or their own coach.

Didn't matter. The way they played, Detroit could have beaten back the Red Army as it advanced on Czechoslovakia. They thrashed the Knicks, all of the Pistons performing like dervishes. It wasn't pretty out there at Delta. The Knicks were ahead, 113–104, with four minutes remaining, when Jimmy Walker went ballistic. He sparked a 14–2 Pistons spree and put Detroit up by two, with thirty-four seconds left. Frazier sank one to tie it, but that wasn't enough. McCoy McLemore, a boxy forward who had made a little noise in the league, hit a fifteen-footer from the foul line an instant before the buzzer sounded, to ice it at 124–122. Even Walt Bellamy, who managed to drag his flabby carcass around for twenty-five minutes, did his share, keeping Willis Reed bottled up under the basket most of the night.

Well, that threw ice water on the Knicks' momentum. After the game, there were the usual high jinks in their locker room, but it lacked a certain pitch, because deep down the fellas knew they'd lost one to . . . the Pistons! Oh, the indignity—it was too embarrassing for words.

"What fool let Walker run off thirty-three points?" asked Dick Barnett, skying an eyebrow at Frazier. "Hmmmmm?"

"I didn't see you break a sweat," Clyde said unemotionally.

"I don't sweat," said Barnett.

The other guys were grinning at the guards as the banter ping-ponged from mouth to mouth.

Johnny Warren was unusually quiet and self-absorbed through the postgame show. He was taking the opportunity to reflect on his performance that night, and what he saw didn't please him. He'd had another so-so game. Four meaningless points in twelve minutes, hardly the output expected from a first-round draft pick. Imagine someone like Derrick Coleman or Anfernee Hardaway scoring four points following a $2 million or $4 million signing bonus; they'd lose a substantial amount of *face*. Whereas Johnny Warren was losing sleep and worried about losing his *job*. Across the locker room, his rival, Milt Williams, wore the same hangdog look. Milt had put up goose eggs in the points column, but he'd played better, he'd looked good out there, hammering away on defense, playing the Knicks' type of game. Could Williams, a long shot, beat him out for the fourth guard spot? Anything could happen, Warren worried. Considering that he was superstitious, how was this for an omen? After their miserable first exhibition game, the Pistons had cut Sonny Dove. His idol! A neighborhood legend. Forget that Sonny was a fuckup—if a team could cut someone like him, what prospects did Johnny Warren have of making it in the league? There was a heap of anxiety emanating from Warren's lonely corner that night. You could be certain of that.

Like most of the Knicks, Warren knew there was a ton of

talent on the club. So what if they had lost to Detroit? You could feel things coming together on the floor, where it counted. They were playing as a team, looking for each other, sacrificing. The missing pieces that had doomed previous years were suddenly falling into place. Dave Stallworth was proving invaluable playing behind DeBusschere. Riordan was making things happen without the ball. Clyde looked superhuman. Willis had gotten tougher to contain. Bradley had regained his touch. Sure, the fans' expectations were high, but the team really was developing into a powerhouse.

As they left the arena, there was some hesitant talk about book contracts that were floating around on the periphery. In the twenty-three years since the Knicks had come into the league, no one had ever written a book about the team. Not a one. Now, suddenly, a beat writer who traveled with the Knicks was moonlighting for Simon & Schuster, and a columnist was negotiating a contract with Dodd, Mead. Marv Albert, the team's announcer—the *announcer*—had a deal. As did DeBusschere, Frazier, Bradley, and Reed. Even Red Holzman was mulling offers for his memoirs. Let it be said: the Knicks were molding into a pack of literary lions.

That's how confident the players were feeling about the coming year. Not only were they getting tighter; there was optimism about what *wouldn't* be there to unhinge them during the year. Of course, the retirement of Bill Russell was their Headache Reliever #1. That knocked mighty Boston out of the box, as far as most people were concerned. Headache Reliever #2: Zelmo Beaty hadn't shown up in Atlanta and was rumored to be signing with the Los Angeles Stars, an ABA team, which would take considerable tooth out of the Hawks' front line. Likewise, Rick Barry—a nasty migraine—was gone. He'd jumped to the Oakland Oaks in the ABA, who precipitately moved to Washington and renamed themselves the Caps. Barry was currently in a U.S. district court trying to have his contract invalidated, but he'd lost round one, and no one on the Warriors expected to see him back in San Francisco soon. And wait—it got better. As the Knicks were traveling to Trenton for their next exhibition game, against Philadelphia, they learned that Rudy LaRusso of the Warriors had retired. *Au revoir,* Rudy! LaRusso had always been a pain in the Knicks' collective butt—he always showed a lot of defensive muscle and was a steady scorer, averaging about twenty a game the last few years. But a nagging backache had put the fear of God in Rudy, and he'd decided to hang it up rather than risk serious injury. No, there wasn't a member of that gang who would be missed. Now, if only Wilt would retire. . . .

The Knicks disposed of the 76ers in overtime without exerting too much effort. It was another game in which they worked on executing fundamentals—moving the ball around the floor, getting everyone involved. All very businesslike. The most exciting moment came when Billy Cunningham, Philly's fearless forward, got ejected for spitting in the ref's eye. Billy C., of all people— a gentleman through and through. Go figure. To make matters worse for himself, Billy came up with one of those I-was-just-skimming-rocks-and-didn't-see-the-car-coming excuses that only gets you deeper into trouble. The way he told it, "[Willis] Reed got me in the Adam's apple with his arm. I was just clearing my throat." Uh-huh.

Everybody was geared up for the next game on the dwindling exhibition schedule. The Knicks were playing host to the Milwaukee Bucks, at the Garden, and they were expecting a distinguished guest for dinner. Lew Alcindor, the Bucks' million-dollar gamble, was making his professional New York debut, and there was a scent of high-octane fuel in the air. Alcindor was a local schoolboy star—he was already a *legend*—who was expected to transpose the balance of power in the NBA. At seven-foot-two, he was taller than most of the big men, and he had all the right moves. But Alcindor had another element in his arsenal of weapons, one that eluded many centers, and that was brains. With

brains, you could outplay any hotshot. Lew was a brilliant tactician. At UCLA, he had mastered all three of Coach John Wood-
en's golden rules—conditioning, fundamentals, and teamwork.
During a game, he was taught, every action had a purpose. As
a result, he could read the court, get a sense of the action, and
make the right move, whether it meant dishing off to a teammate
or skying the ball with that neat left-handed hook he'd perfected.
His ego was never a factor. And he was only a rookie.

Fifteen thousand fans turned out for the game—an exhibition
game, which in those days rarely drew more than a few hundred
diehards—but perhaps no one was more curious than Willis
Reed. At the tip, Reed took one look at Alcindor and quipped,
"They're growing 'em bigger," but it only masked his anxiety.

Reed studied Big Men the way Rockefeller studied the market. They were his client roster, and he was very attentive to
their needs. Each year Willis updated his profiles on the centers
he faced, concentrating on the rookies as the season unfolded.
The word on Alcindor was he needed bulk. Well, he looked
skinny enough, Reed thought, but he knew better than to be
fooled by Lew's appearance. He was going to have to get inside
this guy's head if he intended to stop the Bucks.

As the game proceeded, Willis was able to take a good
look at Alcindor and decided the kid had a lot of promise. He
made a number of good outlet passes, did his best to control the
boards, pulled down ten rebounds, and constantly forced the
Knicks' shooters. Of course Reed wasn't intimidated by the rook.
Nah—Alcindor was a matchstick next to Willis, and years later
the Knicks center lickerishly recalled, "I knew that night I'd
always be able to handle him. He was light and easy to move out
of the paint."

That night, at least, Willis had his way with Alcindor, scoring
a team-high nineteen points and sending Lew home early with
six fouls and a bruised ego, but he might have done something
about the Bucks' Flynn Robinson. While Willis was jitterbugging

with Alcindor, Robinson scored forty points—*forty*—in front of a Garden crowd that had expected more muscle from the Knicks' defensive unit. Robinson was magnificent down the stretch, hitting eleven points to muffle the Knicks' late charge and notch a game in the Bucks' win column.

In the locker room afterward, Barnett wondered aloud, "What fool let Robinson run off forty points? Hmmmmm?"

"Robinson was *your* man, fool," Frazier responded, swallowing a faint smile.

"No, he was your man, sucker."

"Fool."

"Sucker."

Their repartee served to take the edge off the loss, but it was unsettling nevertheless. The season opened in another week or so, and they had to be ready for teams like the Bucks. You couldn't shoot 37.5 percent, as they had that night, and expect to win games, much less a championship. They were going to have to tighten things up.

The Knicks traveled next to Utica, New York, an upstate blue-collar town, where they took on the Boston Celtics. It was an eagerly anticipated game, inasmuch as the Celtics without Russell and K.C. Jones were a tragedy in waiting. The papers were full of such talk. "Celtics Warn Rivals: We're Not Dead Yet," the *New York Post* proclaimed, but everyone knew they already belonged on the obituary page. The Dynasty was a team in decline. They were spiritless. A few Knicks actually felt sorry for poor Henry Finkel. Boston had acquired the seven-footer from San Diego to fill the hole at center, but, as everyone knew, they'd need a flock of Finkels to close that gap. He couldn't cut it as Russell's stand-in. Tommy "Ack-Ack" Heinsohn, Boston's new coach and a former player, insisted that Finkel would "surprise a lot of people," but Heinsohn silently put himself at the top of that list. As Heinsohn knew, Finkel was slow and awkward. He had a deadly shot, which is probably why Red Auerbach had signed him, but he was in constant foul trouble, due in no small part to his obvious lack of finesse. Willis couldn't wait to tango with Finkel. He loved to take big guys out of their game, and Finkel was one man he could shuffle off to Buffalo in time for next year's expansion draft.

As with Milwaukee, the Knicks got much more than they'd bargained for. Boston had instituted a running game to make up in speed for their lack of defense, and it caught New York completely off guard. With minutes to go, the Celtics were still in the game. Well, dammit to hell! Red Holzman roamed the sideline like a general, barking orders at his players. "See your man, dammit! *C'mon!* See him!" What should have been a romp for the Knicks turned into a squeaker, 108–105.

The season opener was drawing dangerously near, and they still weren't rolling over opponents with bone-crushing decisiveness. Holzman wanted to see corpses left in their wake, tall corpses. He wanted a few runaways. Nevertheless, he remained optimistic about the Knicks' prospects. There'd be no major moves in the lineup, he assured everyone, just some fine-tuning. They only needed to concentrate on a few fundamentals—some out-of-bounds work and a better defense against presses. Then the tide would turn.

Privately, Holzman was hell-bent on picking up the slack. His team wasn't showing enough determination on the floor. They were losing their concentration. He had to light a fire under his men if they were going to make a run at the title, he had to pull some tails. Reluctant to crack the whip, however, Red went to Willis Reed, the Knicks' captain, and said, "Look, Willie, tomorrow night I'm gonna get on your ass, even though you haven't done anything wrong. It's for the other guys, but I need to send them a message."

This was the kind of Abbott-and-Costello routine Holzman often staged during his tenure as the Knicks' coach. He'd pick out one of his stallions, someone the other guys respected, and chew him out during a practice. He'd ride the guy hard, maligning every aspect of his game, so that by the end of the session you'd expect nothing short of a murder committed on the floor. This bit really irked some of the players, who knew it for what it was, a confidence-building scheme, but Reed savored his role in the masquerade. He got into playing Holzman's heavy.

So the next evening, before another exhibition game with Detroit, Red strolled out on the floor, nice and casual, while the Knicks were taking their warm-ups. He played kissy-face with Clyde, shot the shit with Bradley. Nodding down toward the other end of the floor, he pointed out how Walt Bellamy, the Detroit center, was so cheap he was still wearing a pair of Knicks team socks left over from his days in New York. Har har har! Good ol' Red, he sure knew how to act like one of the guys. Once the game started, however, he shifted into his Rumpelstiltskin act, roaring and stomping along the sideline. "Get your hands up, *Reed.*" "For God's sake, *Willis,* see the ball." "C'mon, Willis, *jeeeeeeeez.*" These exhortations went on throughout the entire period. You'd have thought Willis Reed was a complete nincompoop.

Then, between quarters, Willis slipped into character for his part of the act. Calling a huddle of the guys, he'd growl, "What the fuck you guys want to do—play tonight or fuck around? You don't want to fuckin' play, take your ass into the locker room, get undressed, and fuck around. Otherwise, I expect you to work if you go back out on that floor."

The way the guys reacted, you'd have thought they'd survived the My Lai massacre. It lit a fire in their eyes. After all, they couldn't let the Cap shoulder all the blame for their play. Sure enough, after the whistle they headed out there *smoking*—lobbing flamethrowers. *Click click click*—they executed like a Rolex, its complete twenty-four-carat jewel movement whirring away, whipping that ball around the floor so hard you could have caught a draft. They gave those Pistons quite a valve job, too—taught 'em a thing or two about team basketball.

Red Holzman was happier than a mudlark. With opening day just a week away, his team was looking sharp. Sharp enough to be . . . to be *good*. They were getting there, as he'd known all along they would.

During the next practice he worked with the guards, refining pass plays to put them in the clear more often. He designed one in which Frazier would pass to Barnett, then they would go downcourt and pick for the forward—either DeBusschere or Dollar Bill—who would pop out. It worked like çlockwork. Very smooooooth. For another play, Frazier was supposed to pass off and go low at the same time DeBusschere popped up. Dave would then double back and pick off Clyde's man while Clyde came around the pick and forced a jump shot. Holzman, watching them pull off these plays half a dozen times, was delighted. They were functioning as a *team* on the floor. A *team!* What a rare and beautiful spectacle. That, he sighed, was the way the game was meant to be played.

Holzman's optimism, however, did nothing to lift the rooks' flagging spirits. The final cut was just days off—on Monday, October 13, a day before the opening of the Knicks' season—and neither Johnny Warren nor Milt Williams was assured of making the club. Both men were still struggling with their respective games. Struggling, hah! They were DOA. Warren was averaging about two points a night, and Williams—poor Milt had seen only five minutes of playing time in two weeks. The outlook for each of them was pitiful.

Williams, sensing the inevitable, had that aura of doom about him that clings to prisoners on Death Row. It was almost palpable. His eyes had lost their luster, his shoulders drooped, his gait was off by a fraction of a step. Around the other guys, it seemed he was sitting just—over there, not quite with them but not really apart, either; he'd begun to separate himself from the inner circle, perhaps preparing for his departure.

Johnny Warren felt no more upbeat about his prospects. The Iceman, indeed! He wanted to crawl in a hole whenever that nickname found its way into print. Who was he trying to kid? Icemen were cool, they delivered relief when things got hot. So far, he was a fizzle.

"Relax, rook," the Cap advised him. "They never cut a first-round draft pick." But Warren wasn't sold. He sweat a river that last week. The Knicks played two exhibition games—in Bangor, Maine, and in White Plains, New York—which were excruciating for him. All that sitting and waiting. All that thinking. Oh, man! Then the team took a few days to get its house in order, during which time Warren saw his confidence erode even further. It wasn't anything management said or did, nothing conveyed by a teammate. It was that lousy self-esteem wriggling around down in his gut, all those demons. There was nothing he could do to fight off the despair. Having a weekend off didn't help matters, either. In fact, all that time on his hands nearly proved—*lethal!*

Monday, the day before the opener, Warren reported for work at Queens College, where the Knicks had scheduled a two-hour practice, expecting the worst. As far as he knew, no decision had been made yet, and even if the news was good he probably had given himself an ulcer the size of a . . . basketball.

"Warren, we need you in here." It was Danny Whelan, the Knicks' Munchkin-faced trainer, beckoning him into a room adjoining the lockers.

Was this how it happened? Warren wondered. Did they isolate you from the rest of the team, drop the bad news on you, then spirit you out a side door so the gloom wouldn't affect the team's surging optimism? Maybe it was staged like a funeral, he thought, where they always remove the casket while the family is otherwise occupied. Let it happen quickly, he decided. Pull the switch and get it over with.

But Whelan had business to attend to. The day before an opener, Danny had to work like an octopus, handling myriad incidentals that needed to be seen to before the season tip-off. Like tape and socks and sweats and shoelaces and—and the *personal stuff* Johnny Warren would need in his locker. Whelan let it be known he was busy, he didn't have all day to wait for Warren to find his voice and tell Danny what he wanted. There were other teammates who needed his attention.

Teammates. Knicks. It finally dawned on Johnny Warren that he had made the club. He was among the *stallions*. How about that! Who knows, maybe in time he'd become a stallion himself, maybe some of the talent on this team would rub off, maybe . . .

A while later, during practice that afternoon, Milt Williams was called over to the bleachers where Eddie Donovan was sitting and was officially thanked for his enthusiasm.

"Sorry, Milt. I wish it'd worked out differently. You did a hell of a job for us, but there's just no room. Maybe next year."

Next year! It seemed like such an impossibly long way off to the Knicks, who one by one gravitated into the locker room that chilly afternoon in October for an impromptu shoot-around. Next year was an absurdity, it strained the imagination, it didn't exist as far as they were concerned.

Tomorrow night they would take to the court for a season unlike any other in their lives, a season that promised to fulfill every competitive expectation that had ever crossed their shadows. This year they could possibly win it all.

Next year be damned.

5 | SHOWTIME

October 14, 1969

T HE KNICKS FELT the heat rise as opening night loomed near, but to the rest of New York City the event was simply another mark on the social calendar. New York is a city of opening nights practically every day of the year, providing yet another excuse for promoters to roll out the red carpet, treat two hundred policemen to overtime pay, overburden the fleet of twelve thousand yellow cabs, fill six hundred parking lots to capacity, mobilize a battalion of tow truckers to rescue (and gouge) disabled motorists, support over two hundred tuxedo-rental shops, two thousand florists, and five thousand restaurants, and deploy an army of columnists, press agents, vendors, scalpers, hookers, hustlers, and street cleaners on their nightly prowl.

The lights around Madison Square Garden were a testament to a hundred similar opening nights. *Promises, Promises* lit up the Shubert Theatre, *Zorba* was at the Imperial, the marquee above the Booth blazed with the news that Keir Dullea and Blythe Danner were starring in *Butterflies Are Free.* Over at the Arvin the crowds were thick for *The Great White Hope* with James Earl Jones, across the street Arthur Miller's *The Price* was at the Morosco, *1776* was bringing tourists to the 46th Street Theatre, *The Prime of Miss Jean Brodie* was packing them in at the Helen Hayes, and slightly farther north, at the cavernous Mark Hellinger, whose marquee was temporarily dark, Katharine Hepburn was in rehearsal for *Coco*. Interspersed among these legitimate houses, the lights of Hollywood flashed seductively outside New York's movie palaces—this was in the days before multiplexes, when screens were still a city block wide and the theaters were lavish and grand—where gala openings had been held for the current slate of blockbusters, including *Easy Rider*, *Midnight Cowboy*, *The Wild Bunch*, *True Grit*, and *Butch Cassidy and the Sundance Kid*. Across town, on Third Avenue, a would-be magazine publisher named Bob Guccione was launching a glossy called *Penthouse*, featuring a cast of gorgeous naked creatures, and in a townhouse in the East Sixties a cast of gorgeous furry creatures named Kermit, Ernie, Oscar, and Grover was preparing for the opening night of "Sesame Street."

The Knicks—their opener was just another New York event on another New York night. Their star was outshone several hundred lumens by the perennially sad-sack New York Mets, who were currently—*miraculously*—engaged in a World Series with the Baltimore Orioles. And yet the Garden pulsed with the tension and excitement of every opening night since Colonel Nicolls took over the territory from the Dutch in 1664. By seven o'clock, a faithful 14,796 fans had filled the graduated, rainbow-colored seats, whose striations denoted a social order on a par with the Indian caste system for its rude taxonomy—the elite filling the red and orange seats near the floor, followed in successive levels of economic diminution all the way up to the untouchables in the green seats just beneath the rafters. In every section, no matter how segregated, beer was flowing, cigars were smoking, expectations were soaring, and the crowd was buzzing as the curtain prepared to rise on a season whose fortunes hung in the balance between greatness—and the pits.

Backstage—or rather, in the Knicks' locker room—the quarters were pushed to capacity with well-wishers, backslappers, hangers-on, politicians, celebrities, and every other species of bloodsucker who had managed to talk his way past security. Dustin Hoffman peeked in, as did Elliot Gould, Soupy Sales, and Alan King. Even Bob Boozer, the six-foot-eight Chicago Bulls forward, stopped by, in street clothes, to announce he'd been traded to Seattle and was starting for them here tonight. The loquacious Adam Clayton Powell, Jr., a local congressman who was under indictment for some ingenious form of graft, bumped from player to player blubbering, "Let it *alllllllll* hang out!" And all the while, in the midst of the belabored chaos, the fox-faced Red Holzman, grimacing as if he'd just swallowed another septic Garden frank, was attempting to communicate his game plan to the starting five.

The Knicks were opening their crusade against the Seattle Supersonics, a hapless expansion team that had finished near the cellar last year, despite a respectable backcourt in Art Harris, Rod Thorn, and Lenny Wilkens, the Boys High star who had been promoted to the thankless position of player-coach. The Sonics had helped themselves considerably in the off season by drafting Lucius Allen, who had starred at UCLA with Lew Alcindor, and grabbing Boozer from the Bulls, but the matchup with the Knicks was stunningly lopsided. Seattle offered little in the way of defense; they were relatively sluggish, only marginal shooters, mostly look-what-I-found rebounders—on the whole, they were half-pints. New York planned to draw blood quickly, then let the Nor'westers hemorrhage through the second half.

At 7:05, a buzzer cut through the low human rumble that stirred the Garden infrastructure, and pandemonium broke loose. The house lights dimmed, creating another forceful, more frenzied reaction, and then spots hit the Knicks bench in a radiant burst, the way they'd hit an inmate at Attica as he was going over the wall. Through the surging applause, the players tried their best to remain blasé, gazing around distractedly or stretching their rubber-band bodies into positions made familiar by carnival contortionists. Bill Bradley and Dave DeBusschere chuckled at a private joke. Nate Bowman elbowed Dave Stallworth playfully in the ribs—*just below his heart.* Cazzie Russell shook hands with someone passing stealthily behind the bench. Bill Hosket bounced lightly on his toes, Mike Riordan chewed gum. Johnny Warren suffered a case of opening-night jitters. On the surface, the team looked earnestly loosey-goosey, but underneath their nerves were a quiver of hatpins.

"Ladies and gentlemen, the New York Knickerbockers are pleased to introduce the 1969 team," announced John Condon, in his familiar magisterial drone, which to most fans corresponded to the voice of God. "At forward, number twenty-two, from the University of . . ."

One by one the Knicks bounded onto the floor to thunderous applause, shook hands with each other, jiggled a little, flexed, sneered, ignored the photographers who crept forward in the dark like enemy snipers. Introductions proceeded routinely, for the most part, until Stallworth's number was called. As soon as Condon blurted out the words "Number nine," the place just erupted. There was bedlam. It sounded as if the train to Massapequa, which originated several levels beneath the Garden floor, had jumped a track, caught an escalator upstairs, and was now tunneling through fifteen yards of concrete on its way into the arena. The fans, in an unusual shower of emotion, were welcoming Stallworth back—from the dead.

Dave the Rave shambled forward and waved tentatively to the crowd. He squinted into the lights, trying to make out the odd human curtain waving tremulously beyond the glare. There appeared to be thousands of people standing, waving, cheering, whistling, shaking their fists, carrying on in a display of wild enthusiasm, which, after several minutes, showed little sign of abating. Well, if that didn't beat all! It seemed to go on forever, too, building in waves as it passed from section to section, echoing off the concrete walls. Stallworth dipped his head appreciatively. Aw, shucks—he was . . . embarrassed. He flashed one of those hairy Richard Pryor grins, his lips stretched elastically back over pink, spongy gums, past his molars, in a mix of amusement and abject horror. And wait, it got worse: his teammates began mobbing him, too, patting him on both shoulders, shaking hands, grinning. Lord, have mercy! He might have survived that damn heart attack, but he was never going to live through this.

Stallworth absorbed much of the endearing hoopla, but he knew he was also a siphon for the Knicks' good fortune. The New York fans were ablaze with pennant fever. You could see it emanating from them, rising from the bleachers like swamp vapor. Even the hard-core gamblers, those antic little termites who sat along the perimeter of the floor rolling their scorecards between sweaty palms, were strangely jubilant. They'd been given ten points over Seattle, and each man took it greedily, sensing the imminent kill.

The game itself was just the kind of send-off the Knicks needed. They acted like bullies picking on five weaklings. They stomped, hammered, and shellacked the woeful Supersonics—ran 'em right back to that beaky little Space Needle on their horizon. The Space Needle, indeed! They couldn't have chosen a more fitting emblem. Why, all you had to do was crane your neck a bit to take in the sturdy New York skyline. The Empire State Building—"empire," mind you—was a few blocks off, and beyond that the Statue . . . of . . . Liberty. Ho boy, the Sonics took some needling that night; they were down by thirty-four points early in the fourth quarter.

The Knicks had come out blasting. Frazier and Barnett ate up Wilkens and Harris; along with Mike Riordan, the New York backcourt scored *fifty* points. Similarly, Seattle's forwards, John

Tresvant, an ex-Royal, and Tom Meschery, were no match for DeBusschere and Bradley. Only Bob Rule, the left-handed center, offered resistance to the charge. Rule had seventeen points in the first quarter, getting position on Reed low in the paint. But Willis was playing his hand like a bunco artist. He let Rule shoot for a while, laying back when the Seattle center bullied his way under the basket. Then he made a slight adjustment, heading into the second quarter, and held the Sonics' big man to ten points the rest of the way.

By the end of the third quarter it was a laugher. Holzman rested his stallions, letting the mules mop up, and the action proceeded to get funny on both ends. With the Knicks up by thirty, Nate Bowman came in, to give Willis Reed a blow. Now, Bowman was a basketball player in name only. In any other profession, a man of his ability would have been on the street looking for work, but Nate was large and powerful, and at six-ten he was taller than half of the starting centers in the league, so inevitably he had made the team, at a salary of $32,000, because his size occasionally proved useful. Trouble was, Nate wasn't really a ballplayer, he was an obstacle. He didn't have a legitimate move in his body, never having been a real student of the game, and for the most part he didn't have to rely on talent. As backup to Willis Reed, he rarely played, and the last job on his résumé denoted a stretch with Philadelphia, where he had stood—or rather sat—in Wilt Chamberlain's long shadow. No, Nate usually came into a game only for damage control, when a big man got hurt or into foul trouble, or, on nights like this, when the Knicks were so far ahead that his presence on the floor wouldn't prove costly to his teammates.

This night was no exception. With the score 105–75, Nate took the ball, stepped around a Seattle forward, and moved to the corner for a shot. He went up beautifully, his launch as clean and swift as a Mercury rocket, but somewhere between trajectory and descent he forgot to let go of the ball. It was still in his hands when he touched down, was still there moments later when he was whistled for traveling.

The fans went berserk. They showered the Garden with hoots and whistles. The circus was still five months off—who'd sent in the clowns?

"Some shot, eh?" Nate asked, grinning. "I was just trying to get better shooting leverage."

So what do you do for an encore? The next shot trickled off his hands and dropped like a dud at his feet. More grins from Nate, more hoots and whistles from the fans. Emmett Kelly, they agreed, had better watch his back. That did it! Holzman had seen enough, and so had the fans. When Nate got yanked, the stands erupted in jubilation.

"I want you to notice, Nate, they applaud you when you come out of the game, not when you go in," observed Dick Barnett as Bowman joined him on the bench.

Despite the limitations of their bench, the Knicks were elated with their opening-night performance. They were on target, they displayed depth at both ends of the court, and they were merciless in their dispatch of Seattle. The game sent a powerful message—not only to the Sonics but to the rest of the league—that they were ready to live up to the expectations that had trailed the team since last year's play-offs. All that noise about "next year"—well, it hadn't been hype.

The Knicks came out of the box like a shot. The next day, they beat the Royals in Cincinnati, 94–89, ruining Bob Cousy's debut as the coach there. The Royals were in a state of upheaval, as a result of Cousy's desire to reshape them in the Celtics' image, and ultimately he went with three rookie starters—Norm Van Lier, Herm Gilliam, and Luthur Rackley—who were in no position to compete against stallions.

Cousy had misread the Royals' legacy. Everyone knew that when you came into Cincinnati your strategy was set in stone:

you spent forty-eight minutes defending against a tactical weapon known simply as O. Most of the Knicks agreed that Oscar Robertson, the Big O, was unquestionably the best all-around player in the game. Since 1960, he'd averaged over thirty points, ten rebounds, and ten assists per game—plus all the others he got by osmosis. For those, you only had to pencil his name onto the scorecard. Once Oscar set foot on the court—*poof!*—a triple double, no questions asked. If he had concentrated less on passing and dribbling, he could have scored—well, that figure was difficult to calculate, impossible to contemplate. No one even wanted to think about it. He gave opponents enough stomach trouble just dealing with what he was, and what he was was a perfectionist. While not particularly speedy, he had stealth; while not a pure shooter, he was accurate; while not a fancy dribbler, he was unerring; while not a flamethrower, he made pinpoint passes. The Big O, it was said, was a machine, and like the most sophisticated mechanisms—like that UNIVAC sitting in the Pentagon—he never made mistakes. He possessed enormous powers of concentration that would have made The Amazing Kreskin envious.

"I am thinking of the perfect pass." *Poof*—a perfect pass. "I am thinking of . . ."

That's the way O played the game. But, while the Knicks swore Oscar was on the floor that night in Cincinnati, they decided afterward that it must have been an impostor. The O they knew would never have stood around like a statue while those rookies—those trick ponies—hogged the ball. Especially when the game was on the line. Down the stretch, when the score got close, the real O would have demanded the ball, he would have put on a scoring clinic, blown the game wide open. But the guy wearing number 14, the chump in the Oscar Robertson mask, had to be a fake, because when he got open, when he called for the ball, when he got the step on his defender and had a clear path to the basket—the rooks ignored him. They looked at him, then away. At one point, the Royals' bench was screaming for the rooks to clear things for him, but nothing doing. The Big O, indeed. An "impostor" was more like it. Walt Frazier, for one, mourned the absence of his nemesis. He loved going against O, it was always a dogfight; to Clyde, that's what basketball was all about. But the stats told the whole story. Next to the name Robertson, in the appropriate box for game points, it said: eight for twenty-six, 18. *Thud!*

The next day, when the Knicks read the papers, they came across a quote that made their scrotes winch. Bob Cousy, in an interview with the *New York Times*, had said, "I think Rackley and Gilliam can get the ball and run, and that's how my teams are going to play the game." That's what he *said*. But what he meant was: Oscar Robertson doesn't figure in my plans. To everyone who read the article, it was a staggering piece of news. Had Cousy lost his mind? The *Post* got him to clarify a bit. "What's the sense of being cute with the veterans if they're not the guys we're going to build with?" Cousy said bluntly. "We're building something, and if the rookies have the potential, well, let's see what happens with them."

"Oscar's not going to sit still for that," noted one suspicious New Yorker. "I'll bet they're shooting at each other next time we play those boys."

Meanwhile, the Knicks tightened their grip two days later in Chicago, stampeding the Bulls, 116–87. Red Holzman had intended to use his starters for most of the game. At the beginning of a season, it was customary to let the stallions test their legs by encouraging them to go the distance, so they could build up their stamina. But Willis Reed, Dave DeBusschere, and Dick Barnett got into early foul trouble, forcing substitutions. It proved to be a mixed blessing. On the one hand, you hate to see the starters forced to the bench, especially against a pushover like Chicago. But it also gave Red an opportunity to gauge the Knicks' depth.

During the preseason, there's usually nothing on the line to warrant a full-scale effort from the players, and as a result, the entire bench comes off looking pretty good. You go into the season an optimist, relying on their availability, feeling comfortably secure. But the true test of bench strength doesn't come until the regular season, usually on the road, and often, when it's too late, a coach makes the rude discovery that a nugget in preseason is actually a lump of fool's gold.

From Holzman's standpoint, the Knick bench was already a known commodity. Every player, aside from Johnny Warren and Dave Stallworth, had been there the year before. He'd seen them in every conceivable situation, under the most adverse conditions. Nevertheless, some question marks remained. Was Cazzie's ankle a hundred percent? Bill Hosket's knee? Stallworth's—for crying out loud, he didn't even want to think about that!

Red lifted his starters and signaled the bench: Stallworth, Russell, Hosket.

He had been satisfied with Stallworth and Russell in the two previous games. The Rave had performed nicely spelling De-Busschere in the home opener, and in Cincinnati, when the Royals made it close, Cazzie had come in for Bradley and run off nine straight points, putting the game out of their reach. No, it was Bill Hosket about whom Red was most curious. Hosket was one of the Knicks' unresolved question marks.

Hosket was from Dayton, Ohio, and by his own definition a hayseed. He was six-eight and blond, with one of those wide-open midwestern faces you see on a mayonnaise jar. He talked with a twang, prompting the Manhattan kids who cornered him for an autograph to ask if he lived in a barn or if he was a farmer—and that just fried Hoss's ass. His real name, Wilmer, didn't help either. On slow nights, when he spelled Reed or DeBusschere, the Garden would echo with whinnies of "Willllllll-ma! Willllllll-ma!"—mimicking that talking glue horse, Mr. Ed. Well, fuck them, Hosket thought. It had been his father's name, too, and no greater basketball legend had ever come out of the Dayton area.

His dad—Big Bill—had played center on three high-school state-championship teams and then had starred at Ohio State when they won the Big Ten conference in 1933. That was before there was an NBA, or Big Bill would have gone on to play pro ball. Instead, he bounced around in semi-pro leagues—those loosely organized outfits where half the men took their shirts off so you could tell which team was which. He was one tough old bird, who needed a police escort to get him off the court on more than one occasion. Little Bill, as Hoss was known, remembered a particular Sunday afternoon game in which his dad was playing against the local Phillips 66 team, whose trademark was to score exactly sixty-six points in every game. The fans loved them for it—counting off sixty-three . . . sixty-four . . . sixty-five . . . sixty-six. *Finito,* game over, the Phillips boys sat down on their haunches, and the place would go nuts. Well, Big Bill thought that was bush, so on that fateful Sunday afternoon, when the Phillips team hit their limit, he called for the ball, drove down-court, and put two more points in the opposing team's basket. Sixty-eight! There was stunned silence in the arena, followed by a wild Ohio fistfight, after which Big Bill was escorted out to his car by the cops.

Hoss trod proudly in his father's footsteps. He'd been a high-school star (on the same squad as his Knicks teammate Donnie May), started at Ohio State, where he was named to the All Big Ten team at two different positions, went to the Final Four, won a gold medal at the 1968 Olympics, in Mexico City, was a first-round draft pick of the Knicks that year, and signed a contract with them for $35,000 a year. Not bad, he thought, for a hayseed. But a lingering knee injury, incurred during his junior year at Ohio State, continued to haunt him. Hoss cursed that damn knee. While doing a simple drill in St. John's Arena, he'd made a little change of direction and heard a muffled *pop* that was his knee—or, rather, what had been his knee. Today, that kind of injury would be no worse than a toothache. A sports-medicine doctor performs a simple arthroscopic procedure on the knee, slaps a Band-Aid over it, and three weeks later you're hauling down rebounds again, business as usual. But in 1965 you were discouraged from having surgery, which might idle you for a year—a college player could lose his eligibility. So Hoss elected to rest the knee as much as possible, and to play hurt. He switched from forward to center because of his limited ability to run, taped the knee in such a fashion as to imitate the cartilage and ligaments that should be holding it in place, and had it aspirated several times a week. The therapy worked—marginally—but it changed the focus of his game, and ultimately the injury destroyed a promising career.

Hosket's first year with the Knicks was a bust. Because of the Olympics, he missed training camp, which took him out of the team's syncopated flow. It also erased him from Holzman's game plan—out of sight, out of mind. And, if the truth be told, he was a nag among the Knicks thoroughbreds. The first day he sought out his old teammate Donnie May, whom he considered one of the best ballplayers he'd ever been on the floor with, to get the lay of the land.

"How's it going?" Hoss asked his Dayton buddy.

May smiled humorlessly, shook his head, and said, "I'm the worst player on this team."

Hosket nearly shit a brick. Impossible, he thought. Donnie's a *stallion*. He must be on . . . No, no, no, Donnie's a straight arrow. This must be his idea of a joke.

As Bill discovered soon enough, May wasn't joking. Donnie was out of his depth. It seemed surreal. Only Donnie wasn't the worst player on the team anymore, Hosket was. Hoss—the Big Ten star and Olympic medalist—became the team's clown attraction, that last man off the bench who played a minute here, a minute there, drawing the fans' horsy guffaws every time he touched the ball.

"*Shooooot! Shooooot! Shooooot!*" they'd holler. "*Haaawwww! Haaawwwwww!*"

And the knee continued to act up. Despite some reconstructive surgery, it was still a fragmented mess. Danny Whelan, the Knicks' equipment man, wrapped it for him all year long—he performed a lengthy process, devised by Ohio State trainers, that involved Ace bandages, a wad of adhesive tape, and a clumsy elastic brace. It kept him in the game. But it wasn't the same as a knee.

This year, however, there'd been some improvement. The knee felt better. It stopped buckling, and Hoss opted to play without the apparatus, for the first time in two years. So when Red Holzman called his name that night in Chicago, with an entire quarter left to play—well, brother, here was an opportunity to make a statement.

Hosket took the bit in his mouth and ran. His man was Bob Kauffman, the Bulls' backup center and not much of a threat. So Hoss decided to exhibit his range. He was a pretty good shot from the outside and proved it by hitting five out of his next six attempts. Well, hot damn! He was on fire.

Then Red put Donnie May on the floor, too, and for a moment it was just like their old Belmont High team. The two Dayton boys played like gangbusters until Hoss inadvertently bounced one off Kauffman's head that went in the Knicks' basket for two points. May laughed so hard that the Knicks had to ask for a time-out.

Stalls added six quick ones, and Cazzie went on a shooting spree that tallied ten points; Johnny Warren came off the bench and hit four straight; Nate Bowman went three for four—yes, *that* Nate Bowman—Mike Riordan worked the ball to the open man, everyone played defense, and before it was over the bench had outscored the starters, 59–57. Dick Motta, the Bulls coach, spent most of the fourth quarter with his head in his hands. "I don't see anyone beating this team," he moaned at the buzzer, as his Bulls dragged their weary carcasses toward the locker room.

For the Knicks, however, the last three games had merely been appetizers. The next night, they were due back in New York to take on the Lakers at the Garden, and they all knew it would give them a good preview of the work that lay ahead. The Lakers were the team to beat. They'd been a powerhouse last season, they were a powerhouse again, and you had to be brain dead not to take them seriously. Everyone was looking forward to the game with a mixture of fear and longing. Seattle, Cincinnati, and Chicago had been easy wins for the Knicks; the Lakers would give them an indication of how good they really were.

Dick Barnett had been a member of the Lakers from 1963 to 1965, playing behind Jerry West and any number of shooting guards—*white* shooting guards—who were brought in to complement the West Virginia Wonderboy. Let's see, there were Frank Selvy, Mel Gibson (no, not *that* Mel Gibson), Jerry Grote (not *that* Jerry Grote, either) . . . Sheeeee-it! Barnett wasn't happy about those peckerwoods. Hell, no—he wanted r-e-s-p-e-c-t. He wanted playing time, he wanted payin' time, and anything else was *booool-shit.*

Sure, he was dissatisfied in L.A. A player with that much talent usually balks at taking a supporting role, especially when some office temp grabs his promotion. And so word got around that Barnett had an attitude. Now, if you were white and had an attitude you were considered gregarious. But a black man who displayed a streak of pride—well, baby, he was trouble. The word front offices used was "disruptive." A man with an attitude disrupted a team's harmony, its karmic flow. Why couldn't Barnett be more like Elgin Baylor? people wondered. That nice fella knew his role, he knew not to bite the hand that fed him. But

Barnett—you could see it in those heavy-lidded eyes of his, affairs that looked like they were sassin' you when he was unhappy. And once you got past his eyes, there was that diction of his. He had a lazy Indiana drawl that bothered some teammates—the way he eee-*nunn*-ceee-ate-ed each word, stretching it out like Silly Putty. And his wit had a subtle sting.

To make matters worse, Barnett was one of the early masters of what is now known as "trash talk." Today, a pro ballplayer had better know how to talk trash almost as well as he plays. He has to get in the face of an opponent, say something rude about the boy's mama or sister that'll disrupt his concentration, comment on the meagerness of his anatomy—or some effective combination. *"Yo, man, you fuck yer own sister for a dime. If you could find it."* You have to be able to dish it—and take it. But in those days such talk was considered impudent. Barnett wasn't the kind of motor mouth that dominates today's game. He wasn't profane, but he did taunt players relentlessly, got in their face—and under their skin.

The chief offending tactic was Barnett's trademark shot—a herky-jerky jumper he launched off his left hand with both feet tucked up under his body, like a leaping gazelle. As he let go of the ball, he'd yell, *"Fall back, baby!"* indicating the shot was on target and his opponent had better head downcourt. *"Fall back, baby!"* It was loud enough to carry into the stands, which rubbed salt in the wound. *"Too late!"* He'd shout that, too, after sinking a twenty-five-footer. *"Fall back, baby! Too late!"* Just who the hell did he think he was—Redd Foxx?

Such slights accrued a kind of negative interest that contributed to Dick Barnett's already precarious reputation. Before L.A., he had played in Syracuse, where he had been the Nationals' first-round draft pick in 1959, and he'd expressed a similar unhappiness there. It was the same story—not enough respect, not enough money. Like any other man, he wanted what was coming to him. In this day and age, if you don't like the terms, you call your agent and renegotiate or demand a trade. But back then the owners offered deals on a take-it-or-leave-it basis, and if you left it, you'd best think of some other profession, because the word quickly got out on the owners' grapevine, and pretty soon you were an untouchable. As far as Barnett was concerned, that was *boooool-shit*. He wanted no part of it. Defying the NBA's slavelike mentality, he jumped in 1961 to the American Basketball League, a renegade league founded by promoter Abe Saperstein, and played for the Cleveland Pipers until the team folded, whereupon he landed in Los Angeles.

The Knicks traded Bob Boozer for Barnett in 1965, in the hope that he was someone who could put the ball in the basket. They were in need of an offensive threat to complement the low-scoring defensive squad they'd assembled, and Barnett seemed to be the man. To many New Yorkers, it looked like a bum deal. Barnett was thirty years old, an old man by basketball standards, and he'd just come off his worst season in the NBA. Boozer was taller, younger, less problematic. But Eddie Donovan saw something in Barnett that clicked with his vision for the team. Diversity, perhaps, or reliability. Barnett was willing to mold his ample talents to suit the team. He'd make the necessary pass, play defense. He had a beautiful touch that delighted the Garden crowd. It seemed like he could hit from anywhere—in the open or under duress, from twenty-five feet out or with a little turnaround jumper. He'd cry, *"Fall back, baby!"* and the place would go nuts. He became a real crowd pleaser on the floor.

More important, the guy had *style*. His wardrobe looked as if it had been assembled by Nathan Detroit—gorgeous threads, wide-brimmed hats, silk ties, wing tips. Now, in L.A., if a black man dressed like that, they called him a pimp; in New York, he was a fashion plate. When Barnett emerged from the Garden in his street clothes, the brothers would converge to check him out. They'd swarm all over him, eyeballing those threads, making mental notes. They dug his style, and they imitated it, too, by running down to the Stag Shop, in Greenwich Village, or to Lester's, farther uptown.

But Barnett would never become a superstar attraction—age saw to that. By 1969, his fourth year with the Knicks, he had developed into a premier role player: steady offense, steady defense, hitting a steady 50 percent of his shots. Steady—how many basketball players could claim that distinction? Most suffered enough downs to complement the ups in their roller-coaster careers, but Barnett's steadiness was a sure thing. He'd become one of the most dependable players on the team. Already this year his points-per-game average was a respectable thirteen. Yet the fans still had their doubts. "He's thirty-three, too old for a starting guard" was their chief criticism. "He's lost a few steps." Then again, Barnett had been hearing that one for the past four years.

Now against the Lakers, during the first half of the game, Barnett seemed to justify the bad rap. He took only three shots and had one point. Jerry West ran him and Frazier across the court like two lab rats. West sank fifteen points in the first quarter (he'd put up forty-two by the final buzzer), and by halftime the Lakers were up by a comfortable margin. But when the third quarter started, Barnett came out firing like a sprightly rook. He hit all eight of his shots, for twenty points, putting the Knicks up by over a dozen and icing the game.

That certainly made the old man feel young again. And beating his former team gave Barnett an extra sense of satisfaction and vindication. A player always feels an inner joy in showing up the team that let him get away. It was like running into your ex-wife with a great-looking babe on your arm. No one disputed that West, Baylor, and Chamberlain were stallions, but the Knicks had shown they could run with them. Could even outrun them. Besides, L.A. had a lot to learn about humility.

Barnett was predictably arch during his postgame rap in the locker room. "Hmmm, West, forty-two," he stage-mumbled, glancing at the stats and then at Clyde. "You some *de*-fensive specialist."

"What happened to Clyde tonight, Rich—he get caught in traffic?" asked Willis Reed. "Don't believe I saw him on the floor."

Barnett shook his head with mock pity. "How'd this guy get forty-two on you? Never even seen that sucker before. Mister *De*-fensive Specialist."

Frazier laughed quietly before flinging his jock at Barnett.

After the game, Jerry West discounted Frazier's defensive performance with a snide shrug. "To be honest," he said, "I didn't know he was there."

Chamberlain was equally dismissive about Frazier's bold play. "You know how I feel about him—I take him for granted," Wilt boasted. As for the Knicks, he continued, "I didn't think they played too well."

The Knicks, not play well? Who was the big guy kidding? They were four and oh and had just decimated a team that the experts picked to repeat as champs. Wilt was Wilt, all right, but he was also a bit of a chump. Jesus, you had to know when to turn it off, brother. What was he trying to do—fire them up for the next time? Someone ought to show him the box score, read those revealing stats. Because everything else was *boooool-shit!*

6 | STREAKING TOWARD BETHLEHEM

October–November 1969

BASKETBALL PLAYERS are an athletic branch of the Legion of Superheroes, and as such they are required to be tall, athletic, coordinated, instinctive, strong, speedy, deceptive, tenacious, and indefatigable. They have to be able to leap tall buildings in a single bound. But deep down, every ballplayer knows that his team owes much of its fortune to serendipity. He realizes that, in the end, much of its success depends on where the chips fall. That isn't meant to belittle a team's abundant accomplishments. It isn't to imply, for example, that the eleven-time-champion Boston Celtics weren't guided by a combination of magnificent athletes who played themselves to victory. But *if* Bill Russell hadn't been part of a fire sale in which St. Louis traded his rights to Boston . . . *If* Phoenix had won the coin toss that sent Lew Alcindor to Milwaukee . . . *If* Bill Bradley had gone to Duke, where he was enrolled as a freshman, instead of switching to Princeton a week before school started . . . *If* . . .

if . . . if—well, study the angles, and you'll see what an iffy game basketball really is.

By Thanksgiving the ifs had started to pile up, wreaking havoc for several NBA teams. Dave Bing and Jimmy Walker, both with knee problems, were early casualties in Detroit, sending the Pistons into a veritable tailspin. Luke Jackson ruptured an Achilles tendon, dimming the 76ers' prospects. Al Attles and Jerry Lucas were sitting on the San Francisco bench with matching broken hands—Blue Cross/Blue Shield must have been having a field day. No team's prospects looked more iffy, however, than those of the Los Angeles Lakers. Picked to win it all, they had come to resemble Charlie Company after the fall of Saigon. Elgin Baylor and Johnny Egan were both nursing groin pulls, Keith Erickson had a bum ankle, and rookie center Rick Roberson had encountered debilitating tendon problems. Still, none of those could compare to a Lakers injury that sent shock waves through the entire league. On November 7, playing a fierce game against the Phoenix Suns, Wilt Chamberlain was driving toward the basket when he suddenly went down with a ruptured tibial tubercle, a tendon high in his right kneecap.

"I'm scared to believe it," said Willis Reed, when he heard that Wilt would miss the remainder of the season, if not of his career.

Sure, Reed was scared. Wilt's injury was a reminder of how precarious the health of a basketball player is. One stumble, one misstep, one *sneeze* can turn a remarkable season into a nightmare. And this wasn't exactly an ordinary player who'd been sidelined. Wilt Chamberlain was the cornerstone of the NBA, he was the league's franchise. He was professional basketball's first real *personality,* the kind of guy who, in years to come, would be pocketing all those rich Pepsi and Nike residuals. He was fierce, fearsome, fearless, and *pffffffffft*—he was gone. Just like *that!* His injury sent an engram to the neural tissue of every player who currently went up against Wilt, which, translated by the brain, came out roughly as "That could have been me."

You'd better believe Reed was scared. The Knicks knew their chances of success were tied to a relatively healthy team. To date, DeBusschere had taken an uppercut to what had once been a fine Belgian nose, Reed had lost a dental plate to a wildly thrown elbow, and Russell was bothered by muscle spasms, but those were minor inconveniences, nothing that threatened their playing time. No, the Knicks were healthy—and on an unprecedented roll. They were an astounding twenty and one, posting a .952 percentage in the standings. What's more, they'd won sixteen straight games—*sixteen straight*—and were one victory away from tying the league record, set by Washington (in 1946) and Boston (in 1959). Red Auerbach, who incidentally had coached both of those teams, attributed the Knicks' success to—serendipity. *Say what?* With their streak on the line, Auerbach contacted several beat reporters and, puffing on that grotesque cigar of his, claimed the Knicks had gotten where they were by riding a trail of lucky breaks. Well, that was just sour grapes. The Celtics were six and thirteen and going nowhere. The dynasty was over. Decimated. Defunct. Auerbach, the Knicks decided, could blow it out his ass.

The Knicks, meanwhile, were going to Atlanta, where they hoped to take a giant step toward erasing that fool Auerbach's name from the record book.

Atlanta had always been a dicey city for the Knicks. It was the Deep South, baby—the scene of some righteous brawls, thanks to a home team that often provoked fights, an arena that was more suitable to gladiators than basketball players, and the cracker mentality of the fans. A year earlier, Willis Reed had been involved in part of a rampage there that the players were still rehashing, like a part of mythology.

It had been one of those nights. Reed had been in a pissy mood to begin with. His knees were acting up, he was battling the onset of tendinitis, and he *hated* playing on Atlanta's floor. *Hated* it! It was old and uneven and dead—there was no "give" to it, which did a number on those already damaged knees. The crowd was loud and obnoxious. The ventilation was nonexistent; it felt like 110 degrees in that sweatbox, sapping his strength. If that wasn't enough, the Knicks were flat, and Red Holzman elected to make Reed his nightly whipping boy, hoping to goad the team into action. From the start, Holzman was all over Willis's back.

"Hey! Willie—c'mon!" Holzman barked from the sideline. His face was warped with dissatisfaction. "Get *on* 'em!"

Every few seconds he'd fire another salvo, at the Knick captain, burping off a string of insults about the center's gutless play. Now, Reed knew better than to take it personally; he knew Holzman's tactic was purely motivational. Reed's work ethic wasn't at fault; Holzman just needed a scapegoat, and tonight that was Reed.

Luck of the draw. Unfortunate timing.

To make it more exasperating, the Hawks were in one of their playful moods. Zelmo Beaty was popping out of one annoying screen after the next, and his brute cohorts—Lou Hudson, Walt Hazzard, Bill Bridges, and Paul Silas—were tweaking the Knicks' frustration. Damn pests! They kept scoring on the screens, too, putting New York down a couple buckets after five minutes of play. To keep the game from getting out of hand, Holzman called a time-out.

In the huddle, he continued to lay into Reed. "You gotta guard your man, Willis. What's wrong with you?"

Bill Hosket, who roomed with Reed, saw the storm looming on the horizon. He could tell by the way Willis was acting that the criticism was getting to him. He wasn't saying anything—which meant he was smoldering—and his eyes were beginning to narrow. Bad piece of business, the eyes. Hosket recognized the danger signs and shuddered.

"You ready to play tonight, Willie?" Holzman cried, before sending the Knicks back into the fray. *"Look alive!"*

A minute later, Phil Jackson pulled down a rebound and attempted an outlet pass that caught Paul Silas on the shoulder. Jackson wasn't trying to hit Silas, but Phil had those enormous gangly arms, like a pterodactyl, that often collided with the landscape. He was like Rodan flying over Tokyo and lopping a few stories off an office tower. Sorry, accident. Only Silas didn't take it that way. He swung on Jackson and missed. Phil's back was turned, so he didn't see the punch. But Willis did.

Reed filed it away for future reference. Moments later, during another time-out, he mumbled, "That's not gonna happen. They're not gonna be swinging on us down here."

"You know what, Willis?" Holzman suggested, "You ought to concentrate on playing. What's with you tonight? Guard your man!"

When play resumed, Reed set a pick for Bradley to run a baseline play. Lou Hudson, the Hawks' scrappy guard, accidentally—*wink! wink!*—hit Reed with an elbow as he came around the screen. Luckily for Hudson, it was only the first quarter and Reed was still feeling merciful. Willis strolled over to the little fellow and said, "Let me tell you something—you hit me again, I'm gonna kick your ass." That was usually enough to do the trick. Reed's reputation, as a result of the Rudy LaRusso massacre, was just a notch above that of a psycho killer, and few players were fool enough to call his bluff. Come the second quarter, however, and Hudson's brain went on the fritz. The Knicks called the same play, Reed set up the screen, and—*thunk!* Hudson didn't even bother to fake an accident this time. He threw a fist into Willis's chest that was tantamount to committing suicide. *Boom!* Hudson took a wicked bounce off the floor.

Often, in this type of contentious circumstance, players leap off the bench, there's some stagy pushing and shoving, a little fingerpointing (*"You!" "No, you!"*), they exchange a few pleasantries about a player's sexuality or about his mother (or about his mother's sexuality, usually in relation to her son), and after a sonic discharge of testosterone, the game resumes. That's what usually happens. But Atlanta's Alexander Arena was a crusty old hole that bred its own hostility. The fans were permitted to wander around right next to the court, and on this night, when Nate Bowman stepped in to cool off the Cap'n, one of them reached over the railing and sucker-punched Nate before springing back into the crowd.

Well, it was a good ol' fight. Willis and Nate took on the Hawks' entire rotation. Hudson was already down, Zelmo Beaty went down, then Bridges. Reed, just warming up, cruised the Hawks' bench in search of his next victim. Actually, he was looking for Silas, to get even for the blindside he had thrown at Jackson, but Silas was nowhere to be found.

Richie Guerin, the Hawks' pugnacious coach, was pointing at Reed and yelling, "Go after that guy! Go after that guy!" but the bench players wisely shrank back.

"C'mon—all of you!" Reed taunted them.

Eventually Willis got a police escort to the locker room.

"M'man Will took no prisoners tonight," Dick Barnett observed, as the crowd hollered and booed.

Later that night, back in his room, Reed was in a reflective mood, visibly unnerved by the fight. He sat on the edge of the bed staring into his hands and slowly shaking his head.

"Well, if nothing else, that took care of a lot of racial stuff," he told Hosket, who was packing for the flight back to New York.

The comment caught Hosket completely off guard. Willis usually acted color-blind. It wasn't like him to raise the specter of racial hate.

"What do you mean?"

"I got in a fight in L.A. a couple years ago."

"Yeah, I read about it," Hosket said. Everyone knew the LaRusso saga inside and out. It was practically required reading.

"Anyway, some people implied I went after those guys because they were white. Tonight, they were all black. So, if nothing else, Wilmer, I resolved that problem."

Hosket smiled at the cockeyed logic. It was just like Reed to unload a piece of racial baggage like that, he thought. Quietly, privately. The big guy was sweet to the core. Still, the ferocity of the fight haunted Hosket.

"Willis," he said, "that brawl was real scary."

"Yeah. But I'm not that tough. In college, I couldn't even whip my roommate."

"Who'd you room with?" Hosket asked.

"Buck Buchanan."

Then on October 28, during the Knicks' first tango with Atlanta of the new season, Bill Bridges, who was widely known as a guy who liked to mix it up, had gotten testy with DeBusschere and had to be aired out. And Walt Hazzard—well, everybody knew about Hazzard. The guy was a freaking termite. He'd let a player go in for a lay-up, then uppercut the guy; while the player was still airborne, he'd crawl in under him in order to draw a dangerous foul.

Apparently that's the way they ran things in Dixie. The Hawks had a siege mentality, so the Knicks were prepared to do battle. On the other hand, the Knicks were incredibly loose, buoyant, almost giddy at the prospect of winning number seventeen. Before the game, the emotional state of the locker room was lighter than cotton candy. Dick Barnett, who idolized comedian Redd Foxx, loved to entertain the guys when they were in this kind of a mood. He'd get up and do some shtick or make a wry observation that would send the team into peals of uncontrollable hysteria. One of his great comic bits, a send-up of the mania for all-star teams, was what he called his NBA All-Ugly team, a squad made up of the league's most scrofulous-looking players, and a half hour before game time he rose to conduct a ceremonial draft for this squad.

Gumming an imaginary microphone, Barnett announced, "The Atlanta Hawks select . . . Walt Hazzard!"

Well . . . my God, as you can imagine, a howl billowed through the room as the players shouted their approval. Naturally, Hazzard! What a felicitous choice. Keep going, Rich. Wind 'em up, baby!

Barnett set himself and proclaimed, "The Seattle Supersonics select . . . Bob Rule!"

Ah, yes—perfect! The Knicks doubled over as they flashed on Rule, a fearsome-looking guy with muttonchops and a hard, rangy face. He was a natural choice, and the guys responded appreciatively.

Bob Rule was, in fact, one of Barnett's favorite whipping boys. When the Knicks played Seattle, he performed a hilarious TV parody before the players took the court for warm-ups. He waited until he had everyone's attention, then stood up on a bench in front of his locker. Assuming a smooth, euphonious baritone reminiscent of Don Pardo, he cooed, "Join us next week on 'American Sportsman' when Willis Reed will be in the Pacific Northwest hunting for . . . Bob Rule." The guys laughed so hard they could hardly see straight. As the laughter died down, Barnett spotted Reed by his locker and said, "Willis, man, that guy's so ugly you just have to put his head on your den wall."

In Atlanta, the guys howled so hard it hurt. How could they play basketball after such a priceless piece of burlesque? *Har, har, har!* Barnett waved his hand, urging them to quiet down.

"The New York Knicks select—" An expectant hush fell over the room. *"—Cazzie Russell."*

Well, that did it! Players keeled over onto the floor holding their sides, they toppled into each other, lobbed wet towels. And, of course, Cazzie, who was on the other side of the room lacing his sneakers, jumped up screaming, "What do you mean—*Cazzie Russell?*" He was irate. *"What!* Now, wait a—I'm gonna—"

Even Walt Frazier, ordinarily a cool customer, was convulsed with laughter. Clyde gave Barnett a high five as he slipped his street clothes into the narrow locker. Leave it to Rich to take the edge off, he sighed.

Frazier had been raised in Atlanta, and earlier that afternoon he'd gone to his mother's home, the upper half of a simple two-family residence on East Avenue in northeast Atlanta, for some rest and an honest southern meal.

There was nothing like a visit to the old homestead to humble the superfly Clyde. In New York he was the cat's meow, sly and studly, with sumptuous threads, hot wheels, a babe on each arm. My, oh my, the man cut a precious figure, gliding down Broadway after dark; he oiled a smooth reputation. But in Atlanta the real Frazier resurfaced. The southern Clyde. Well, he wasn't even Clyde down there, he was Walt. And, truthfully, he wasn't even Walt, he was . . . *June.* Walt Frazier *June*-yer. Now, if that wasn't a mighty plunge! In fact, the name June probably suited Frazier best. He was a shy, quiet, guileless soul, content to ruminate behind a mask of pure impassivity. He was righteously introspective, self-contained, a confirmed loner, unfathomable. Come on to him with some hokey jive and—stand back. Those almond eyes of his would go dead, the smile turned plastic, the glide disappeared. He'd throw up sheets of armor even a blow-torch couldn't penetrate. When the subject was basketball, however, he'd relax again, still vigilant, but the charm would return, he'd radiate confidence, become animated in the way that all ballplayers do when they talk about the game. That Clyde business was nothing but a decent piece of public relations someone had dreamed up.

No, Atlanta brought out the June in Frazier, and that was fine by him. He loved going home—*loved* it. He was the oldest of nine kids—the others were Mary, Brenda, Janice, Brezita, Renita, Ethel, Phyllis, and Keith—the most successful by far, but the gang intuitively didn't push the hero baggage in his face. They were far too sharp for that. Maybe it helped that the local media virtually ignored Frazier on his home turf. If he had been anyone else, you could bet the farm on a few columns in the *Atlanta Constitution*—a profile of the studly "Clyde" linked to a story about the Knicks' current success, accompanied by a piece on his playing days at Howard High. A glorious spread, perhaps an entire page. Figure the phone would be ringing off the hook. But even now, with the Knicks' streak on everybody's lips, there wasn't a word about Frazier's hometown heritage in any of the Atlanta papers. Clyde paged through the *Constitution* on the off chance that—but, no, some things just never changed. And anyway, he was well aware of the reason. You could alter Atlanta's image, throw up a few dazzling skyscrapers, build an international airport and a media empire, improve education, and call it the New York of the South. You could call it anything you like for that matter, but a black man in the Deep South, even a top professional athlete, was still a nonentity there in 1969. The Confederate flag that flew atop the state capitol alongside the Stars and Stripes just about said it all. The powers that be— those Rebels in their silk suits—still yearned for Dixie, where a white man was a man and a black man was a boy . . . if you get the drift.

Frazier had lived in an all-black neighborhood, gone to all-black public schools, and been considered the best *black* basketball player in Atlanta. He didn't know where he stood in the overall picture, since he wasn't allowed to compete with any white players. "It was the *South*, man," he says today, recalling the disenfranchisement that was then the status quo. "We'd go to the white games and have to sit in the last row of the bleachers. They had a small section there where blacks could sit and stay out of sight. And we'd watch those guys play, with all that fantastic equipment, and thousands of screaming fans. Man, it was another world."

Frazier's world was dirt-poor, literally. He learned basketball on a playground behind Forrest Elementary School, where the surface was strictly sun-hardened earth and most of the dribbling was performed on a patch of wild tundra that included ruts, divots, and the random sedimentary rock. The game came easily to him, as did baseball and football. From the start, he could pass, rebound, and dribble with either hand. And he was tall—already six-two in the ninth grade. In tenth grade, he played varsity football, starting at quarterback and throwing seventy-yard bombs from both sides—righty and lefty—which should have made him a natural for the pros. But Frazier, already cool in the way he could sum up a situation, knew that black men weren't meant to be pro quarterbacks—not yet, anyway. Barking orders at white guys in the huddle would never wash—not in his lifetime, anyway. So he declared for basketball, with mixed results.

Frazier would have loved to go to one of the local sports emporiums—like Georgia Tech, whose teams he followed like a loyal puppy, or the University of Georgia, which Fran Tarkenton was turning into a respectable attraction. But they'd have needed a National Guard escort to get him on and off the court. Sadly, the white schools in Georgia were strictly off-limits to men of color. Of the black schools, Clark played its basketball games in a vacuum, and the programs at Morehouse and Morris State were a joke. There was always Tennessee State, where Dick Barnett had gone, or Grambling, Willis Reed's alma mater, but those particular black schools attracted the smartest athletes, and Frazier's grades weren't up to snuff. So, at that point, it was looking bleak as far as college went.

The September after his graduation from high school, Frazier still hadn't gotten into a college. It was getting late, and he was afraid he was going to wind up like many of the 'hood's other athletic hopefuls, haunting the bars along Auburn Avenue. That might well have been his fate, too, if a patron saint hadn't materialized. An Atlantan named Samuel Johnson, who did charitable work for one of the local black Christian fellowships, had suggested Frazier apply to a few of the integrated schools up north and had offered to do the necessary legwork. Well, that was about the most ridiculous idea Frazier had ever heard. Play basketball with *white* kids? In the *North?* That was practically a foreign country.

Frazier was skeptical, but Johnson just wouldn't go away. He popped up a week later with some news. Indiana wouldn't take him, due to his shabby grades, Johnson said, but there was another school, Southern Illinois— Well, hold it right there, brother! Southern Illinois? Come off it! Was that one of those schools they advertise inside matchbook covers? What conference were they part of—the Little Ten? Johnson had to be joking. "Hey, man, I never heard of this place," Frazier told him. "Is this on the level?"

The next thing Frazier knew, he was on a plane heading north. A *plane,* for Chrissake! The whole idea of air travel scared the shit out of him. It was his first flight, and he caused a bit of alarm on the runway by asking a stewardess to show him where the parachute was. He slobbered the whole way, too, and when the air-conditioning gave off a faint puff of condensation, Frazier saw God and assumed the proper position for the moment when the damn ship would nosedive and hit the ground in an amazing ball of fire.

Actually, the plane landed smoothly in St. Louis. Carbondale, where the school was located, was a tiny blip on the map ninety miles away, and the assistant basketball coach, George Iubelt, met Walt at the airport. As soon as their car turned from the airport onto Route 13 and entered rural Illinois, Frazier knew he'd veered about as close to The Twilight Zone as he was ever going to get. Why, the towns en route were only a stoplight or two long. Blink, and you just might miss Pinckneyville, Swanwick, Winkle, Marissa, Meridian, Coulterville, Murphysboro, or any of the other wicks, villes, or boros off the main road. This was the sticks, baby! Frazier thought. Must be what Poland looks like. He was blown out by the hayseed scenery. He didn't say a word for the entire two hours. Iubelt did all the talking. Telling Walt about how the great Harry Gallatin, who had coached at SIU, and Chico Vaughn, currently with the St. Louis Hawks, had played there. All these tidbits registered with Frazier, but he couldn't find a way to respond. He kept thinking, Where am I? What am I doing here?

As it turned out, Southern Illinois was a blessing in disguise. The school was the "Little Engine That Could." It was a Division II team, which is like saying you were first-chair cello with the San Luis Potosi Symphony Orchestra, but that didn't put the brakes on its ambitions. Jack Hartman, the stern, hard-boiled basketball coach, was a man with a single objective: to tweak his team into Division I, and to that end he often would rent his team out at well below the going rate. He would convince Division I schools to play his team, but on grossly inequitable terms, such as giving them a sweetheart two-for-one deal: SIU would play two games on their campus for every one game they played in Carbondale. It's what any self-respecting school called a handout, and most would have done it as soon as they would have worn hand-me-down jerseys. But a lowly joint like SIU wound up playing quite a few powerhouses, such as Oklahoma State, Texas Western, Louisville, Kansas State, and Iowa—and actually *beat* more than a few of them, while they were at it. Quite a few legends got to see Walt Frazier play (and a handful of pro scouts, too, Red Holzman among them), and most knew right away that they were looking at a hot model loaded with extras.

Frazier was a comer, all right. He was a great team player, completely unselfish, who could run, jump, rebound, and shoot. And *strong!* What a body, a real piece of work, muscles in places

they haven't even identified in *Gray's Anatomy*—Hartman had
never seen anything like it before. It was like one of those movies
in which an angel sends someone to earth with a mission to
transform the worst team in creation into champs—like the Devil
in *Damn Yankees*. Frazier was his Joe Dobbs. The kid was a
natural. First year out, Walt led the team—the Salukis!
(*really!*)—in rebounds and points . . . despite the fact that he
felt like a foreigner.

Today he looks back on Carbondale and says, "It was an
adjustment for me." But that is so much understatement. Frazier
was completely out of his depth at SIU in just about every way.
Academically, he was lost, helpless. Math, English—forget it;
he had what amounted to a grade-school equivalency at best.
Also, his speech was slurred, preventing him from expressing
himself in class. There was no way he could do the work. He
was already quiet and shy, but now he became a complete introvert in order to avoid embarrassing himself.

On the social scene, he was no better off. Integration, such
as it was, threw Walt for a loop at first. Black and white together?
He had to hand it to them—it was a helluva concept. Dr. King's
dream, Bobby Kennedy's mission, a lot of his idols worked hard
to push it through. But in reality, you'd probably see it only on
the printed page. Some things would never change. Then, during
orientation, a white girl with a big friendly face volunteered to
help him register. *A white girl!* Imagine that. And black kids sat
with white kids at lunch, side by side. They took the same classes,
went to *mixers*. (Now, there was an appropriate name!) No one
at SIU seemed to give it a second thought. Ironically, the worst
bigotry he encountered there came from a clique of northern
black students who looked down on their southern counterparts.
"Brother must be from outer space," they scoffed.

Once basketball started, however, it was the whole Clark
Kent routine for Frazier. He'd change into the uniform, step into
hi-tops, fly onto the court, and the transformation was complete.

There wasn't anyone or anything that could compete with him. For games against the Salukis' chief rivals—Kentucky Wesleyan, St. Louis University, and Evansville, with the great Jerry Sloan—Frazier played both ends of the court. The guy was unstoppable. Score nineteen, twenty-four points, pull down a dozen rebounds. Switch to small forward at the drop of a hat. He was magnificent, invulnerable. But, like Superman with his nemesis of the deadly green kryptonite, Frazier encountered two near-catastrophes that threatened to strip him of his magic cape.

The first was a pox called academic probation, and it hit him sophomore year, in the form of a letter from the dean. It was the usual bureaucratic crap about standards and excellence. Walt skimmed it to determine the degree of fallout, but only four words stood out: ". . . ineligible to play basketball." Well, it might as well have said, "You have been sentenced to hang by the neck until dead." He was benched for the season. *Thunk!* But Frazier resorted to a tactical maneuver that probably made his career. Unable to play competitively, he spent the year serving as an extra body at practices—what was called "red-shirting." He spent all his time scrimmaging, playing defense, so the varsity could get a good workout. In the process, he mastered the Art of D, those facets of the game that most players hate because it eats into their point stats—shot blocking, rebounding, boxing out, setting picks, Frazier refined them all. He perfected passing the ball to teammates, working the clock, making outlet passes. Hartman also encouraged him to practice petty thievery—stealing the ball, stripping it from an opponent's hands, picking a pocket or two. Imagine the invaluable little package that created—taking a pure shooter like Frazier and turning him into a defensive specialist. How many coaches laid awake at night, dreaming of such a superbeing! Matter-of-factly, Frazier took a potential disaster and turned it into a blessing.

He wasn't so lucky in handling the second crisis.

She was a grad student from Chicago, and if that were the

long and short of it he would have been all right. But she had a hidden agenda that rivaled *Fatal Attraction* for sheer spookiness. First off, she faked a pregnancy to lure Frazier into marriage— she convinced him to do "the right thing," which he did, and then she went and got pregnant after the fact. Okay, he could live with that. Marriage, fatherhood, that was coming sometime anyway. But not only was his new wife deceitful, she was insanely jealous. Any female so much as glanced at Walt—well, in her eyes that meant they'd practically done it! She waited outside practices to make sure he came right home, followed him to classes. If he stayed late to see a prof, they were obviously doing it. Stopped to buy a textbook, he was doing it with the cashier. Patted the head of a dog, he—well, you get the idea. She wouldn't get off his back.

Then it got worse.

One night Walt's buddy Ed Zastrow stopped by their place on his way to practice and found Walt with his hand swaddled in a surgical bandage. Seems his wife had accused him of doing it with God knows who and had come across the table with a fork. Stabbed him right in the hand, too, like it was a piece of brisket. Another night, Walt and Zastrow stopped in a local joint called the Club for a beer. She was waiting outside when they left and caught Walt in the back with a dull kitchen knife. Then she went home and smashed his trophies. Glenn Close couldn't have played it more convincingly.

Somehow, despite this nightmarish turn of events, Frazier managed to stay focused on the court. Following his reinstatement, he continued to work hard, to play his game, and even to make a national name for himself. In this, his third year at SIU, the Salukis ran off fifteen straight wins and went to the NIT— at Madison Square Garden!—where they dispatched St. Peter's, Duke, Rutgers, and Marquette, to win the entire tournament. A nothing school like SIU! It was unheard of. Not coincidentally, Frazier grabbed the MVP trophy, in front of a packed house that included just about every pro scout in the country, including Red Holzman and Eddie Donovan.

Well, you can imagine the stir that created back in Carbondale! There were rallies and parades and receptions and . . . offers. Representatives from Baltimore, Seattle, and Chicago all inquired about his status. His status! If that didn't put a whole new spin on things, suggesting to Frazier that he might skip his senior year and turn pro instead. In the end, it was the lure of money that drew him into the draft. A poor black kid from Atlanta, with a wife and a kid to support. How could he refuse a lucrative employment opportunity? Not an opportunity to play basketball, anyway. Screw the diploma; school could wait.

Everyone, including Frazier, expected Seattle to take him in the first round in 1966. The Sonics needed a playmaker like Walt to spell Lenny Wilkens, and they'd already made a pitch to him. But the Knicks picked ahead of the Sonics, and Dick McGuire, their ill-fated coach, loved the Salukis' all-around guard. He *loved* him. In a strategy meeting with Ned Irish, his partner Freddy Podesta, Eddie Donovan, and Red Holzman, McGuire trotted out all of Walt's merits—his touch, his speed, his defensive play. This kid Frazier reminded him of . . . Jerry West!

Donovan and Holzman didn't need any convincing. They'd both been to Carbondale, had done the whole scouting bit. Talked to the coaches, looked at film, kept a record of Frazier's progress. McGuire was right, they agreed, Frazier would fit right into the program the Knicks were developing. Irish and Podesta listened with keen interest.

"Did we think Frazier was going to be great?" Donovan asks today "No, he'd played too much small forward, he was coming from a nowhere place like Carbondale to New York. It'd be a tough adjustment all around. But he was loaded with talent. Red liked the way he looked, too. It just felt right. There was little disagreement that he was our man."

Detroit picked ahead of the Knicks, who knew the Pistons

were taking Jimmy Walker. Then, in succession, Baltimore selected Earl Monroe, Chicago grabbed Clem Haskins, and Detroit
(with a second first-round pick) went for Sonny Dove. When it
was New York's turn, Dick McGuire pounced. Walt Frazier
became a Knick, and the team came across with a hundred grand
to seal the deal.

A hundred grand for three years—talk about a sweet deal.
For practically a pittance, the Knicks got the cornerstone of their
franchise: an outstanding playmaker, scorer, and defensive expert
rolled into one. By only his second year, Frazier had shattered
Dick McGuire's team record of 542 assists by nearly a *hundred*
points. He'd learned how to control the pace of the game. In
1968, when Red Holzman replaced McGuire as the Knicks'
coach, he made Frazier the springboard for most of the team's
offensive plays. Now people were talking about him in the same
breath as Oscar Robertson!

Well, Oscar was the penultimate player, but Frazier proved
to be that and more. He was even developing a persona. A *persona,
for Chrissake!* Today, that's almost a given for a basketball star.
Every rook comes out of college trailing a fancy rep. He's got a
marketable nickname or a shaved head or a recording contract.
Or all three. He ascends to the pros with a whole entourage.
But in 1968, the concept of a persona was something that hadn't
yet reared its ugly head. Sure, there was Wilt Chamberlain—
Wilt the Stilt—but he hadn't cultivated the nickname; in fact,
he hated it. And besides, Wilt wasn't human, he was . . . Wilt.
God. You had to hand it to Frazier. This persona business—it
was original, it was brash, it was noisy.

He became *Clyde*—so named after Clyde Barrow of the in-
famous Bonnie and Clyde stickup team. The Knicks' equipment
man, Danny Whelan, gave him the *nom de théatre* when Frazier
began spending his salary on fancy threads. We're not talking
about the occasional silk shirt or alligator shoe, either. This was
the whole nine yards—a makeover from top to bottom of that

statuesque six-four frame. Walt laid out a real chunk of change in developing the Clyde persona, too. The outfit usually required a wide-brimmed hat, aviator glasses with tinted lenses, a silk scarf knotted at the neck, an incandescently colored suit with lapels recalling the wingspan of a DC-10, silk ankle-length socks, hundred-dollar shoes with Cuban heels, manicured nails, and hair that wasn't just cut but sculpted. In the winter, Frazier—make that Clyde—would drape a full-length fur coat over his shoulders to make his way to his . . . limo. Sure, it was a persona, but considering that only two years earlier he'd emerged from a life-style that fell significantly below the poverty line, it demonstrated a fair bit of hubris, too. Well, this was New York City, and Clyde had decided to do the town in style. Uptown style. Those northern SIU students had called it: he was from outer space, all right—the brother from another planet.

In the process, Frazier unloaded his wife and became the man-about-town (a title he shared at the time with Jet-setter Joe Namath). He was a fixture at all the current hot spots. Wore a babe on each arm—and not just a babe, but a *babe!* The guy had amazing luck with gorgeous women. Inwardly, Walt Frazier, Jr., may have remained shy and soft-spoken, a conventional introvert, but when he put on the clothes—and, brother, he could put on the clothes—and became Clyde, he was *out there.*

Walt . . . Clyde . . . Walt . . . Clyde . . . the guy seemed to be able to turn it on and off at will. Still, it must have been a relief to him to be back in Atlanta. Back home again, he could cool his jets and reset his clock to the pace of the sleepy Old South. It was reassuring to leave the Clyde persona packed away in his suitcase for a while. He had enough pressure just worrying about the Hawks. They weren't going to be a walk in the park, not with a sixteen-game winning streak on the line. No team liked going into the record book as a goat, and the Hawks would not do so voluntarily. Those birds were going to put up a fight.

The Knicks stayed downtown, at the Marriott, and Frazier checked in with the rest of the team. They'd been on a night flight, and everyone craved some sleep. Around noon, Walt took a cab to his mother's home and wolfed down one of her mouth-watering southern spreads—fried chicken, collard greens, thick brown gravy that congealed into a molten paste, the works. Most ballplayers eat a good meal, usually a steak or something equally fortifying, before game time, but this fare had the density of a manhole cover, and it made Frazier feel gassy and leaden. Man, he was having trouble keeping his eyes open. If anybody had asked him, at that moment, if he felt like a game of horse, he would have declined. It was hard to figure how he was going to get up for a game. And not just any game, but The Game. Maybe he could just skip this one, could phone Red at the hotel and say, "Listen, Coach, about the game tonight—I've decided to sleep in. Let Johnny Warren have a shot." Maybe *not!* But, Christ, he was going to need a blood transfusion for this one.

Eula Frazier watched her son through steely slit eyes. He was dragging his feet, lollygagging. The mother of nine, she'd seen this routine before. What did he expect—a note from her excusing Walter junior from the Game? She'd have none of that. June, Clyde, whatever he was calling himself now, it made no difference.

"Walt," she said sharply, "don't you let those Hawks beat you!"

This is yo' mama speaking! Well, it had the effect of a double shot of Pepto-Bismol. *Whoooooosh!* Adrenaline flooded into those weary chicken-stuffed limbs, murder crept into his heart. Frazier grabbed his coat, headed to Alexander Arena, the old Georgia Tech field house, and fired up the engines. "Let's get 'em! Let's get 'em!" he said, percolating on the locker-room bench. *"Let's get 'em!"* He was pumped.

Willis Reed already had his game face on. He'd be going against Jim Davis, who was a gamer but no one he couldn't handle. At six-nine and 235 pounds of gristle, the two were exactly the same size and weight, and both were around the same age. But that's where all comparison stopped. Fact was, Davis had played behind Zelmo Beaty for so long that he was still getting his sea legs. With the demands of leadership thrust on him, he wasn't much of a scoring threat, was only an average rebounder, and wasn't strong enough to fend off a bulldog like Reed. Willis would be able to flick him out of the box like a flea. What's more, Davis had a weak side that Willis could exploit. There'd be an opportunity for him to put some points on the board tonight. "Let's go!" Reed shouted, cracking his impassive facade.

Bradley and DeBusschere wandered in together and talked up the temperature further, clapping their hands and whooping.

"You got to want it!" Barnett cackled. Up until now, he'd seemed impervious to the streak, and had maintained a cool composure. Then, before finishing warm-ups tonight, he'd run into Bill Bridges, Atlanta's feisty forward, who warned him about celebrating too early.

"You guys aren't going to set any records against me tonight," Bridges growled.

"Why not?" Barnett asked. "Aren't you playing?"

It was vintage Rich, a real knee slapper that quickly made the rounds of the Knicks bench before the buzzer. " 'Why not, aren't you playing?' Good ol' Rich! Har, har, har!"

No one was certain what did the trick—Clyde's mama or Barnett's barb. But, going into the third quarter, with the Knicks holding a tenuous seven-point advantage, all hell broke loose. Willis Reed hit a jumper from the corner that lit the proverbial powder keg under his team. *Boom!* The Knicks exploded, going on a 12–0 run, followed by a 14–0 run, outscoring the pitiful Hawks 33–5 in the quarter. It was a punishment of humiliating proportions.

The Knicks were brutal in their orchestration of deliberate, flawless basketball. They put on a clinic, executing plays with such delicate precision that even Red Holzman was impressed. *Click, click, click*—you could almost hear the gears falling into place, it was that mechanical. They not only outplayed the Hawks, they abused them. To give you an indication of the carnage, the Hawks penetrated to the basket a total of *three times* in the quarter. Two of those times, the drives ended in steals when Frazier and Bradley took the ball away from Walt Hazzard and Joe Caldwell, respectively. It practically brought those old birds to their knees. Frazier made seven steals in the quarter and finished with fifteen for the game. *Fifteen steals!* Three of them came on successive drives by Hazzard. Clyde flicked the ball out of Hazzard's hands as if he were defending against an amateur. (Afterward, the usually taciturn Red Holzman told a reporter, "It's a good thing they didn't have any gold fillings in their teeth, because he would have taken them, too.") And he threw in thirty-three points on top of that, just to prove that he occasionally played offense.

Clyde may have given the hometown crowd a dose of humility, but he was abetted by the combined efforts of his teammates. Reed matched the guard's hefty point total with another thirty-three, Barnett grabbed a dozen loose balls and converted each of them, Russell ran off a perfect ten points in five minutes of play, and Bradley handcuffed Lou Hudson, holding the man with the second highest point total in the league to a pair of foul shots. You could actually see Atlanta's frustration at work on the court. They were flailing around spastically, kneading their brows, looking toward the coach for a clue. The Knicks almost felt sorry for them.

Almost.

Any fool could see it was over after the third quarter. Red Holzman pulled his starters and let the bench have some exercise. Even with that, the Hawks couldn't break the code. They were stuck in a bad dream. In the end, it was a romp, 138–108, and the Knicks had tied the record for consecutive wins at seventeen.

For the New York Knicks, the flight out of Atlanta was a typical low-key affair. There was no strutting, no woofing. The lopsided victory generated mostly satisfied smiles, but no one mentioned the streak. As a subject, it was taboo. "We play them one at a time and take them as they come," Willis Reed reminded his teammates. If anything, the streak loomed precariously over them, like a curse. The players felt that if they acknowledged it, they'd jinx it. Anyway, it was bush to play for a streak. Instead, the guys slept or played cards, leaning out into the plane's narrow aisle where the kitty—and their drinks—were strewn.

They had a day off before the next game with Cincinnati. The Royals were doing their good-neighbor bit by playing this one in Cleveland. It was referred to as a "neutral floor," and for the Knicks it was a particularly itchy piece of luck. Last year, they'd been five-and-one on neutral floors, with their only loss coming in—that's right, Cleveland. Well, they'd have to make the best of it—take the day off there, get acclimated to the town. As a rule, no player liked being in Cleveland, much less being in Cleveland on Thanksgiving, which it was.

"It's an insult to turkeys everywhere," Barnett said, accompanied by a chorus of lewd gobbles.

To celebrate the holiday, Danny Whelan organized a team dinner at a local restaurant, where the mood was relentlessly upbeat. Lots of chatter. Everyone giddy as a Girl Scout. Red Holzman was particularly chatty, no doubt stimulated by the copious supply of twelve-year-old scotch on hand. And such a marvelous feast! Enough food on the table to end hunger in our time—not too bad, by road standards, either. The guys rarely ate a meal together, even when they were on the road; players had different feeding schedules, different routines. So it felt good to shoot the shit for a few hours, to eat and drink with true soulmates.

Still, the conversation inevitably edged back to Cincinnati. The game with the Royals was foremost on everyone's mind. It was a milestone, certainly, but a sense of foreboding had crept in around it. DeBusschere, for one, voiced concern that the Royals could stage a coup. He figured they had enough elements to surprise you on any given night. Most of the Knicks feared Oscar Robertson—Oscar could single-handedly sink their ship. And, to a man, they were curious to see Bob Cousy in action.

Cousy's story was getting wackier by the day. In the beginning of November, after the Knicks had their first look at Cincinnati, Cousy began shaking up his sorry team. They wouldn't be re-building with veterans, he announced, and to prove it he shipped superstar Jerry Lucas to San Francisco, in exchange for reserve players Bill Turner and John King. It was an unpopular deal, to put it mildly. And when King promptly broke his leg, he was lucky the Cincinnati fans didn't take him out behind the barn and shoot him. Cousy's reaction to the misfortune was—well, preposterous. The Royals' rookie coach decided to come out of retirement and activate himself as a player. What the fu . . . ? The Cooz hadn't played in seven years—the guy was forty-one, practically a relic. Everyone suspected it was some kind of crack-pot stunt.

For what it was worth, Bob Cousy was an uncontested NBA legend, maybe the finest player to ever appear on the court. He was the Michael Jordan of his day. A sleight-of-hand artist, he could dribble the ball behind his back—on the run—without breaking rhythm, could fly through the air, then stretch hang time into a spell that resembled a holding pattern at Logan Air-port. In thirteen years with the Celtics, the Cooz had performed supernatural feats with stunning regularity. Christ, maybe he was the Messiah. The Boston fans sure treated him like one.

This present stunt, however, had unmasked Cooz as nothing

but another charlatan. His old coach, Red Auerbach, in particular, was displeased. Cousy—*his* Cousy—in a Royals uniform?
Over his dead body! Auerbach notified the NBA commissioner
Walter Kennedy that Cousy was on the Celtics' retired-player
list; no way he'd play for another team without suitable com-
pensation.

Say . . . what? What did Auerbach expect—a player from
Cincinnati? Well, exactly. The way he saw it, Cousy was a Celtic
player for life—or until Auerbach chose to set him free. There
were conditions, of course, that might facilitate such an outcome.
Auerbach wouldn't be unreasonable. Heh, heh! He'd be willing
to part with Cooz for, say, Connie Dierking or Luthur Rackley
or . . . Wasn't there a rumor that Oscar was unhappy?
Hmmmmm? Oh, and there was one other thing Cooz could do
to motivate ol' Red. Auerbach tried to extract a clause stating
that if indeed Cousy was activated, he wouldn't suit up against
Boston.

Well, the commissioner finally put his foot down. He'd have
no more of this monkey business. Bob Cousy, he decided, worked
for Cincinnati now, and he could do as he pleased with the Royals.
Auerbach could smoke his cigars and otherwise keep his mouth
shut. The matter was closed, as far as the NBA was concerned.
The way the Knicks read it, Cousy would be in uniform for their
critical game.

A crowd of 10,438 turned out to see the Knicks' flirtation
with history. It was one of those chilly northern Ohio nights that
rattle the bones, the wind sweeping down off Lake Erie with an
ominous *shwoooosh.* "Fit for neither man nor beast"—it was a
phrase that described both the weather and the Cleveland Arena.
The Knicks hated playing in that dump. It was built around the
time the Pilgrims landed at Plymouth Rock, which was probably
when it last saw any maintenance. The halls were filthy, the
floor was worn and decrepit. The locker rooms were in worse

shape than some recently condemned Bronx tenements, with collapsed ceilings and exposed rotting pipes. Half the lights were blown. Incongruously, the NBA had announced that Cleveland would get the next expansion team to be admitted to the league, and so the city was frantically trying to make improvements to the building. Planks of wood were propped against walls. Construction tools littered the place. A sign out front proclaimed "Home of the Cleveland Barons"—one of the Midwest's low-rent hockey teams. Well, sure, that made sense.

Still, the old arena buzzed with anticipation. Eighteen victories in a row—it'd be a fantastic achievement. *Eighteen!* Earlier in the year, a man had walked on the moon, so why not? But *eighteen?* In a row? Highly unlikely, they bubbled, moon walk or no moon walk.

Even before the game started, a few of the Knicks were sure it wasn't going to happen. Not tonight. The guys felt lifeless, flat. All that food the night before—it was still lying there in the old breadbasket, like undigested cud. Nothing was moving properly. Arms felt heavy, feet were sluggish. The warm-ups, you could tell, lacked the proper spark. The Knicks needed sleep!

Once the game started, it looked like the ship had hit an iceberg. They were sinking. No one was going full tilt. The action had a slow-motion stickiness to it. Guys were walking the ball up the court, daydreaming. Did someone say the word molasses? Shots weren't falling. Passes flew out of bounds.

"Everyone into the lifeboats!"

The Royals were going to be spoilers. The *Royals!* A team of water treaders, of also-rans. And in Cleveland, at that. How ignominious could it get?

Oh, pretty ignominious. Oscar Robertson tap-danced on the Knicks' grave. The Big O scored thirty-three points, added ten assists, and had himself what was turning into a tidy little defensive night. Then, with a minute-forty-nine to go and Cincinnati safely in front, a strange thing happened. Oscar picked up his sixth foul and got the hook. Okay, good riddance. Cousy looked down the bench for a sub, hesitated, then got up and jogged over to the scorer's table.

Down at the Knicks' end, Donnie May jabbed Bill Hosket in the ribs and said, "Hey, get a load of this! Cousy's putting himself in."

The Cooz stood up and peeled his warm-up shirt over his head. Well, the place went nuts. The Cleveland fans were going to get to see The Great Cousy play. Talk about rubbing the Knicks' noses in it. Having their streak stopped by a mediocre team that throws a forty-one-year-old geezer at you in the final seconds! If that didn't beat all!

Cousy's mission was simply to eat up the clock. That normally requires a good deal of talent, a calm head, and steady nerves, especially against an unflappable team like the Knicks. The Cooz, however, had made time killing an art in the West. He was a master practitioner. Even at his age, in his shape, having been away for seven years, Cousy knew exactly what to do. He took his time bringing the ball down the floor, then made one of those trademark hook passes of his—a dart that looked like it was coming from behind his hip—to Norm Van Lier, who buried it from the right side for two points. Immediately afterward, Bradley fouled Cousy, and he methodically sank both shots, putting the Royals up by five, 105–100.

You could read the reaction on the Knicks' faces: We're out of it. It's over. Sixteen seconds left, down by five. Lord, let it be quick and merciful.

Then Tom Van Arsdale fouled Willis Reed, who made two, and Cousy called for a time-out—Cincinnati's last—which would give the Royals the ball at midcourt when play resumed.

Holzman waved his team over quickly. "We're still in it," he said, although no one took him seriously. "Just play 'em tight. Stay up their asses. Don't give 'em any room."

On the fringe of the huddle, where the subs grazed, Bill

Hosket shook his head dejectedly. "It doesn't look too good," he mumbled, shuffling his feet like a disappointed child.

Danny Whelan clapped him on the shoulder. "Hey, Hoss— no problem, baby. We hit a few free throws, grab a couple of steals. This thing isn't over!"

The guy's a fucking space cadet, Hosket thought. He's still circling somewhere over Atlanta.

When the breather ended there were thirteen seconds left on the clock. Not much you could do with that. Holzman sent in Mike Riordan, along with Frazier, Bradley, DeBusschere, and Reed. Cousy prepared to put the ball in play at midcourt, and Riordan, New York's resident pest, moved right into his face. This gave Mike, whose high-school coach was in the stands, an opportunity to take a good look at one of his all-time heroes. He peered at Cooz, trying to rattle the old man. Nothing doing. This guy has supreme confidence, Riordan thought. At his age! Mike moved in as close as he could get without standing on Cousy's toes. I don't know, he thought, if I were Cousy I would have let Odie Smith or Van Arsdale take it out. They have the size to look and pass over the defense. But, hey, this is The Great Cousy. He must know what he's doing.

Cousy's eyes scanned the floor. The Knicks had their respective men covered. They'd left him no breathing room. The play had been set up so that Connie Dierking was supposed to break free and circle out, but Reed had him by the waist. Finally, in the nick of time, Cousy saw Van Arsdale get open and flicked him a bounce pass, but DeBusschere swept in between them and picked it off. Dave looked for Clyde or Bradley downcourt, but he saw only the Royals' Johnny Green, edging toward the line, so he switched course, lowered his shoulder, and took it in by himself for a lay-up. Now it was 105–104, with six seconds left.

This time, Cousy found Van Arsdale on the inbound pass, and Van Arsdale promptly brought the ball up the right sideline. He was a solid, reliable ball handler. His brother, Dick, had played for the Knicks from 1966 to 1968, and together they had registered considerable fraternal leverage among the league's offensive ranks. Tom Van Arsdale was the right man to play out the clock. He rarely made a mistake.

Rarely.

Willis Reed shot an eye at the clock—*five seconds showing*—and reacted impetuously. He had been shadowing Dierking, the Royals' big man, but that tactic was fast proving irrelevant. Van Arsdale wasn't fool enough to pass the ball, not with his team up by one point and only four seconds left. He'd hold on to it or try to take it in himself. So Reed made the kind of split-second decision that becomes mythologized as intuition: he left his man and went for the ball. He descended on Van Arsdale like a storm trooper, causing the small forward to lean away from the unexpected pressure. Somehow, Reed anticipated the seachange and swatted the ball into the air. And somehow destiny brought it down into the hands of Walt "Clyde" Frazier.

With two seconds left, Frazier didn't have time to think, either. He was operating on pure adrenaline now. He dribbled dangerously behind his back in order to get past Van Lier. Then, driving the other way, he launched a jumper from the top of the key that didn't quite have the direction. *Clank!* The ball hit the back of the rim, bounced out over the airborne heads of Dierking and Reed, both of whom were slow-dancing in the paint, and . . . into the hands of Walt Frazier! Talk about luck! In one motion, Clyde went up with the ball again and took aim but was knocked slightly sideways by Van Arsdale.

No time left.

Whistle!

Foul.

Could this be true? All 10,000 fans jumped collectively to their feet, hooting at the refs. The five Royals on the floor wore the same expression: *Wuh?* Cousy was livid. He pleaded his case to the ref, appealed, was overruled, appealed again, threw himself on the mercy of the court—nothing doing. The Knicks were alive.

Frazier walked resolutely to the line. He glanced at the scoreboard—Royals 105, Knicks 104—and felt a zing of self-doubt sluice through him. "Why *me?*" he sighed, bouncing the ball maniacally on the floor. A week earlier, against Philadelphia, he had been in a similar spot and had choked. With fifteen seconds left, the score seesawing at 94–91, Frazier was fouled by Hal Greer and made only one of his attempts. Then, five seconds later, he was fouled by Matt Goukas and again made only one. Luckily, the Knicks managed to pull that one out, but shooting blanks like that hadn't helped the cause. Damn, this was an annoying spot. He looked over at the bench. The entire New York team was on their feet, waving joyously like children.

He stopped dribbling and aimed. *Please, God, don't let me fuck up!*

The ball looped through the air and fell sweetly through the net. *Swoosh!* Tie score.

Based on recent history, however, the odds now shifted away from the Knicks. Frazier's clutching in Philly—well, you had to like the prospects of overtime here in Cleveland. Again, Frazier tattooed the ball against the floor—five, six, seven, eight . . . If he kept dribbling, maybe the situation would just go away. Maybe they'd call the game on account of curfew. Instead, a remarkable thing happened. The screaming, the arm waving, the relentless pressure—Frazier couldn't hear, see, or feel a single distraction anymore. It all melted away. Only the ball and the basket occupied a hundred percent of his focus. He could see it so clearly now. The flight path was directly in front of him. Unimpeded. He could almost reach out and touch it.

Frazier didn't so much as hesitate. He arched his back, dipped his ample behind a few inches for rhythm, and let the ball go. The second it left his hand, he knew. No need to even look. A perfect shot, all net. 106–105. *The Knicks won it!*

Ned Irish *(left)* and Dick McGuire *(right)* hover as Red Holzman conducts business during the 1969 NBA draft.

The official 1969–70 team picture. Standing *(left to right)*: Coach William (Red) Holzman, Phil Jackson, Dave Stallworth, Dave DeBusschere, Captain Willis Reed, Bill Hosket, Nate Bowman, Bill Bradley, Chief Scout Dick McGuire, and Trainer Dan Whelan. Seated *(left to right)*: John Warren, Don May, Walt Frazier, President Ned Irish, Chairman of the Board Irving Mitchell Felt, General Manager Ed Donovan, Dick Barnett, Mike Riordan, and Cazzie Russell.

Above left: Dave DeBusschere shows perfect form as he puts two points on the scoreboard.

Above right: Dick Barnett demonstrates "fall back baby" to an unidentified Hawk.

Right: Willis Reed outmuscles Boston's Dave Cowens.

Facing page: Earl Monroe and Walt Frazier, two masters of speed and skill.

Right: Red Holzman reviews a critical play with Stallworth, Frazier, Bradley, Riordan, and DeBusschere.

Below: Willis Reed flicks off rookie Lew Alcindor in a clear drive to the basket.

Left: Cazzie Russell drives
on the Bucks' Greg Smith
in the second round of the
play-offs.

Below: The players toast
Walt Frazier's play,
following the Knicks'
defeat of the Milwaukee
Bucks in the second round
of the play-offs.

AP Wirephoto

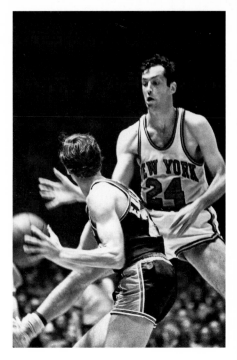

Above left: Willis Reed rejects Wilt Chamberlain's shot during Game One of the NBA championship series.

Above right: Bill Bradley soars above LA's Keith Erickson in Game One of the NBA championship series.

Below: Willis Reed writhes in pain following an injury in Game Five of the NBA championship.

Above: The
Garden crowd
goes wild as
Willis Reed
appears moments
before Game
Seven of the
1969–70 NBA
championship.

Left: Victory—
at last!—as the
Knicks defeat
the Lakers
for the NBA
championship.

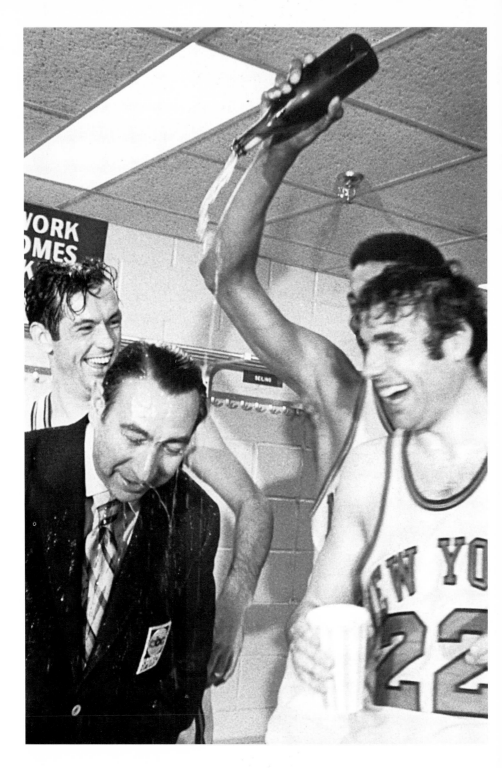

Nat Bowman *(hidden)* douses Howard Cosell with celebratory champagne to the amusement of Bill Bradley *(left)* and Dave DeBusschere *(right)*.

Frazier shot his hand into the air, double-pumped, and danced toward the sideline. They'd done the impossible—won eighteen in a row! They'd broken the record and left the Royals standing shell-shocked on the ratty Cleveland floor.

On the way into the locker room, Cazzie Russell hugged Frazier and . . . kissed him! "You did it, baby!" Russell shrieked. Then Red Holzman clapped him on the back. "Way to go, Clyde!" Bradley was there, too—"Beautiful, beautiful!"—and Reed and Barnett and Riordan and . . . Everyone was around him, and the momentum carried them up the ramp, around the obstacles, and through a pack of wild-eyed reporters.

The locker room was a swirl of complete pandemonium. The whole squad squealing, pushing, hugging, slapping each other's shoulders. Someone handed Frazier a bottle of Johnnie Walker Black, which he took a pull from and passed to Barnett.

"I got ice water in my veins," he said, holding his hands aloft as evidence.

Shouts and squeals echoed off the walls. Someone put his fingers to his lips and pointed at the plywood divider separating the Knicks from the Royals in the arena's makeshift quarters. On the other side of that board, maybe a quarter inch away, sat The Great Cousy, languishing in defeat.

"That ol' *chump!*" yelled Nate Bowman, taking his turn with the bottle of scotch. The guys howled their approval.

"*Suck*-ah!"

"Yo, *baby!* You gotta be *young* to play this game!"

Frazier stood up and waved across the room at Dick Barnett. "Can I get my cement hands back, baby?" he said, grinning. Barnett rolled his eyes. "I got a new title, baby. Just call me Ice Water Veins. The ball never touched the net!"

The Knicks celebrated in those cramped quarters for more than two hours, reliving every one of the last sixteen seconds in minute detail. Across the way, the Royals showered, dressed, and left in silence.

On his way out of the arena, Tom Van Arsdale stopped for a moment in front of New York's door and listened to the laughter emanating from inside. Van Arsdale's heart sank. He was a die-hard competitor, and he felt the Royals should have won the game. It's like a nightmare, he thought. The Knicks had stolen one. Then he stared at the door and flashed on the familiar faces of that mighty New York squad.

Nah, he thought. It's their time. The gods are with them.

7 | BOOGALOO
DOWN
BROADWAY

November 29–December 24, 1969

WHEN THE KNICKS got back to New York, they were given the full star treatment. The Royals game had been on TV, and throughout the telecast the drums beat steadily along the fashionable metropolitan grapevine—from pleasantly stoned Greenwich Village up through Chelsea, spreading east into Gramercy Park and the no-man's tundra dividing the Bays (Kips and Turtle), spiraling up posh Park Avenue through the nouveau-riche Upper East Side, across town into Hell's Kitchen, farther north among the tweedy environs of the Upper West Side, and reaching into deepest, darkest Harlem and the South Bronx—reminding smart New Yorkers that their star-making machinery was spitting out celebrities. Gradually, grudgingly, the city's resident scene makers began turning up at the games.

"Harriet, darling, check out these gorgeous athletes, will you. They're like . . . gazelles. Warrior gazelles."

"My *God,* these men have potential."

"Doesn't that Barnett fellow look positively Babylonian?"

"Is it true, Doris, that men of that size have bigger—"

Hold it right there, Doris! Get a grip!

In something under fifteen minutes, the city was caught up in a basketball frenzy. The Knicks captivated an audience whose capricious attention that year had already been joggled by a prime crew of luminaries out beating the pavement for attention. Neil Armstrong, John Lennon, Mario Puzo, Lauren Hutton, Philip Roth, and Bob Dylan fought valiantly for their piece of that rich New York minute, but the Knicks clearly won the day. They were your basic instant media darlings—straightforward, pliant, uncorrupted. They were interdenominational, multiethnic. The leading New York P.R. factories couldn't have churned out a hotter product. There was plenty of meat on their bones, too. Everyone wanted a piece of them. Advertisers, marketing bureaus, and politicians were collectively in heat. Law firms fought over dusty packets of season tickets that, up until now, had lain fallow in a receptionist's desk drawer. Investment bankers, speculating that they might raise a little capital at the games, shelled out a bundle for courtside seats. Socialites practiced saying, "I just *cahn't* make the curtain at the Met next Wednesday. *We have Knicks tickets.*"

How wonderfully vulgar. How deliciously . . . camp!

You could actually go to a game and feel like you were at the *thee-a-tuh.* Have dinner beforehand at a nearby bistro, catch a shoeshine in Penn Station. You didn't have to sit outdoors in a remote stadium, on a bench invariably flecked with pigeon shit. You didn't have to freeze your ass off or be stranded in driving rain or snow. For a couple of bucks, a New Yorker could cab to the Garden, cheer his brains out for a tidy two hours, then disappear again into an anonymous box of rooms forty-six floors above the flow of traffic and human squalor. And if you weren't one of the righteous 19,500 with a ticket to the game, there were bars along the East Side of Manhattan that had remote, closed-circuit TV, where, for a nominal cover, you could watch from a booth and feel almost as if you were there.

Yes, basketball players had become lusciously de rigueur in New York. The Jets may have won the Super Bowl that year, but, aside from hunky Joe Namath, those football players were considered ground chuck. Similarly, the Mets had won the World Series, but baseball players were viewed suspiciously as hayseeds. On the other hand, there was something uncommonly stylish about basketball players. They had a certain cachet. You could invite them out, and they'd actually show up in a suit. And not one of those Robert Hall jobs, either. These fellows knew how to dress to impress.

Besides Barnett and Frazier, other Knick stallions were emerging as potential clotheshorses. Nate Bowman found God at A. J. Lester's, one of the brothers' favorite uptown boutiques specializing in outrageous threads, and over at Leighton's, a shop close to the Garden, where he could pick up something a little more conservative—like, say, a gold-plated medallion. Bowman and Dave Stallworth dabbled in capes, yes, *capes!*—even in Nehru jackets, which were all the rage. Barnett was the first to wear the Nehru, and the stir it caused would have provoked jealousy even from Gandhi. The man looked *mighty fine* in that sleek tunic. So Bowman bought a Nehru, and Frazier, too. They even got one on Johnny Warren, a reluctant participant, who was initiated into the world of haute couture by his roomie, Cap Will.

Reed was one of the meatier entrées on the Knicks' fashion plate. At six-nine, he wasn't lean and lithe, like those beaky guards and forwards, but stout, all tooth and gristle. You might see one of the well-proportioned centers, like Chamberlain or Nate Thurmond, in street clothes and think, "There goes a well-put-together man." But you wouldn't say that about Willis Reed. Reed, like Wes Unseld, had more density, more bulk. He was built like a Volvo—big and boxy. So you wouldn't necessarily want to see Willis in a Nehru. And, yet, he knew what to do with what he had. He dressed up that mean physique in eight-hundred-dollar suits that were so dashing they drew attention from clear in the next state. You could stand somewhere in western Connecticut and admire Will as he crossed Times Square.

Reed, who had a closet full of these fancy suits, "suggested" to some of the Knicks urchins that they'd do well to follow his example. Consider the team image, he said. Loosely translated, that meant "How about some class, bozos?"

Johnny Warren was a typical Reed makeover candidate. Warren cut an appropriately sly figure, thanks to a mushroom-shaped Afro that carried some clout on the street, but when it came to clothes the guy was hideously off the rack. He wore slacks with *cuffs,* for Chrissake! Willis frowned on his roommate's prehistoric form. "Hey, rook," he warned Warren, "you gotta get rid of those cuffs." Well, the thought of dropping good money on something as functional as clothes drove a stake right through Warren's heart. He was studying in the off season to be an accountant and was already tight with a buck. On the other hand, he lived to please Willis Reed. Warren anguished over the mounting dilemma: Reed? Good money? Reed? Good money? In the end, his decision was obvious—painful, but obvious. Reluctantly, he agreed to have the Cap escort him on a shopping expedition to the garment center—particularly to a second-floor showroom on West Thirty-seventh Street where Reed was a well-known customer.

"You gotta have a few suits made," Reed advised Warren.

"Few . . . made . . ." Those words, Warren knew, were code for *expensive.* He pleaded with Reed, even reminded him that Bond's was just down the street—they had dozens of suits there at a fraction of the price, blazers, pinstripes, quality stuff. Nothing doing. Reed held firm, and Warren walked out of that joint,

having placed an order for two suits at more than a week's salary. I must be out of my mind, he thought.

A week later, Reed showed up with a full-length sealskin coat, and Warren nearly had a stroke. "No way, man," Johnny said. "Don't even think about it!"

Reed didn't have the heart to tell him the coat was free. Ben Kahn, a furrier in the West Thirties, had given Reed and Frazier "promotional coats"—all they had to do was wear them, which was a pleasure considering that the weather had turned cold. Frazier chose a sleek brushed, short-haired number—pin seal—that looked fabulously rich on his frame, while Reed's was long-haired and uncut. The guys thought he looked like an Alaskan grizzly in it, and they'd get on him about it. "Willis, m'man—good thing there's no hunting in Manhattan. Right?"

Aside from Phil Jackson, the team hippie, the white guys dressed pitifully. Jackson's appearance wasn't exactly sharp, but at least he had his own style. He wore crazy flowered shirts with huge lapels, fringed vests, and wide-wale bells, maybe a strand of love beads or a leather choker around his neck. He even "accessorized" with beaded Indian belts and doeskin mocs. Not exactly chic, but very groovy. It was a look that attracted a certain kind of chick, a hippie chick, to be precise. You had to hand it to Jackson. He knew what he was doing.

The rest of the Knicks, though, were hopeless. Mike Riordan was strictly working-class Queens. In the morning he put on a shirt and a pair of pants, and that was that—he was dressed for the day. DeBusschere, a part-time stockbroker, took the conservative Wall Street approach, sticking to dark suits. Hosket and May were from Ohio, which more or less said it all. And anyway, Hoss knew he'd never be the worst-dressed Knick as long as Bill Bradley remained on the team.

By comparison, Bradley was a horror show. Really! He dressed like one of the derelicts who slept under the Garden in the tunnels that led to Penn Station. His shirts were dirty, frayed, and invariably missing buttons—he often relied on paper clips to hold his cuffs together. And his pants were chronically wrinkled.

"Yo, Dol-*lah,* you *pay* somebody for those pants?" Barnett once asked him with a straight face. "Really—you shittin' me? Some motherfucker took real money for them?"

Bradley's shoes were scuffed, with holes in the soles and tape to keep them from falling apart. And that beige raincoat he always wore—the guys were so offended by his filthy London Fog that one time they actually trashed it and chipped in for a new one. Just goes to show, they thought, a guy could go to Princeton and Oxford and still couldn't dress himself properly. Bradley's teammates eventually gave up trying to figure it out. He was making good money, people respected him—didn't he have any pride?

The fact was, Bradley didn't give a spit about clothes. Fashion simply wasn't a part of his agenda. But he was smart enough to sense that his style, or lack of it, offended some of the other guys. In an effort to maintain team unity, Bradley appealed to Dick Barnett for help. One night after a game he handed Barnett a check for $2,000 and said, "Pick me up tomorrow and we'll go shopping."

Before the next game, Barnett reported in with the results. "Yeah, we went," he told his skeptical teammates. "I spent that bread in a hurry, too." He picked out an entire wardrobe for Bradley—three suits, shirts and ties to match, and a full line of accessories. It took a while for the alterations to be made, but when Bradley finally showed up in one of his new outfits he looked *smart.* He looked *dignified.* He looked *debonnaire.* With that square-jawed, midwestern face and athletic physique, he might have stepped out of the pages of a recent issue of *GQ.* What a sight for sore eyes! Naturally, he took a lot of heat from the other guys, who made him model—walk an imaginary runway through the locker room, lean and bend like Twiggy—as they whistled and howled their approval. Each of them took a turn running a hand up and down his lapels, checking the labels, handling the material as delicately as they might a Fabergé egg. It was all too good to be true. Within two weeks, however, Bill had reverted to form, wearing the wrong shirt with the wrong suit, missing crucial buttons, wiping stains from ties. Barnett was openly frustrated and declared the whole experience a disaster. "He's hopeless," Rich said, with a final shrug.

From the fans' perspective, it didn't matter how the Knicks dressed. Their play alone was worthy of devout worship and adoration. So far, it had been a spectacular ride. But now, with twenty-three games under their belt, with an eighteen-game winning streak on the line, the fans and the players alike grew realistic about the situation. Technically, there was nothing to stop the New Yorkers from extending their unbeaten streak. As long as they'd won eighteen in a row, why not twenty-eight or thirty-five or some other infinite exponent of greatness? There were precedents for it, and right in their own backyard. Nobody had to be reminded of Joe DiMaggio's fifty-six-game hitting streak or Babe Ruth's sixty home runs—New York was fertile ground for establishing durable sports records. Realistically, however, the chances were not good because of the human element that needed to be figured into the equation. The Knicks were not a machine; they weren't infallible. And unlike DiMaggio or Ruth, they couldn't rest between swings of a bat. Basketball demanded that players expend an atomic burst of energy every night. Some guys would be out there for the entire forty-eight minutes, hustling up and down the court, banging bodies, suffering endless wear and tear on those fragile, stalky limbs—not to mention the wages of mental stress. Sooner or later, fatigue was bound to set in; they'd blow a spark plug. Eventually, it had to happen.

Eventually, it did. And sooner, rather than later.

On the surface, their first game back in New York figured to be a walk. It was against the Pistons, a team the Knicks routinely ate for dinner, and the fans had turned out specifically to express their appreciation for the record-setting streak. The New York players were greeted by a four-minute standing ovation marked by uninterrupted applause and cheers, applause from the bottom of the heart, spectacular applause. The fans were having an overheated orgasm! Throughout the salute, which began spontaneously as the buzzer sounded and lasted, well, forever, it seemed, the eleven prize stallions stood locked in place, grinning like fools, while the 19,500 spectators went ballistic. You could see the guys cutting glances from either end of the bench up at this massive quivering spectacle. These weren't the usual screams and cheers that went with a spectacular play, like when a guy sinks one at the buzzer to win a come-from-behind game or hits a grand slam in the bottom of the ninth or drops a hole-in-one at Pebble Beach. No, there was something unarguably implicit in the outpouring of emotion, a note of rapturous hysteria that signified something far greater, and more frightening, than anything they had ever experienced before. It was a flash of recognition that the Knicks—a team defined historically by ineptitude and loss—*were going to win it all!* Yes, that was it! The crowd, in what could only have been a *folie à dix-neuf mille cinq cent,* had simultaneously glimpsed the future and come to that startling conclusion. With fifty-nine games remaining to be played! No matter, the vision had been divined. What a blessed event! How perfectly . . . embarrassing.

The Knicks waved at the crowd in appreciation, but they knew they'd been jinxed. They knew it, and they felt it. The road games that contributed to establishing the streak had been enervating. The pressure had taken its toll. The players were physically and emotionally exhausted. As the game began, the Knicks realized they didn't have it tonight. They were flat. The Pistons ran off six straight points, avoiding the defensive traps that usually worked for the Knicks and sending a signal that augured poorly for another come-from-behind win.

The Knicks actually kept it close until the fourth quarter.

The lead changed hands a total of twenty-one times. Usually, you could count on New York to give it some gas in the waning minutes and put their opponent away, but tonight that killer instinct was gone. New York never took control of the game, they didn't rally. Usually there was someone who could come in off the bench and give them a spark. But no matter who the Knicks threw out there tonight, they only sputtered. In thirteen minutes of play, Stallworth couldn't put up a single point. Riordan managed only two in fifteen minutes. In fact, for more than five minutes *the Knicks didn't score at all!* At the nine-minute mark of the last quarter, Detroit finally broke it wide open. Howie Komives, the ex-Knick who had gone north in the DeBusschere trade, combined on two three-point plays to put the Pistons ahead for good. Ouch! . . . that hurt. And it goaded Detroit into another six-point surge. The fans—the same fans who two hours earlier had showered the Knicks with cheerful love—began edging toward the exits.

Detroit, a relentlessly mediocre team languishing in sixth place, rear-ended the Knicks' streak by beating them, 110–98.

Oddly, the Knicks weren't wounded by the defeat. They were relieved. It had to happen sometime, they insisted. Their luck was eventually going to run out, and now that it had, they could concentrate on winning individual games again, instead of worrying about keeping the streak alive. As they walked off the floor, the New York players held their heads high. They shook hands among themselves, congratulating each other on the magnificent run. They even got some applause from the fickle crowd.

"This only proves that we're human," Willis Reed said, elbowing his way into the locker room. Human. Well . . . exactly, Willis. "I think we can be beaten."

Each Knick took a few minutes to eulogize the streak, delighting the crush of newspaper, magazine, and TV reporters squeezed into the cramped, sweaty quarters. You could see the players competing for sound bites. "I guess you can't win 'em all," Frazier said, applying an ice pack to an aching left ankle. DeBusschere agreed, shrugging, "This wasn't our night." And Bradley, the team philosopher, chipped in with these inspirational words: "One voyage is over, now another one is going to begin." Hallelujah and amen, brother. Let it rest.

Red Holzman watched from the far end of the room. When it was his turn, he said; "Tomorrow is Sunday, a day off. If the streak hadn't ended, I would have had a few drinks and watched the football games on television. But since the streak is over, I'll have a few drinks and watch the football games on television."

He glanced at his players, who had grown quiet and reflective as the reporters left to file their obituaries. What's with the long faces? he wondered. No one expected we could win 'em all.

"You know, you guys *stink!*" he said, fighting back a grin.

For Holzman, it was an unusually coy line, considering his record of postgame remarks. He had the reputation for being a man of very few words, and those he parted with were remarkably wan and colorless. "Sure we played a good game—but so did they" was a regular comment of his. Other nights he came across with stuff like "You've got to hand it to [name of losing team], they gave us a run for the money," or "It was a close one out there tonight." Well, gee, thanks, Red. The beat reporters knew they'd never get anything quotable from Holzman, and as a rule they left him alone. He was the worst copy in the league, hands down. You could have a bench-clearing brawl, blood spilled from one end of the court to the other, and afterward, surrounded by a pack of truculent reporters with pens poised to register some pithy observation, Holzman would come up with a conversation stopper like "I think it was a good all-around effort tonight."

Jesus! You could get juicier stuff from a pomegranate! What was it with this guy? Most coaches were stand-up when it came to the press. They knew what was expected of them, and they could be relied on each night to provide a pungent, readable quote. Not a lot of long-winded bullshit about the finer aspects of basketball. No one wanted to hear that stuff after sifting through the details of a thrilling game. The reporters wanted something thoughtful, something brief and abstract, something wry. How could it hurt? Cousy and Jack Ramsay always did their part. So did Lenny Wilkens. Dick Motta, in Chicago, was a regular comedian with his one-liners. Atlanta's Richie Guerin always had a nasty word to say about everybody. Joe Mullaney of the Lakers—he was only a rookie coach, for Chrissake, and you couldn't turn him off. And Van Breda Kolff in Detroit—the guy said something completely nutty almost every night of the week. Here you've got a guy like Red Holzman, a noted basketball tactician, sitting in the media capital of the world, with a team just begging for copy, and he maunders on like a damn priest.

"I thought both teams performed nicely tonight."

Have a heart, brother!

Well, Holzman wasn't inarticulate, nor was he a simpleton. He had his own theory about interviews, which served his purposes, and he stuck by it throughout his entire tenure as a professional coach. Basically, what it came down to was job security. Holzman wasn't interested in seeing his name in print, and, more to the point, he wasn't interested in his employers' seeing his name in print, either. How would it look, he wondered, if Ned Irish or Freddie Podesta opened the paper each morning and saw their coach's philosophy set out in a moronic headline? If your team wasn't winning it was certain death for a coach, and even during a good year you were taking your career into your own hands. Self-serving publicity had gotten more than one coach dismissed from a good job.

Holzman liked his work. He liked his employers, too. Besides, he was a company man, in the strictest sense. He'd been with the Knicks since 1958, first as a scout—his dream job—and then, in 1967, taking the coach's position when management demoted Dick McGuire. If any one thing symbolized his loyalty, that had. Coaching the Knicks, after all, was a dead-end job; it was a springboard to the unemployment line. The team stank, the players ignored professional advice. They ate coaches for breakfast. Red had viewed the opportunity the way most candidates for the job had: thanks, but no thanks. He wanted no part of it. That would have been it, too, had Ned Irish not insisted he fill the vacancy. Mr. Irish wanted someone from within the organization to take charge, someone familiar with the players. No one was more familiar with them than Holzman. He had scouted every one of them, from the time they'd played college ball. So McGuire was shifted to scout, a job he was more suited to, and Holzman took over the team. To say it was a job *he* was more suited to would be inaccurate, especially since Red was a scouting legend. But something clicked. He took a team of spare parts and built a lean, mean machine with them. In less than two years, they were on the verge of a championship. So, no—he wasn't going to sacrifice that for a few noisy graphs in the *New York Times* or the *Post* or the *Daily News*. He didn't need a scrapbook full of clips to remind him what a good job he'd done. And he certainly didn't intend to upstage his players. The spotlight belonged to them. The reporters? Granted, they were vampires, they drank human blood, but Holzman actually liked most of the guys on the beat. He occasionally ate dinner with them or invited one out for a scotch after the game, as long as it was off the record. But for the most part, they were predators and the less they got from him, the better it would be for all concerned.

Holzman's business was basketball. The game obsessed him. Even after a streak as beautiful as the one the Knicks had just run off, he was determined to fine-tune the machinery. The day after the defeat by Detroit, the guys got a Sunday off to unwind. But Monday morning, December 1, bright and early, Holzman scheduled a practice at a training facility called Lost Battalion Hall, in the Elmhurst section of Queens.

Lost Battalion, where the Knicks worked out when the Garden needed its ice for hockey games, was a hall in name only.

The place had been built in the Jurassic era, when athletic dinosaurs dribbled stones. Come to think of it, the gym resembled a cave. The floor was worn practically to the concrete pilings, the benches were filthy, and the backboards . . . it's almost too shameful to admit . . . were made of wood—plywood, if you can believe it. Guys would go up for a shot, try to bank one in for a bucket, and you'd hear a *bonk.* Instead of dropping through the hoop, the ball would glance off at some crazy angle and sail through the air like a wicked golf slice. That kind of stuff drove the guys mad. Here they were, at the top of their game, heirs to the Celtics' crown, and they had to practice in a shithole. It was pathetic. There was no weight room, no real trainer to speak of, no place to watch film of an opponent. The locker area looked like a public toilet. Still, no one complained to Red. Everyone generally acknowledged he had a job to get done and needed this extra work if the team was going to stay this incredible course.

While no one actually said it, the practice was staged to prepare for two upcoming games—one against the Bullets, in Baltimore, on December 5, and the other the following night, against the Milwaukee Bucks, back at the Garden. Of the other thirteen teams in the league, only Baltimore and Milwaukee had a prayer of catching the Knicks. The Bullets, after all, had finished first in the league last year, ahead of both the Knicks and the 76ers. Earl Monroe was at the top of his form, Gus Johnson was having another sensational year, and Wes Unseld, whom everyone compared to Willis Reed in the middle spot, seemed undaunted by his own astounding rookie performance. You only had to follow the box scores to realize the kind of threat a guy like that posed. For example, the night after New York's loss to Detroit, Unseld put on a typically animated floor show against the Cincinnati Royals, scoring thirty points and grabbing twenty-one rebounds, despite being double-teamed by Connie Dierking and Oscar Robertson. A game like that pointed to Unseld's superstar potential. Besides, the Knicks knew that Baltimore was quietly on its way to posting another superb season. The Bullets had their own respectable nine-game winning streak going and had won sixteen of their last twenty-three games. Had they not been completely overshadowed by the Knicks, you could bet they'd be drawing more attention. And the Bucks were creeping right up their asses. As expected, Lew Alcindor had turned the Milwaukee franchise around, and pairing him with Bobby Dandridge, the team's rookie subaltern, gave the team a powerful one-two combination. Dandridge had become the Bucks' shadow force. He routinely scored twenty or more points a night, making Milwaukee a dangerous competitor any night of the week. So the Knicks were taking nothing for granted.

As a tune-up for those games, the Knicks welcomed a rematch with Seattle at the Garden on December 2—nothing like a waltz before tango time. There were some jitters in the stands during the first half of play. The Knicks looked sluggish, uninterested. Nothing was going in for them. After twelve minutes, Frazier was two for seven, Barnett and Bradley were both one for six, Reed and DeBusschere were showing slightly better stuff, but on the whole the team's frustration was evident. Those hot hands had gotten frostbite; the guys couldn't find their rhythm. Come the second quarter, they began overcompensating, and it got ugly.

The Knicks weren't the only ones who panicked. Several season-ticket holders decided to vent their disappointment.

"What's the matter with you bums?" screamed one man with twin-engine jowls seated a few rows behind the bench. He was obviously from Brooklyn, because it came out as *"Whatsamattahwitchewbums?"*

One of the reserves flipped him the finger. Fucking moron! We lose one game, and this clown thinks he can turn on the steam.

"I've seen monkeys make better shots!" another guy yelled, using his rolled-up program as a megaphone.

Monkeys. Now, there was an analogy that brokered team enmity. At halftime, as they were leaving the court, the Knicks threw some pretty hard stares into the crowd.

"Did you hear that shit out there tonight?" asked Nate Bowman, pulling off his sweaty jersey.

"Motherfuckers are heartless," said Stallworth.

"Forget those assholes," Reed told them. "We can win this one. It ain't over yet."

Maybe it wasn't, but if the Knicks were going to turn it around then Reed was going to have to do something about his man, Bob Rule. That ugly mother was giving him ulcers. Rule had scored thirteen quick points against Reed, almost at will. Somehow Seattle had been able to get the ball to Rule down low, and he'd just nudge Willis out of the way. Rule was using his body to keep pushing Willis farther and farther out. He was relentless, a damn bully. Barnett was right, Reed thought, he should have put that beast's head on his den wall when they were up in Seattle. Now he was going to have to deal with him here. First, however, he had to get past the coach.

"I never saw so much shit out there!" Holzman shouted before the Knicks returned to the court. "You guys need a fucking enema! For Chrissake, Willis, this isn't Chamberlain or Thurmond out there. What's the matter with you? Rule's eating you alive. Move him off his spot, give him a goddamn game!"

He unloaded his wrath on Frazier next, then on Bradley, while saving his choicest words for the bench. The way Red was laying in to them, it was embarrassing. But when the Knicks came back out for their warm-ups, it was obvious they were a changed team. They were angry, they looked determined, they wanted revenge.

They got it without delay.

Reed and Frazier came out blazing with both guns. Each man rattled off a quick ten points, and Willis managed to put the cuffs on Rule. He crept up under Rule each time he got the ball, forcing the big fellow off his mark, and DeBusschere helped out down low by cutting off a path to the basket. With Rule in check, Bradley and Frazier started a nifty little play-action that broke it wide open. Circling without the ball, Bradley would look for an opening, then come out and get the ball from Clyde. The second it hit Dollar's hand, Frazier would cut to the basket, Bradley would hit him perfectly, and he'd take it in for two points. They worked this play repeatedly, like a confidence game, treating the Sonics like a bunch of rube tourists out on Broadway. New York shot a collective eighteen for twenty-seven from the field and limited Seattle to eight measly points in the third quarter. In addition, the Knicks stole the ball eighteen times. By the end of the quarter, they were up by thirty-three points. The bench took over and cruised to another lopsided victory.

Baltimore wasn't going to be as easy. The Bullets were a kennel of angry dogs still howling about last year's play-off fiasco. That blowout had punctured a few egos, and what with another thrashing by the Knicks earlier in the season, they were aching for vengeance. Baltimore was six and a half out. They needed a win desperately, not only to narrow the gap but to prove to themselves that they could handle New York should the teams meet up again in postseason play.

The Knicks were looking forward to this game. They especially loved playing the Bullets because of the matchups: Reed/ Wes Unseld, DeBusschere/Gus Johnson, Bradley/Jack Marin, Barnett/Kevin Loughery, Frazier/Earl Monroe. The symmetry of it was beautiful. Each New York player felt he was going up against an opponent of similar talent who would give him a game. That's what real ballplayers relish. You pick your teeth with teams like Seattle, take the win, and go home. But great teams long for a challenge, they want to play against someone who makes them work for a victory. When it came to these teams, the Knicks and the Bullets, they were equally aggressive, scrappy, stubborn, crafty, tireless, and determined to win.

The day of the game, Reed devoted part of his afternoon to thinking about Wes Unseld. It was going to be another dogfight, he decided. Of all the Bullets, Unseld was the most unselfish, was the only Baltimore player willing to sacrifice his own offense in order to let an open teammate take the shot. So, in that respect, Reed could relax a bit. But Wes was a great rebounder, with a deadly outlet pass. Reed always did his level best to block the man out, but Unseld had one move that waxed Reed's tail. He would hold his hands up, shove his body against Willis's chest, and just walk the Cap under the basket. The refs wouldn't call it, because it didn't look like he was doing anything illegal. He had his hands up, he was body to body. And he was so good at it, he didn't even bother to turn his back to the officials. Reed would look up and see nothing but the open mouth of the net as Unseld grabbed the rebound and flicked it downcourt. So Willis was going to have to find some way to contain him. He couldn't give up any ground. And he couldn't count on DeBusschere for help.

DeBusschere had his own problems to worry about. After the last game with Baltimore, there had been published reports about how Gus Johnson had had it with the way his teammates hogged the ball. Now, you play on a team with Earl Monroe and Kevin Loughery and chances are there'll be a lot of boisterous oinking on the court. *Gimme the ball! Gimme the ball!* Neither Bullet guard was particularly a team player. Their sole purpose in life was to shoot out the lights. What had disturbed Johnson most, however, was watching the Knicks hit the open man—and win. To Johnson, it was like having relativity explained to you by a three-year-old. You work the ball around the court until one man has an unobstructed shot, and that's the guy who puts it up for two points. There it was—basketball in a nutshell. Simple as that. Johnson took one look at the Knicks' unselfish style of play, then at his teammates', and flashed: I'll never win a ring playing with these hot dogs.

Hell, Walt Frazier could have told him that much. Frazier disdained playground specialists, the flashy street guys who put on the moves, go one-on-one, and take it in every time. Acrobatics! Any moron with an ounce of ability could do that. He'd watch those guys try to stare down their man, talk some trash, give a little shoulder shake, execute a spin move, and *leappppp* into the stratosphere. Showtime!—the crowds loved it. But those cats were showboats. They didn't know a thing about fundamentals. And they played for themselves. Yeah, Frazier knew all about them. Now Gus Johnson knew it, too. He also knew he'd never tame Monroe or Loughery. So tonight he'd be looking for the ball with a vengeance, and that meant it would be up to DeBusschere to bite the Bullet who could single-handedly wound the Knicks.

The Baltimore Civic Center—a hangarlike stockade with a floppy pancake roof—was rockin' almost an hour before the bout was to begin. The Temptations came blasting over the public-address system—"I know you're gonna leave me/ but I refuse to let you go"—then Sly & the Family Stone, Tommy James, the Delfonics. It was party time in the stands. The happy crowd— a sellout of 12,289—represented a comfortable ethnic mix, with some dignitaries from D.C. seated grotesquely down front. George Romney, the Secretary of Housing and Urban Development and former governor of Michigan, was there to root for DeBusschere and Cazzie Russell. Secretary of Labor George Schultz came to watch Bradley, a fellow Princeton alumnus. A swarm of minor congressmen flocked to the cameras like moths to a flame. Only Tricky Dick himself seemed to be missing.

To top things off, some P.R. genius got the idea to handing out thousands of free buttons with the slogan "Kick the Knicks" emblazoned on them. *Kick the Knicks!* Well, they'd have to see about that.

A few minutes before game time, Nate Bowman strolled into the locker room with a handful of the navy blue buttons and distributed them to the guys. "We ought to take it to those suckers and wear 'em ourselves," Bowman suggested, pinning one on his jersey. Stallworth and Warren quickly followed his example.

"What it is, is . . . *bool-shit*," Barnett added.

"Yeah, it is," said Holzman. "But you're not going out there with them on your uniforms." Bowman started to protest—he had his rubber-band face on—but Red cut him off. He'd had it with the fun and games. He wanted his players to concentrate on the Bullets and forget about the distractions. It was time to get serious.

There was so much going on in the stands that night, the game seemed almost secondary. Once the buzzer sounded, however, the focal point was unmistakably basketball.

A palpable tension gripped both teams from the opening tip. As the centers jumped for the ball, Unseld threw a subtle hip into Reed and knocked him sideways out of position. Before Willis could recover, Mike Davis (who was playing for the injured Kevin Loughery) broke downcourt and hit an open jumper for two points. It happened so quickly that the Knicks were stranded at midcourt. Baltimore was off and running. In fact, the Bullets reeled off seven unanswered points on fast breaks, taking the Knicks right out of their game. After ten minutes, the Knicks were down by thirteen, their largest deficit all year. This had been Coach Gene Shue's strategy all along. He knew that if his team let the Knicks set up defensively, the game would be a blowout. The Bullets couldn't penetrate with New York defenders blocking the lanes. So Shue had designed a series of plays that kept his men in perpetual motion: quick outlet passes, behind-the-back dribbles, spin moves, long jumpers—the old run-and-gun mentality.

The Bullets put the Knicks through a hellish first quarter, overpowering them by twenty-one points, and the crowd was right in it with them. The fans were on their feet throughout the entire twelve-minute stretch. They were screaming, stomping, whistling, and needling any New York player who picked up an itinerant foul—*"You! You! You! You!"* The season-ticket holders in Baltimore were hostile to begin with, especially those who sat behind the visitors' bench. There were two guys in particular—two wild men—who never let up. The Knicks bench warmers knew them by sight—Heckle and Jeckle, they called them. Both were obese, swinish, sweaty, balding men in their forties, clutching beakers of beer in each paw, who acted as if the Knicks were responsible for the spread of the bubonic plague. They were there every time the Knicks were in town and spent the night spewing obscenities toward the bench like confetti. They never let up. Goddamn *termites*. Usually, Nate Bowman got into it with them. He'd throw them a ferocious sneer, then flip a finger or mouth the word "motherfucker," with the accent on the third syllable, the way the brothers said it, so that it struck the appropriate chord. But nothing worked on those two. They paid their $5.25 admission expressly for the privilege of annoying the New York bench.

Tonight, however, Bowman paid no attention to those clowns. He tuned them out. Instead, throughout the first quarter, he, Stallworth, and Russell sat huddled together trying to fracture the Bullets' deadly strategy. They knew it was only a matter of time before Red sent them in, and they wanted to formulate a game plan to help turn this beast around. In reality, it didn't take much figuring out. The Knicks, they decided, hadn't tested the Bullets' defense; they weren't pushing those gunners to guard against the drive. Barnett's passing wasn't crisp enough. The guys weren't taking the ball inside to the hoop. Meanwhile, Baltimore was doing a great job of doubling Clyde and Bradley. This nonsense had to stop.

Five minutes into the second quarter, Red called for the Minutemen. He sent in Russell, Stallworth, and Riordan for Bradley, DeBusschere, and Barnett, with instructions to shake things up. Within moments, Cazzie went into his antic Superfly routine. Russell had the touch tonight. He hit a quick four for five, igniting the offense and pulling the Knicks to within six.

Bowman was the next man off the bench. He got up and wandered over to the scorer's table, waiting for a break in the action so he could go in and give Reed a blow. When the ref whistled the play dead, Nate broke for the floor but heard Holzman calling him back. Reed, it appeared, was hurt. He'd jammed his pinky finger in a crowd under the basket, and was searching for the perp. Normally any coach would pull an injured player right away. You'd want to get him out of there before he did any serious damage to himself. But Reed was a special case. When he got injured he got angry, and that spelled trouble for the opposing team.

"Let's see how this plays out," Holzman told Bowman as the Snake took a seat.

Mike Riordan could have predicted the outcome. He walked past the Cap, saw a pair of murderous eyes flashing in futility, and took off in the opposite direction. No use sticking around for this, he thought. Willis was intent on punishing the culprit. But since he couldn't determine who'd hit him, he chose to take it out on the entire Bullets team. When play resumed, Willis went on a tear down low. He hit three quick baskets, grabbed four tricky rebounds that should have gone the other way, and stole two passes, which the Knicks converted for four additional points. It was halftime before he settled down again, but by then the Knicks were up by six.

Baltimore was clearly frustrated. You could see it on their faces as they headed for the locker room. They'd had those suckers . . . *right there!* But the tide was shifting and they knew it. Their game was out of control. Unfortunately, the Bullets let it fester while they rested and tried to regroup. There was a lot of grumbling, a lot of finger pointing between halves. In trying to assign the blame, the Baltimore players drove a stake through the composure they'd shown in the first quarter.

As the second half began, New York seized control of the

game. Frazier shut down Earl Monroe, the Bullets' most explosive scoring threat—took him right out of his game by coercing him into pressing the ball, which confused the Pearl. Then Clyde picked off a pass from Wes Unseld and dished off to Bradley, whose basket sparked a 15–2 run by the Knicks. Actually, Frazier had learned something crucial about Unseld that gave him a clear advantage over the powerful Baltimore center. It was Unseld's eyes—they gave him away. Frazier had spotted it in the play-offs last year, then had tested his theory in the first meeting with Baltimore, back in October. Wes would glance toward an intended receiver a split second before making his pass. It was a dead giveaway, affording Clyde enough time to make the appropriate adjustment in order to thwart Unseld's plans.

In the fourth quarter, Riordan came in to spell a weary Frazier. "Unseld—watch his eyes," Clyde whispered as they passed on the court. With the score at 97–88, Mike dropped off his man, Fred Carter, and doubled Unseld. Frazier was right, he thought, the guy's telegraphing. As a result, he intercepted two of Unseld's passes, which ultimately put the game out of reach for Baltimore.

Kick the Knicks! Yeah, in your dreams, sucker.

The name of the game was finesse. Baltimore had five men in double figures, they outrebounded New York, yet the Knicks defeated them by a score of 116–107, running their record to 25–2. It was an amazing start. Only the old Philadelphia Warriors had done better, posting a 26–2 margin in 1966. More impressive, however, was a streak that had gone largely unsung: the Knicks had won all twelve of their road games. Imagine that! Today, most NBA teams hope to win fifty percent of the games they play away from home. All that traveling tires them out, the players complain. Hotel life is debilitating. The crowds take them out of their game. The weight-training rooms are inadequate.

The Knicks were feeling invincible now. "At no time did I think we'd lose," DeBusschere said, on the plane back to New

York. Clyde felt the same way: "I knew if we caught them, we'd pull it out."

Reed had his own theory, but he kept it to himself. He'd decided that if the Knicks were within ten in the final five minutes, they'd prevail. "We just had too many weapons," he said years later. "Barnett or Cazzie could get hot, or Riordan, or Stallworth. Even Nate. There was always someone who could come to the rescue when push came to shove. And that knowledge gave us a cushion of confidence."

The next night, it was Bradley and Frazier who did it against Milwaukee. Each man had twenty-nine points, but it was Bradley, hitting six of seven from the field in the first quarter, who set the tempo. It was uncanny the way he kept unhinging himself from a crowd, finding an open spot on the floor, then doing something pivotal. Moving without the ball was Bradley's specialty. He'd circle the floor, darting here, then there, cutting to the baseline or across the key. Providing a decoy. Studying the opposition. Looking for options. It allowed him to screen a man, then run an opponent off the screen into a pick in order to get free. That usually left him open in the corner, from where he was virtually unstoppable, or it let him sail in for an easy lay-up.

Among the five Knick starters, Bradley was probably the hardest to contain. He was constantly on the move, covering great, ground-breaking distances regardless of the errant forces or velocities that tried to counteract or impede his progress. It was amazing; it was Newton's Law in reverse. But off the court he could be closed and enigmatic, which made him seem ice-cold. The other players had some difficulty in getting close to him. "The guy has no soul," said one critic who demanded chummy, dim-witted conviviality from his teammates. But others saw in Bradley's personality an unconscious defensive apparatus designed to keep at bay the media vultures pecking at his bones.

Bradley had started out in the NBA as the Second Coming

of Wilt Chamberlain. That is to say, he entered the league as an established phenom, a former college star, already trailing a retinue of rabid fans and advisers, a string of seemingly insurmountable records, a fat salary, amazing hype, intense speculation, and the brains to cash in on any deal within the limits of the law. Chamberlain had been the first player to make that kind of disquieting splash. And Bradley, if you're counting, was the second. That's hard to believe, considering the ferocity of today's bull market. Since Julius Erving broke the mold, in 1973, hype and contractual intrigue have dominated practically every first-round draft choice's transition from college to the pros. Today, if you don't have a press agent, a recording contract, and your own line of sneakers before your rookie season begins, you're dogmeat. But in 1967, Bradley's first season, the game was still a gentleman's sport, euphemistically speaking. It thrived on the gene pool of young college grads who were grateful for the very privilege of playing in the pros. At the time, basketball wasn't prepared for a guy like Bradley, whose popularity gave him the muscle to negotiate a ball-busting contract, then put on a uniform and shuffle onto the court and shoot out the lights.

Bradley grew up in Crystal City, Missouri, a dinky manufacturing town situated halfway between the state's oldest settlements, St. Louis and Ste. Genevieve, on a tributary of the Mississippi River. Crystal City was a company town, and practically all of its 3,600 residents at some time in their lives labored at Works No. 9, a showcase factory owned by the Pittsburgh Plate Glass Company, where plate and later float glass was manufactured for various automotive, architectural, and furniture uses. Bradley's father, Warren, a self-taught man who became the town's principal banker, handled many of the company's financial transactions, and Bill might well have inherited the old man's chair at the Crystal City State Bank had it not been for the bluff determination of his mother.

Susie Bradley was one of those larger-than-life southern numbers, a big buttercup of a woman you'd expect to encounter in a
Tennessee Williams play. She wasn't a belle, by any stretch of
the imagination; more husk, less juice. A lot of it was ordained
by her stature. At five-foot-seven, she was an imposing figure,
with the personality to match. She was driven, gracious, self-
centered, beguiling, passionate, effortlessly outgoing, completely
at home anywhere and in any situation. And she wanted it all
for her only child, Bill.

Bradley was groomed to be a thoroughbred. He took piano
and trumpet lessons, learned how to speak French, how to dance,
swim, play tennis, and shoot a respectable round of golf. There
was Palm Beach every winter, for good grooming. And of course
there was basketball, too. It wasn't a genteel game, like croquet.
But Susie herself had played the game when she was a student
at Herculaneum High School, and, after all, the boy was growing
at an alarming rate. He was already six-three, and only in eighth
grade. So she had a hoop nailed to the side of the garage and
turned him loose.

Bradley wasn't the kind of kid who just dribbled the ball
around while daydreaming, or who played horse with the neighborhood tomboy. No, he was a serious young man—serious about
school, serious about church, serious about family, and *very* serious about basketball. Very. Serious. He set up a rigid schedule,
practiced *eighteen hours* a week. Day and night. Alone. Mastered
the lay-up, the jump shot, the running hook, the set shot, and
the free throw. He didn't just *shoot* them, like most kids. No,
he studied the mechanics of each shot—how to place his hands
most effectively on the ball in order to release it, taking into
consideration the energy exerted, the resistance brought to bear
against the ball, even the density of the air; where to plant his
feet for maximum stability; the best alignment of his torso in
relation to force and motion; the trajectory of the ball; the effect

of torque as it applied to the perpendicular distance from the line of action of the force to the axis of rotation . . . As you can see, it was a scientific enterprise.

Dribbling the ball was another matter, less dependent on experimentation and the study of data than on impulse and perception. Dribbling, he concluded, wasn't scientific but practical. It simply required a great deal of concentration. Nevertheless, Bradley devised what engineers call "an optimal disciplinary device" to take care of that. He bought a pair of ski goggles and taped cardboard to the bottom of the frames so he couldn't see the ground. That way, when he dribbled, he would be forced to rely solely on his instincts to know where the ball was at all times instead of just watching it. In effect, he was training himself not so much to dribble as he was to make it an unconscious action, thus enabling him to do other key things—such as think, run, see the action, plan, and project—all at the same time.

The way he went at it, you'd think the boy was training for a NASA space flight. He set up an obstacle course on his court so that he could dribble against imaginary opponents; he loaded his sneakers with ten pounds of lead pennyweights to increase his stamina; he played at night, so that bad lighting wouldn't distract his concentration. All that was secondary, however, to his routine. With nothing but a regulation basketball, he worked his way systematically around the court, and from each spot he hit a cluster of set shots, hook shots, and jump shots, not moving on, however, until he had sunk ten of thirteen. *Ten of thirteen!* That kind of consistency, in and of itself, is beyond the means of most pros. Today, a kid earning $4 million a year as a starting forward for an NBA team has trouble hitting 60 percent of his free throws. (Bradley, by the way, was regularly in the high 90 percentile from the line.) And he performed this warm-up every day, throughout his adolescence, through high school, and later in college and the pros.

Well, people began to talk. That Bradley boy must be some

kind of a machine, they said. He never missed! In high school, starting for the Crystal City Hornets, he ran off incredible strings of consecutive baskets. Just incredible! Thirty, *forty-five!* People eventually lost count. This was before they kept statistics on shooting percentages, but the folks there still declaim Bradley's deadly accuracy. *Boy must have radar or something!* Radar—well, exactly. Intuitively, he knew the precise distance between the ball and the basket from anywhere on the court. He could feel it. He had the touch.

Word soon spread around the provinces. "You've got to see this boy from Crystal City play ball." They didn't say "see him jump" or "slam dunk" or "shatter baskets" or perform any of the hot-dog stunts perpetrated by today's grim-faced "super-stars." No, just "see him play ball." Simple as that. Bill Bradley could . . . play ball. Missouri may be known as the "Show-Me" state, but when it came to Bradley the folks there were anything but skeptical. They knew a legend when they saw one. And here he was, right in their own backyard.

Word eventually worked its way from the provinces to other states, too, and before long Bill Bradley was something of a na-tional sensation. This was years before newspapers wrote stories about schoolboy phenoms, years before Shaq and Kenny Ander-son and Donyell Marshall were making headlines. No, Bill Brad-ley's reputation was handed down much like a folk song. A team would play Crystal City one night, the next week maybe they'd be up in Beaucoup, Illinois, and someone would say, "Last week we played this kid Bradley . . ." It wouldn't be "We played Crystal City" or "We played the Hornets," but "this kid Bradley." Then, a week later, maybe someone from Beaucoup would play a team from Perrysburg, Indiana, and would repeat the story. Then Perrysburg played Altoona, Altoona played Rockville Center, Rockville Center played Myrtle Beach, and before long Bradley was a household name. High-school hoop stars from Maine to Monterey became acquainted with his exploits, however exaggerated many may have been by this time. John Garber, who later roomed with Bradley at Princeton, remembered a National Student Council convention he attended in Janesville, Wisconsin, in the summer of 1960, when word spread that Bill Bradley was there, and every seventeen-year-old basketball player present, including Garber, dropped what he was doing in order to catch a glimpse of the legend as he made his way into the hotel.

It was national news, then, when Bradley announced he'd be entering Duke University in the fall of 1961. The school had an outstanding history department, which was Bill's intended area of study. And who could say enough about those Blue Devils? They were an eastern basketball power, a Division I school in the NCAA's elite rank. He'd fit right in with their style of play. Which is why John Garber was so astounded to encounter Bradley standing on the corner of Nassau and University Place, in Princeton, New Jersey, on the day freshmen were to report for registration.

Bradley explained that he'd had a last-minute change of heart. He'd been to Europe that summer, spent a lot of time thinking about the world, knew about the high reputation of Princeton's Woodrow Wilson School, and had decided to place education above athletics. Face it, you didn't go to Princeton because of its basketball program. It was the Ivy League, for Chrissake! Local legends avoided it like the plague. Princeton didn't even offer basketball scholarships, so what phenom in his right mind would consider playing ball there? Princeton had always had what in polite company would be called a less-than-forgettable team.

Four years later, the Princeton Tigers were as eminently important as the Kentucky Wildcats, the UCLA Bruins, the Michigan Wolverines, the Indiana Hoosiers—and . . . the Duke Blue Devils. Bill Bradley had put Princeton on the basketball map, and in doing so, he had established or broken every local record on the books. He held personal records for Most Points in a Season (936 in 1964), Most Points in a Game (58, against

Wichita State, 1965), Most Field Goals Made in a Career (856), Most Field Goals Made in a Season (338 in 1964), Most Field Goals Made in a Game (22, against Wichita State, 1965), Most Field Goals Attempted in a Career (1,969), Most Free Throws Made in a Career (791), Most Free Throws Made in a Season (273 in 1965), Highest Free-Throw Attempt Average per Game/ Career (20.1), Most Rebounds in a Career (1,008), and Most Points in a Career (2,503). What's more, he led Princeton to the Final Four in 1965, got the All-Tournament Team MVP, and set a tournament record of 177 points in five performances there that lasted for twenty-four years, until Glen Rice topped it in 1989.

From 1962 until his graduation in 1965, Bradley was the best known, if not the best liked, student on the Princeton campus. He was dedicated to the intellectual experience, and he was also the most exciting college basketball player in the country, and yet he didn't seem smug or arrogant about it. He looked like a taller version of the All-American Boy Next Door—which, come to think of it, he was. He had short, dark hair that he wore neatly combed to the side, and he was very handsome, with the same knifelike, intense good looks as his father. His eyes were deep set and guarded, making him seem reserved and observant and giving him an air of cool, emotionless judgment as he looked out on the world.

Handsome, reserved, observant, cool—these words described the public face Bradley put on each day during his tenure at Princeton. But beneath that thin candy-coated shell was a young man who was best characterized as driven. For him, the school motto—"Princeton and the Nation's Service"—was a serious matter, and he channeled all his energy into meeting the school's rigorous standards.

He took killer courses, and he studied all the time. After basketball practice, he studied in the library, and when the library closed at midnight he'd hole up in a room upstairs in the student center until two or three in the morning, hitting the books. During one stretch—after his freshman basketball season ended in March and continuing over the next three months, until his last exam was finished—Bradley studied every waking hour that he wasn't in class, getting maybe five hours' sleep a night.

If basketball was going to matter, he decided, it would have to take care of itself. The same could be said for socializing. He joined Cottage, one of the eating clubs on Prospect Street, but his affiliation was strictly for tradition's sake and he seldom attended. Around his dorm, Little Hall, he remained guarded and a little distant, like a man who would be more comfortable with a basketball in his hands. He wasn't what you'd call one of the guys. His roommates recall that he rarely seemed relaxed around them, except for the few times, late at night, when he'd do imitations of radio broadcasters. He'd grab an imaginary mike, conjure up a memorable St. Louis Hawks game, and mimic the sports jocks of his youth, with their stark midwestern accents and inscrutable commentaries.

"Cliff Hag'n brings the ball up*cart*. Sees Pettit on the *bees*line. There's *Sleeter* Martin. Passes to Pettit. Spins. Pops. Two *pints!*"

The guys would roar with laughter, not because they identified with his performance or his timing, but because it was Bradley, acting goofy. A rare unguarded moment.

It was the same with women. There really weren't any to speak of. Oh, he occasionally had a date with a girl from one of the Seven Sisters schools. And there was a girl named Kathy, from a college in Connecticut—a thin-faced, streaky-blond number—who kept turning up unannounced and had to be warned off by the school's proctors. Otherwise, he pretty much kept to himself and studied.

That's the way he was at Princeton—and the way he was with the New York Knicks. For all his gutsy play, Bradley wasn't considered one of the guys. He was different from most conventional basketball players. Serious different . . . complicated different, aloof different—*rigid.* One time, the team was offered the opportunity to appear together in a Vitalis commercial—which the guys viewed as both lucrative and a hoot—but Bradley declined. Principles, he said: he didn't endorse commercial products. Well, give it a rest, Dollar! You didn't have those principles when it came to soaking the Knicks for that juicy contract of yours, *n'est-ce pas?*

Ostensibly, the commercial offer wasn't affected by Bradley's refusal to participate. The Knicks decided to go ahead with it anyway. The incident didn't help to sow team harmony or erase Bradley's image as an eccentric. Some teammates perceived him as being aristocratic—and now insensitive. One idea behind appearing in the commercial had been to advance the team's soaring popularity. The guys were already New York heroes, they were recognized on the street. The Vitalis spot, however, would run nationally, ensuring them a broader appeal. It meant Reed's family would see it in Louisiana, Russell's in Illinois, Frazier's in Georgia; May and Hosket would be beamed into Ohio, DeBusschere into Michigan, Barnett into Indiana, and Stallworth and Bowman into Texas. For most of them, it meant recognition beyond their wildest expectations. Madison Avenue had flirted with sports figures before, but never with an entire team. The spot would put a popular face on the Knicks.

The problem, as the advertising agency saw it, was "team image." The Knicks were known by their starters—Frazier, Barnett, Reed, DeBusschere, and Bradley. The way the spot had been conceived, they'd have to function as a unit to pull it off.

The storyboard was simple. Fade in to Madison Square Garden. Time: a game night in 1970, moments before the opening tip. The Knicks are being introduced to the crowd. "At guard, wearing number ten, from Southern Illinois . . . Walt Frazier. [*Cheers and applause.*] At the other guard, number twelve, from Tennessee State . . . Dick Barnett." Then DeBusschere and Reed. Finally Bradley is announced, and as the guys slap palms they look at Dollar and recoil. Did he cut one? No, it's worse than that. His palms—*they're smeared with that greasy kids' stuff!* Dollar, you greaseball! He hangs his head, an outcast, and drifts back to the bench. At which point Red sends in Mike "Vitalis" Riordan as a replacement.

Well, it was a cute idea. The guys were into it, Holzman went along for laughs, and the Knicks' management gave its blessing. The rest of the team would serve as extras, and everyone, including Danny Whelan, stood to make a nice piece of change. Now Bradley had gone and backed out. You can imagine how that went over with the guys. *Principles!* Why couldn't he loosen up? Make an exception once in a while? Instead, Dollar was always thinking about what was best for Dollar. Mr. Rhodes Scholar. Might have figured as much!

As it turned out, the ad agency was willing to salvage the spot. They'd survive without Bill Bradley. Substitute the one of the other guys. No one would know the difference. In the final print, the guys are introduced—Frazier, Barnett, Reed, DeBusschere, and—*Donnie May?* What the fu . . . ? May is a *scrub!* And not even a primo scrub. Next to Warren, he's the last guy off the bench. How bogus, how . . . embarrassing. All across America, people would be scratching their heads and saying, "Donnie *who?*" What happened to Cazzie Russell, an All-American out of Michigan? Or Dave Stallworth, Mr. Come-Back-from-the-Dead?—he was a great sentimental story. But Donnie May? Starting for New York? Who were they kidding?

The black members of the Knicks knew the answer to that. Those TV people needed to sell their Vitalis, and you could bet they weren't selling it to the brothers. A guy watching the commercial in Iowa or South Dakota sees four black faces staring back at him, in the privacy of his living room, he's going to freak out. To him, that's a pretty scary image. He might look at it and decide . . . *Brylcream!* The agency couldn't take that chance. They wanted another white face on screen. So send in Donnie

May. Sure, they figured, that's what happened to Cazzie and the Rave.

As it was, Cazzie had already felt the pinch of racial polarity. In his eyes, he should be starting ahead of Bradley at small forward. All you had to do was compare the two players' abilities. Bradley wasn't as good a shooter, he wasn't in as great physical condition, he wasn't as exciting. What Bradley was, however, was *white*. No doubt that did figure into the equation. Russell maintained a game face when the subject came up, but in private he made his feelings known. In his eyes, it was still a white world, even on the basketball court.

Russell's problem wasn't limited to Bradley, either. He'd already had it out with Mike Riordan. Following one game he'd confronted Riordan with the accusation that Mike was making brothers look bad on the court. On two occasions, Cazzie concluded, black players were open on plays, and Riordan had intentionally ignored them. He'd passed to white guys instead. It was obvious what was going on.

Well, Riordan heard that and he was flabbergasted. Race a factor? Cazzie was obviously out of his skull. Race was the last thing on Riordan's mind. In fact, he particularly admired Cazzie for serving in a National Guard reserve unit on weekends during the season. Cazzie was a patriot. The doves, like Bradley and Phil Jackson—Mike had trouble with them. He was a blue-collar guy from Queens and didn't hold with that protest crap. He believed a guy ought to do his duty and keep his mouth shut, even where Vietnam was concerned. America—love it or leave it. That was one slogan he could get behind. Some nights, during the playing of the national anthem, Riordan would look up in the stands and see those hippie bastards sitting down, and he wanted to go up there after them. Read 'em their rights, teach them a thing or two about respect. But Cazzie—man, he had nothing but respect for Cazzie when it came to patriotism, and those same feelings carried over onto the court.

The racial stuff upset Riordan's gentle soul. There was a lot of that shit flying around, too. He got an earful from Nate Bowman, and from Dick Barnett. Rich was one angry Negro, Riordan thought. He believed that the black man was always being exploited and that Vietnam was just another example of the black man being sent to fight a white man's war. Did you ever hear such crap in all your life?

This was in the years when the Vietnam War was being fought not only in Southeast Asia but in the press, on college campuses, and everywhere else. The country was clearly divided about American involvement in the war. There were large-scale protest marches in every large American city. In New York, construction workers went on a rampage through the streets, carrying the flag and assaulting anyone who looked like a hippie to them. Yet the Knicks seemed to steer clear of the uproar. They were preoccupied with playing basketball. There were any number of political discussions, but they were respectful. Jackson and Bradley were the obvious doves. They were outnumbered by the hawks—Riordan, DeBusschere, Hosket, and May. And the brothers—aside from Russell, you couldn't tell how they felt.

Once the whistle blew, however, everybody—black and white, hawk and dove—pulled hard for the team. The guys were busting ass, especially now that it looked like they had a great shot at the championship. Despite the everyday frictions, the bonhomie was tremendous. Playing pro basketball, being a New York Knick—these were the essential luxuries in life. The real world, what went on outside the arena, beyond the locker room, was only a distraction. Racial equality, war, patriotism, the life-and-death struggles of ordinary folks—they'd all have to wait until June, until after the last basketball dropped through the hoop and one team remained standing.

8 | ROAD WARRIORS

Late December 1969

B Y CHRISTMAS, the Knicks had fallen back to earth. A four-game losing streak to mediocre teams had clipped their wings, and for a time there, the locker room was a gallery of long faces and suspicious minds. Players started moaning about fatigue and injuries. Reed had a sore toe. Frazier pulled a groin muscle. DeBusschere got a fat lip that led to some light-headedness. Bowman turned an ankle. It was a dicey scene. Then, for encores, Reed jammed his ring finger and Frazier dislocated a pinky. To some of the guys, it felt as if the chronic complainers were jaking it. No one actually said anything or accused anyone of lying down on the job, but you could see it in their faces. Players regarded each other with squint-eyed expressions that said, "Okay, what's wrong now? Where does it hurt, baby?" Next thing you knew, Johnny Warren or Donnie May would be grumbling about bench sores.

What the hell was going on here? Danny Whelan felt as if he was running a M*A*S*H unit. The guys were falling faster than flies. Under the best of circumstances, Whelan was over-taxed. Officially, he was the team trainer, but if you were injured—and not with a rinky-dink nosebleed or a shiner but a genuine injury requiring more than first-aid treatment—you'd better hope like hell Danny wasn't the one who came to your rescue. Not that the guys didn't like Danny. He was a lovable character, a jouncy little troll with a voice like Jon Lovitz, who entertained them with tales about his days as the clubhouse boy for the San Francisco Seals, a minor-league baseball team. In fact, "Minor League" would have been a fitting nickname for Danny, considering his dearth of medical training—if he wasn't already called "Big Time." Big Time said in such a way that it meant "Small Time." The guys knew Danny wasn't a medic, or even a very good trainer. He was okay with gauze and bandages, or a few aspirins if your head hurt. He also had a can of Freon he sprayed on everything. But for serious injuries, the accepted policy was: Never let Danny within a foot of you.

DeBusschere knew the score. One night, against the Lakers, he took an elbow from Rick Roberson and felt his nose shift a few degrees west, to a spot behind his ear. Danny was on him in a flash, wanting to minister to the wound. "C'mon, Dave—lemme pop it back in place," he whined. "Lemme have a whack at it." DeBusschere took one look at the flecks of blood splattering on the floor, glanced at Danny's eager face—*"Lemme have a whack at it!"*—and nearly passed out. Over my dead body! he thought, demanding an escort to the hospital.

As DeBusschere knew, Danny's knowledge of the human body was limited to a numbered medical chart of the muscles and skeletal system that hung in the Knicks' locker room. It was his sole frame of reference. Whelan's dependence on that chart was demonstrated one time when Bill Hosket got kneed in the side. Danny hovered over him dramatically, crying, "Hoss—what's wrong with you, buddy? Did you take one?" The guy had obviously seen too many John Wayne movies. Hosket, who was in pain and wanted to save the time it would take Whelan to consult his chart, replied, "Yeah, Danny, I did—I pulled a number nineteen."

When it came to serious training, Big Time Danny Whelan was something of a liability. Basically, his job was to keep the guys loose, keep them happy. But even Whelan's airy personality couldn't lighten the gloom. All of a sudden the record-setting streak, with its fifteen minutes of celebrity, seemed like no big deal. For the month after it ended, the Knicks were playing just a notch over .500 ball. It was stupefying. They started to take it out on each other, throwing hard fouls even during practice. Like complaining they didn't get the ball when they were open. Like tightening the racial boundaries. The Knicks had become the least bit prickly, and it wasn't limited to the guys on the floor.

After the fourth loss, the team went to Chicago for a game against the woeful Bulls. Chicago—that rot bog of head winds and deep-dish pizza—was actually a good place to lift the Knicks' spirits. The Bulls, relatively new to the league, were still shuffling their lineup in an attempt to find a winning combination. Bob Love and Al Tucker had just been brought over from Cincinnati, in an attempt to give them more offense, but they needed time to fit into the Bulls' style of play. Tom Boerwinkle, their big man, was no match for Reed; Willis pushed him around the court like a chess piece—like a rook. Clem Haskins and Chet Walker played respectably when they got enough help. Only Jerry Sloan posed a real threat.

Sloan was the Bulls' only true All-Star—a great ball handler and a scoring machine. He was unnervingly fast. He could control the rhythm of a game, explode for thirty points, or give your guards a dose of jitters by switching gears to tighten the defense. Or all three. Frazier knew Sloan well. They had been college rivals and had played against each other often, going head to head for forty-eight minutes at each meeting. For all the souped-up rivalry, however, they were fairly evenly matched, and they loved playing against each other. It made them work like bandits and raised the level of their respective games to new heights.

Frazier should have been up for this one. He was angry over the four losses and sought to avenge them, but he arrived at the arena feeling bloated and lethargic. He had wolfed down a big dinner, topping it off with extra helpings of pie à la mode, and they were currently detonating depth charges in his intestinal tract. Then he spied some fans wearing those damn "Kick the Knicks" buttons. Well, the gimmick had seemed funny in Baltimore, when the team was winning, but now he found it annoying. Kick the Knicks, eh? I'll kick your chump asses. The food, the buttons, the fans—man, he hadn't counted on all this. Damn! The last thing he felt like was battling Jerry Sloan.

Frazier came out slowly and had an untypically awkward start, letting Sloan rattle him and shooting a miserable 20 percent from the field. Then, late in the fourth quarter, Holzman got on his case. During a time-out, Red lit into him for not taking Al Tucker out of an easy play. He screamed at Clyde, picking apart his character, trying to push the emotional temperature up a few notches.

"You in the game or what?" Red yelled. "Block your fuckin' man or get him off the boards."

Whuh!—

Frazier checked the clock. There was slightly under two minutes left, and the Knicks had pulled sufficiently away from the Bulls to assure them of the win.

"What do you want from me, Red? I'm not doing any worse than anybody else. And, hey, man, the damn game is over anyway."

The damn game is over?

Well, Holzman nearly had a stroke. He nearly came across the huddle at Frazier and committed a punishable crime.

"I'll tell you when the fuckin' game is over!" he shouted.

"You're not the coach, I am." Frazier felt like a mingy newt. He felt . . . disgraced. Still, he wanted to mollify Red, say something conciliatory, but Holzman waved him off. "Just shut the fuck up. Okay? *Shut up!* I get the last word, and the first word, and all the rest of the words in between."

You could have grilled a T-bone over the flames that shot out of Frazier's eyes. His blood was boiling. Red had left him no way out, no way to save face. It wasn't like the old man. Fortunately, Clyde was still dwelling on an earlier incident that had knocked him seriously off balance. In the second quarter, trying to contain an unruly Jerry Sloan, he and Riordan had combined to squeeze the Bulls guard off stride. They double-teamed Sloan, trapping him between their bodies, and next thing they knew Sloan went down—hard. He crumbled to the floor, and Frazier knew right away it was serious. Sloan wasn't a dive-bomber. He never took an unnecessary flop. You had to know Jerry Sloan as Clyde did to appreciate his tenacity. The guy'd rather take a bullet than be dropped to the floor. Frazier had watched as Chicago's trainers helped Sloan limp off the floor and thought, That could have been me. You tear something crucial and—*pfwiiitttt*—the season goes bust. Just like that. He had to keep himself in check, he decided. He had to stay healthy. Red could go haywire, he could blow off all the steam he liked—it wouldn't mean a whit if Clyde stayed focused.

The very next night, Frazier took his frustrations out on the Bullets. Baltimore still harbored fantasies of taming the beastly Knicks, but New York brought them rudely to their senses. The Knicks, continuing their seasonal torment of the Bullets, routed them, 128–91. Frazier led all scorers with twenty-nine points, also racking up fourteen assists and eight rebounds, but the key ingredient was a team effort that, as one paper reported it, left Baltimore "disorganized, demoralized, and defenseless." The Knicks hog-tied the dud Bullets. At one point, New York was up by forty-one points—with subs Johnny Warren, Bill Hosket, and Donnie May on the floor. And the team had seventy-three rebounds, compared with their opponents' paltry forty-nine. It was the kind of lopsided victory that made Red Holzman want to frame the stats.

Whoever had had any doubts about Holzman's ability to lead the team had dismissed them by now. He finally had all the components of the New York Knicks playing together in one glorious fanfare. He might almost have been conducting an Italian opera—emotions were exploding unexpectedly from his cast members, their cumulative petulance was producing sparks, and it took steely nerves and a steady hand to steer them toward the last act. Ned Irish, who had flirted with a full-scale shake-up of the Garden's pro basketball program—meaning that he'd been ready to dismiss some of the top management as well as a few of his pricey stars—was blissfully content. Finally the team was winning games and breaking attendance records, heading for a 700,000 season total. Yep, Holzman had been an inspired choice to turn things around. There'd been plenty of skeptics around when Irish picked him to take over for Dick McGuire. How can you appoint a former scout? they argued. The guy's nothing but a traveling salesman. Irish told them that if they wanted to second-guess him, they should audition for a quiz show. He rarely bothered to answer his critics, but when he did, he usually stopped them dead in their tracks.

Now, on Christmas Day, Ned Irish was in his usual seat at the Garden, a few rows up behind the bench, to watch the Knicks play a grudge match against the erratic Detroit Pistons. The Pistons seemed to have the Knicks' number. True, there were all those games when the Knicks had spanked their little heinies, but that was to be expected of two teams with such disparate degrees of talent. It was the rare game in which Detroit prevailed that stuck in New York's throat, and there had been a few of them since training camp broke. The last time, in fact, had been when they stopped the Knicks' winning streak, so there was a bit of a score to settle.

Then, of course, there was that loudmouth coach of theirs—Butch Van Breda Kolff. The guy was a piece of work. He's got a team that's playing .382 ball—as opposed to the Knicks' .829 percentage—and he brags about their being fearless giant killers. The nerve of that sucker! He'd practically claimed sole responsibility for stopping the Knicks' streak by directing Howie Komives to run Frazier away from the ball. In fact, what happened was that every time the ball came to Komives, he moved to the other side of the court, and if Clyde didn't follow, then Komives would badger the ref into calling a zone infraction on Frazier. That was some brilliant strategy of Butch's! The Pistons couldn't play with the Knicks, so they resorted to stunts designed to rattle the cage. And now, Van Breda Kolff was popping off in the press about how he had shown Cincinnati, Philadelphia, Seattle, and Atlanta—the victors during the Knicks' mini-slump—how to beat New York, by keeping Clyde off the ball. The guy had massive chunks of spleen—he didn't know when to turn off the b.s.

For all the bickering, the Detroit game was fairly unspectacular until the last *one second* of play. The score seesawed throughout the first forty-seven minutes. First the Knicks were up by eleven, then the Pistons by one. In the third quarter the Knicks regained the lead, 88–83, but Dave Bing, just back from a dangerous knee injury, scored seven straight points, followed by a basket from Walt Bellamy that put the Pistons up by four. The Pistons were leading, 109–108, when Bradley hit a twelve-foot jumper with fifteen seconds to play. Momentum was shifting in the Knicks' favor; it seemed they were going to pull this one out. Besides, Detroit wasn't exactly known for finishing close games. They'd dropped a number of squeakers, and with the emotional incentive they had, the Knicks figured to put this one in the "win" column. Yet somehow the Pistons pushed the ball down-court to Bellamy, who drove through his old teammate Reed to make it 111–110, with one second left on the clock.

One second!

Holzman called for time. "There's not much we can do," he acknowledged, as the guys hovered glumly near the bench. "We're gonna run the one-second play."

The one-second play—it was like calling for volunteers to take a bullet. Pure suicide. A Hail Mary, if ever there was one. The Celtics were the only team that had ever run it effectively, and that had been with Bill Russell in the lineup. They'd clear out the lane, and one of the Jones boys would lob it to Russ from out of bounds, a beautiful arcing shot that Russell would dunk without ever putting the ball on the floor. It was a showstopper that required great hands, split-second timing—and Bill Russell. The Knicks had never gotten it to work. In practice, Clyde would aim for Reed's head—and wind up tossing the ball over the backboard. *Clank!* The last time they'd tried it, against the Atlanta Hawks in overtime, Clyde wasn't even close; Joe Caldwell anticipated the play, deflected the ball perfectly, and it came down somewhere south of Savannah.

Holzman pointed a finger at Dick Barnett. "Rich, you're my key man," he said. "You've got to take your man down low, swing around a screen to get behind Bellamy, and set a pick so Willis can go to the basket."

Barnett nodded automatically. Sure, sure, whatever you say. Count on me. But, like everyone else, he knew it was hopeless.

So did Van Breda Kolff. He knew what was coming. You could see him pantomiming it for his guys, down at the other end of the floor—one hand tracing the trajectory of the ball, the other representing the Knicks center as he stuffs it through the hoop. Got that? Butch seemed to ask, because everyone nodded and laughed. No fucking way!

Frazier took the ball at midcourt and surveyed the situation.

Everyone was in place. Reed was positioned a few feet behind Bellamy on one side of the basket; Barnett was fencing with Komives; Bradley and DeBusschere were clogging the lane; and Jimmy Walker, Clyde's man, was free-lancing, ready to leap in any direction to swat the ball away. The clock wouldn't start until the ball touched a player's hands in bounds.

Clyde slapped the ball. Like clockwork, Barnett swung around, losing his man, and set a screen that picked off Bellamy. Reed took two gargantuan steps toward the basket and leaped skyward as Clyde lofted the ball diagonally toward the hoop. Time stopped dead. The crowd was stunned into silence. The ball seemed to hang in the air for an hour—weightless, lingering, wavering—until Reed stabbed two hands toward the projectile, grabbed it right on the word "Spalding," and guided it gently through the net.

What a finish!

The buzzer drowned out most of the exultant screams. Reed leaped into the air again, raising both fists in victory. Cazzie Russell hoisted Frazier into the air and paraded him triumphantly past the dumbfounded Pistons bench. Van Breda Kolff buried his head in his hands, refusing to acknowledge their presence, but he knew they were there all right. They seemed to be saying, Share that piece of strategy, Butch! Merry Christmas to you. Sayonara!

"A one-in-a-million shot!" Holzman warbled as the guys galloped past him. It was a sweet way to win.

Following that game, the Knicks took off for a road trip that would be a true test of their mettle. The itinerary included three stops in as many days—in Los Angeles, Vancouver (for a game against Seattle), and Phoenix—taking them on a wild 7,200-mile tour before landing them back in New York ninety-six hours later. It was a particularly dense part of the schedule, with games shoved up against each other shoulder to shoulder. That was nothing new; they'd get through it. The Knicks' primary objective was to get a good look at the Lakers, a team they figured to face when play-off time rolled around.

The Lakers were a beleaguered team. Wilt Chamberlain, their go-to guy, was sidelined with that dicey knee injury. Elgin Baylor nursed a nagging groin problem. Johnny Egan, who wore a knee brace under the best of circumstances, was banged up and near the end of his career. Dick Garrett, a six-three rookie who was starting at point guard, had played behind Frazier at Southern Illinois and was hardly worthy of the assignment. Willie McCarter, another rookie, was a marginal pickup. The Lakers were barely treading water. With Wilt on ice, the chores at center fell to a rookie out of Cincinnati named Rick Roberson, who brought new meaning to the word "flake." Roberson talked to himself, all the time. And he was irrational. He had been known to destroy metal lockers—following a Lakers *win*. When Chamberlain was still healthy, Roberson, enraged over his supporting role, had gone to management to complain about his playing time. Imagine that!—a backup center, a lousy rookie, trying to displace the great Chamberlain. It later turned out that Roberson simply wasn't equipped to carry the load. He was inexperienced and inconsistent and immature. Mel Counts was picked to fill in at the center position, but he was basically a forward, with all the limitations of that position.

Still, the Lakers were a threat thanks to one man—the incomparable Jerry West. West practically carried the team by himself. He was as intense a competitor as anyone who had ever come down the pike. He operated at maximum thrust every night of the week, played nearly the whole forty-eight minutes each night. Led the team in scoring, rebounding, and assists. Functioned as the primary playmaker. Played injured. Inspired his teammates. Practiced unselfishness. He was a one-man show. "Pressure makes me want to play harder," he once boasted, and faced with the rigors of the current season, West had turned up his game several megawatts and was operating in another stratosphere.

He was unnaturally quick—not speedy, but instinctive in a way that allowed him to scope out situations and make split-second adjustments. He could anticipate what was coming. In baseball, a batter senses when a pitcher changes speed and makes the appropriate correction to his swing every time he steps to the plate. West handled each possession of the ball in much the same way. Depending upon the team he faced and its lineup for that night, West altered his moves and shots, going so far as to change the arc on his jumper to counter the defensive style of a particular opponent. That's how he averaged twenty-seven or twenty-eight points a game. And in play-offs, when players normally tightened the screws, he scored over thirty points a game—and had pushed it to an astounding 40.6 points in his eleven play-off games of the 1964–65 season.

West could do it all when he had to, but it was clear he needed a supporting cast. The newest—and most pivotal—addition to the team was its rookie coach, Joe Mullaney. A former FBI man, Mullaney had been a teammate of Bob Cousy's at Holy Cross and was later the varsity coach at Providence College, where his teams had produced a herd of NBA stallions, including Lenny Wilkens, Johnny Egan, John Thompson, Jimmy Walker, Ernie DiGregorio, and Mike Riordan. With those horses, Mullaney took Providence to the NCAA every year. In fact, during a championship round at Madison Square Garden in 1963, Ned Irish had offered him the job of coaching the lowly Knicks, which Mullaney had been smart enough to refuse. With his record, he figured he'd eventually get to the pros.

Riordan said that Mullaney coached the same way he played the ponies, relying on wily strategy and good percentages. "He used to make the analogy that if he had Ted Williams on a team and the game permitted it, he'd bat Williams twenty-seven times," Riordan recalled. "In basketball you can do that. You feed the hot man until the defense doesn't allow it anymore, then you go to the next best percentage man, and that's the way he coached."

Trouble was, when he looked down the Lakers bench, there wasn't any next best. Los Angeles was idling as a one-man team. Mullaney pleaded with Laker GM Freddy Schaus to bring in some help. There was plenty of trade bait on the roster. Mel Counts, a gangly seven-footer, who was nicknamed "Low Counts" due to his meager productivity, was expendable, and Mullaney had seen enough of Billy Hewitt, a slight forward from USC. Hewitt just wasn't good enough in his book.

Initially, Schaus tried to make a deal that had Mullaney salivating—Mel Counts for Gail Goodrich, even up. My God! Goodrich, who was with Phoenix, was a local favorite—he'd played at UCLA—and he could shoot; he'd do the trick nicely. There was also a special relationship between the Lakers and the Suns that would facilitate a deal. Schaus and Jerry Colangelo, the Suns' coach, were friends and often pooled information on scouting and the draft. Today that would be collusion, and illegal. Nevertheless, they sat down together a few times each year and assigned "power ratings" to the available players. But Colangelo couldn't move fast enough, and in the end he refused to part with Goodrich. Then Schaus dangled Counts in a swap for Atlanta's Joe Caldwell.

"Great!" Mullaney said, envisioning a powerhouse. Caldwell had always been a defensive nightmare for Jerry West, he was a good defender, he could run, he was graceful, tough, not much of a shooter, but an *athlete* nonetheless. "What are you waiting for? Do it," he said. But Atlanta chickened out.

Schaus came back with a far less tantalizing proposition: Hewitt for Harold "Happy" Hairston, the former NYU star, who was functioning as Detroit's third or fourth forward. Wellllllll, it wasn't exactly what Mullaney had in mind. Hairston was a strange cat. He was moody, resentful, outspoken—trouble. Van

Breda Kolff wasn't happy with him in Detroit. Hairston had dared to criticize his strategy in the press. When Butch called Hairston lazy, Happy took it as a racial slur. It went back and forth like that. Mullaney called Bud Shackroe, Detroit's trainer, who happened to have been the assistant hockey trainer at Providence when Mullaney was there, and asked for the lowdown on Hairston. The word came back: He's in great athletic shape, keeps to himself.

"I don't know why," Shackroe added, "but for some reason no one likes him—the white guys don't like him, the black guys don't either. He seems to be a loner. But he's ready to play tomorrow."

Mullaney was still undecided. On the one hand, he needed a big body and wanted to unload Hewitt; on the other, he already had his share of head cases. And Mullaney had already had a strange encounter with Hairston, whom he had known from his college days. It was after the third game of the season, when the Lakers were in Detroit, and Mullaney got a phone call at his hotel from an agent named Don Grinker. "Hey, Joe, how you doing?" he said. "I represent Happy Hairston and need to talk to you." Mullaney said fine and told Grinker to come on up.

Well, Grinker arrives a few minutes later and—he's got Happy Hairston with him. This is an odd situation, Mullaney thought; Hairston's in my hotel room, and we're playing them tonight. It doesn't say much about appearances. The former FBI man began to sweat, thinking it might be some kind of setup. But no, Happy was merely making a personal pitch. He hated Van Breda Kolff, loathed Detroit, and wanted to play in L.A., where he could get into show business and acting. Mullaney didn't know what to say and gave them the brush-off. The next day, in Baltimore, he asked Wilt Chamberlain for his opinion of Hairston and got two thumbs down. Wilt personally wasn't fond of Happy. But . . . well . . . now Chamberlain was out for the season . . . Hewitt wouldn't do them much good . . . they needed another big man . . . Mullaney called Schaus and said, "Make the deal."

Immediately Hairston made the Lakers a stronger team. He gave them more height, a scoring punch, and offensive rebounding—and he'd prove troublesome for DeBusschere. With West and Garrett in the backcourt, Roberson at center, and Hairston and Counts on the wings, the Lakers actually had a chance to make a little noise.

The Knicks landed in L.A. at 6:30 in the morning, went to their hotel, and were ready to play by four that afternoon. It was a grind, to be sure, but the guys found that overnight travel often tapped a hidden source of energy. You hit the point of no return, when you felt the energy bottom out, then ran on the vapors, switched over to automatic pilot, letting adrenaline carry you until you didn't even have to see the ball to know where it was and what you had to do with it. The Knicks called it Zombie Time. You didn't think or feel—you just did.

It was Zombie Time.

By 6:30 P.M., a crowd of 17,219 had filed into the Forum, the only pro arena besides the Garden where the audience was that large and that loud. It was one factor, along with the hundreds of transplanted New Yorkers in the stands, that gave the Knicks an extra boost. Of course, there were a few minus factors giving them a boost, as well. For one thing, Elgin Baylor sat on the bench in street clothes. Baylor was feeling nearly a hundred percent and ready to go, but the team doctor, Bob Kerlan, had held him back at the last minute. And Wilt Chamberlain was standing in a runway near the basket.

But Chamberlain's presence was noteworthy, inasmuch as he had stayed away from basketball during his lengthy recuperation. Detractors said Wilt couldn't bear to watch a game he might never be able to play again, but the truth was he'd been too busy fielding other interests. Notably, there was the mansion he was building on the Pacific, which demanded his constant attention. It was a massive contemporary structure—an endless warren of rooms, all arches, vaulted ceilings, loggias, and cornices, specifically designed to house the world's most famous seven-footer. And he was obsessed with his return to uniform. After an overall examination, Dr. Kerlan had determined that Wilt was finished for the year. It was an educated prediction, which it was entirely reasonable for the Lakers to take at face value. Wilt had suffered serious damage to the knee, and if basketball was to be in his future, a lengthy rest followed by intensive physical therapy was necessary just to restore the big guy's basic ambulatory skills. That was the doctor's prognosis. Chamberlain, as was his way, had his own ideas. Exercising his mouth like a megaphone, he had announced publicly that he'd be back on March 13. March 13? He'd obviously chosen the date because it was the number he wore on his back. Well, it was wishful thinking. The smart money said he was nuts. Few people ever came back from the kind of injury Wilt had sustained, and those who did often took years. But March 13? Yep, circle that date, Chamberlain insisted. It was going to be a humdinger.

Willis Reed had passed Wilt earlier in the afternoon and thought he looked remarkably well for what he'd been through. He was standing on the bum leg, flexing it a bit, and he seemed reasonably fit and muscular. You had to hand it to Wilt, he'd kept himself in tip-top shape.

In fact, Chamberlain had suffered through a rehabilitation that few ordinary human beings could have endured. It was like something out of *Dr. Terror's House of Horrors,* although in this case, the torture rack was a contraption approved by the AMA. Following the knee operation, Wilt began taking daily whirlpool sessions to warm up the leg; then he manipulated it in a regimen of range-of-motion exercises, free of resistance, in order to initiate some motion. It was the basic exploratory exam to determine if he'd ever walk again, and that part wasn't so bad. He'd do the motion exercises, called muscle memory, several times each day—straight-leg raises, knee extensions, and flexes. Towel off, take a little more whirlpool. It was an almost pleasurable ordeal. Eventually, he grew comfortable with the way the leg was responding and graduated to more complicated resistance training. The Lakers' trainer, Frank O'Neil, prescribed sessions on a stationary bicycle, but a check of all the manufacturers revealed that no one made bikes to support a creature Wilt's size. So they resorted to resistive-weight exercises, in which Chamberlain sat on the edge of a table and lifted seven-pound sinkers with his lower body. Even for Wilt, it was a struggle. He'd had considerable muscle atrophy near the knee, and there was a danger of tearing scar tissue, and that would do far more damage than if you did absolutely nothing. But Wilt was adamant. He wanted to show progress, and was willing to take some risks if he was to meet that target date of March 13. So O'Neil increased the weights incrementally, and cracked the whip across the big guy's back. More sets of exercises were ordered, more repetitions. By the middle of December, Wilt was pushing, pulling, stretching, flexing, mincing, slicing, chopping, dicing—he was the human Veg-o-Matic. It was pure hell. But he was starting to show some progress. O'Neil would ratchet up the resistance, hold the leg down, and have Wilt go through the motions, and Wilt could feel the strength coming back. It was incredible—practically a miracle. At that point, against his better judgment, O'Neil went to management and conceded that, no, Chamberlain hadn't been off his rocker when he'd boasted he'd be back. He was on some kind of schedule. And, yes, doctors were sometimes wrong. Sometimes, they went too much by the book. With Chamberlain, however, there was no book that described his servomechanism— why, you needed a whole fucking encyclopedia. This guy, he was no ordinary mortal. He'd be back. Maybe not on March 13, O'Neil said, but he'd play again . . . this season . . . Count on it.

From the way Chamberlain looked, Willis agreed. The team the Lakers were preparing to put on the floor that night was essentially an appetizer, a little something for the Knicks to nibble on while the big guy rested. The Knicks would be ready, they'd give it a hundred percent, but Reed sensed that if they met again in April, in the play-offs, the man in the middle would put a completely different face on the game.

Tonight, it looked as if the Knicks were going to eat this version of the Lakers alive. New York came out playing as though they'd been sunbathing on Zuma Beach for the last six days. They hit an incredible 56 percent of their shots in the first half and shut down the Jerry West scoring machine. Jerry looked dazed and confused. He took a number of jumpers that ricocheted off the rim, lost the ball off the dribble, passed out of bounds. He let even Barnett, his old teammate, creep up his ass and give him hemorrhoids every time the Lakers had possession in their zone. West had obviously blown a fuse. As the game progressed, he began muttering to himself and badgering the officials. To say he wasn't exactly on his game would be an understatement. Mullaney sat him down for a few minutes, but the damage was evident. At halftime the Knicks were up by a comfortable thirteen-point margin, largely thanks to West's horrible performance. He was only two for nine from the field, with eleven points, and seemed headed for one of the most dismal nights of his career.

But whatever they did to West during intermission should be patented and bottled and studied at every university research facility in the country. When the teams came out again, the guy was physically transformed. You could see it from the first in-bounds pass. He took the ball, charged downcourt, pirouetting rapidly around Barnett, and made a difficult basket over the heads of three scowling New York defenders. Well, you had to sit up and take notice when something like that happened. West was sending a message to the Knicks that the first half was history—it had been a fluke. You had to take this guy seriously.

Within minutes, West changed the rhythm of the game. He hit with jumpers from outside, he drove to the basket, in both cases inflicting damage on the bug-eyed Knick defenders. Barnett and Bradley, for example, played right into his hands. They tried to trap and double-team him off a zone press and got themselves into serious foul trouble. Riordan came in and fared no better. The guy was unstoppable. He threw in twelve in the third period, and when he ran into traffic there was always an open man— Keith Erickson, Dick Garrett, or Mel Counts—lurking nearby to whom he could pass for an easy lay-up.

The Lakers eventually caught the Knicks, at 85 all, and then it was all Jerry West down the stretch. He pumped in another seventeen, giving him forty points, and Los Angeles pulled away to an unexpected 114–106 win.

The Knicks left Los Angeles the next morning on an 8:30 flight to Vancouver. They were still mumbling about the way they had lost the game, still crying about The Jerry West Show, but there were some other stats that were troubling their reflective coach. Five Lakers had wound up in double figures, with Counts, Roberson, and Hairston together picking off a whopping forty-one rebounds. Hairston also scored fifteen points and gave DeBusschere migraine headaches under the board all night long. It was clearly a preview of things to come, Holzman concluded.

"I'll tell you one thing," he said. "If they get Baylor and Chamberlain back, we're going to really have our hands full."

Baylor . . . Chamberlain. The likelihood of their both returning this year was slim, as everyone knew. Surely Red wasn't dwelling on such a long-shot possibility. And yet just the gentle spin of that scenario was enough to spook the stallions. Even now, cruising at 32,000 feet above sea level, the guys could almost feel the earth trembling. A great shifting of the sands was taking place in the treacherous Los Angeles basin. You could feel the solid standings being re-evaluated, maybe reshuffled, even though those two legends hadn't done a thing except show up to watch a lousy ball game.

In Vancouver, the Knicks mopped up late, squeaking narrowly past the Supersonics, 119–117. The team was clearly exhausted by their insane schedule, and things only proceeded to get worse. They were awakened at 5:45 the next morning for a six-hour flight, which made stops in Portland, Los Angeles, and San Diego before landing in Phoenix at 4:00 in the afternoon. How was anyone expected to play basketball after that? You have to figure that a normal body needs to replenish its energy after a plane trip like that, especially considering the intense dehydration that takes place on such an excursion. And these weren't normal bodies. These were titans in the mid-six- to seven-foot range. They needed water, they needed food, they needed to stretch their long legs, they needed *sleep*. Instead, after they checked into their hotel, Danny Whelan herded the guys onto a bus heading to the Veterans Memorial Coliseum, in the Arizona State Fairgrounds, for a slugfest with the Suns.

For visiting teams, Phoenix wasn't exactly the warm, sunny place it was cracked up to be. The fans there were goddamn animals. They treated opponents like early Christians being sacrificed in an arena. They howled and hooted and cursed, and they threw things at the players. Called them names you wouldn't utter in a public urinal. The last time the Knicks had played there, the fans went berserk when Dick Van Arsdale got called for a technical, and they pelted the refs with ears of corn! For Chrissake, they must have been out in the desert sun too long.

The Knicks were asleep on their feet when they entered the aptly named Coliseum, but the crowd woke them up. Damn savages gave the guys an extremely hard time during warm-ups, so by game time they were revitalized and gunning for the Suns.

Phoenix may have been 15–22 on the season, but they put an interesting team on the floor. Like Milwaukee, they had suffered through miserable growing pains throughout their first years in the league, and, also like the Bucks, they'd drafted a player with the potential to lift them from unparalleled wretchedness to nobility, practically overnight. Connie Hawkins wasn't as tall or as dominant as Alcindor, but when it came to talent, the guy could shoot out the lights. His secret weapon was what he called the hesitation hook, which seemed indefensible by NBA standards. Here's the way a writer for *Sports Illustrated* described it: "Hawkins sweeps toward the basket with long strides, veers to the right, leaps high, holds the ball outstretched for two heartbeats and at last flips the ball through the rim." That was it in a nutshell. It was beautiful to watch—a lovely, unconventional piece of ballet that left defenders standing with their mouths open as the ball pierced the net. Hawkins was a *premier danseur* of the intergalactic order. He was uncommonly supple for a six-eight man—and elegant. My God, he had style! He could extend and glide through the air like no other man alive—like an eagle, perhaps—and he'd arrived in town with a vapor trail of press that would fill the scrapbook of most ten-year veterans.

The Hawkins legend was a cautionary tale that basketball players and fans alike knew by heart. He'd been a legend at Boys High in New York City, and the envy of every NBA scout. But during his freshman year at the University of Iowa, he'd been barred from ever playing in the NBA for allegedly not reporting a bribe. It was all based on innuendo. The league's investigation was considered a hatchet job, but the betting aspect left an indelible stench, and Connie was banished to basketball Siberia. He was blacklisted. For a while he barnstormed with the Harlem Globetrotters, whose audiences laughed at his antics. What a waste of pure talent that had been. The man was probably on a par with Oscar Robertson, and here he was doodling on the court as part of basketball's most famous freak show. Well, that didn't last long. He played next for the Minneapolis Pipers of the defunct American Basketball League, ending up with Pittsburgh in the ABA, where he led all players in scoring for two years straight. That would have been it for Hawkins, too, had he not gotten some good advice: a lawyer encouraged him to sue the NBA, which he did, and won reinstatement, beginning with the 1969–70 season, along with a $1.5 million settlement.

Holding the rights to Hawkins, Phoenix, got lucky. They needed a big scoring threat up front, and, even though he was already twenty-seven years old, even though he was known as damaged goods, he was still capable of greatness. As far as scoring went, he was averaging in the mid-twenties—certainly nothing to sneeze at. The first time the Knicks saw him, back at the Garden on October 21, he hit twenty-seven and tortured De-Busschere, benching Dave early with foul trouble. DeBusschere was flabbergasted at Connie's anatomy. "He's got the biggest hands I've ever seen," Dave remarked after their introduction on the court. "He handles the ball like a baseball. And he's deceptive. He doesn't run, he floats or sort of glides."

Back in October, Hawkins still hadn't shaken out all the mothballs, but he was cruising now. And he was on a team of rabble rousers who were worthy of his elastic grace. The Suns had picked up forward Paul Silas from Atlanta, a move that complemented Hawkins and gave them rebounding strength, and the backcourt was solid, with Van Arsdale and Gail Goodrich. For now, there was a traffic jam at center, with the very capable Jim Fox upset over sharing the spotlight with rookie Neil Walk, who'd been drafted number two, behind Alcindor. Eventually that would have to be sorted out. It was causing all sorts of havoc on the floor and in the locker room. But Red Kerr, the Suns' affable coach, wasn't up to handling it. What the team had, however, was potential. They had tons of potential.

Still, all the potential in the world wouldn't have saved them from the Knicks' brand of tight-knit, aggressive play. In the second half, just when the Knicks might have been expected to curl up and hit the sack, they exploded, scoring forty-five points in the third quarter alone and sinking an astounding 72 percent from the field. That was a record for the Coliseum. Connie Hawkins's thirty-one points was wiped out by the Knicks' bench; Russell had a seventeen-point second half, while Riordan drilled fourteen. And Willis Reed proved that one center of his immense ability was enough for any team.

Reed had one lousy basket in the first half, and it seemed as though the whirlwind traveling was catching up with him. He was sluggish, way off the mark. The Suns tagged him for three quick personal fouls. Then, in the third quarter, he picked up his game, hitting a perfect eight for eight, with four free throws, for twenty points, and he finished with thirty-two.

Across the league, teams were talking about the year Reed was having—but not all they said was kindly. Most experts agreed that New York had assembled a team whose chilling productivity allowed Willis to concentrate more on scoring and rebounding, and so he had finally come into his own. There were others, however, who said he was playing way over his head. Who was right? Actually, the question oversimplifies the debate and obscures the bigger picture. Had Reed finally come into his own? No question about it. He was cranked. He'd literally dictated the course of the Knicks' play for the first half of the season and had demonstrated plenty of confidence to go with it. Was he playing over his head? Certainly. If you judged strictly according to the stats, he was. He was having the best year of his career, pure and simple. But since joining the pro ranks, in 1964, Reed had endured such a herky-jerky ride that it was difficult to peg his overall performance.

For years Reed was the Rodney Dangerfield of the Knicks— he didn't get any respect. It had started even before he arrived in New York. He'd been a standout at Grambling College, guiding the Tigers to three Southwestern Athletic Conference titles, along with teammate Charlie Hardnett, who later played with the Baltimore Bullets. Reed was Grambling's all-time biggest

basketball star, but Grambling was a football school by reputation
and therefore off the beat of most pro basketball scouts. Basketball
operated in virtual obscurity on the Grambling campus. That
hadn't kept Red Holzman away. Red got an early whiff of Willis
and then set Eddie Donovan on the scent to Bramley, Louisiana,
with instructions that they consider Reed come draft time.

Donovan was aghast. Do I really want to go down there? he
wondered. This was the early 1960s, and the South was sim-
mering with racial unrest. There'd been a few scattered incidents
of violence near the campus, and Donovan's white ass would no
doubt provide a winsome target for the instigators. Welllllll . . .
But Red insisted. The kid was a real prospect, he said. The
Knicks had a jump on the other teams. Eddie really owed it to
them to take a look. At the airport, as Eddie waited for his flight,
word drifted through the waiting room that all hell had broken
loose in Bramley. Oh, that's just fine, Donovan thought. They'll
tar and feather me. They'll make a TV movie out of this and
have Robert Wagner star . . . as Willis Reed. Eddie couldn't deal
with it. Then, as luck would have it, the flight was canceled.
This was turning into a nightmare assignment. Somehow,
though, Donovan did get to Grambling in time for the game he'd
come to see—and three minutes into the first quarter Reed
sprained his ankle.

Luckily, Donovan got a few minutes to talk with Reed as they
drove back to the airport. That was one of Eddie's objectives
when he scouted a kid—to measure his personality. To determine
if the kid had what it took to play in New York. Eddie had learned
that lesson early in his career, after the Knicks drafted Darrall
Imhoff as their first choice in 1960. Imhoff was a big, tough kid
out of California who promised to solve the Knicks' woes at
center. Donovan was coaching the team then, and he was excited
when they signed Big D. The only problem was, Darrall was
. . . sensitive. Well, that threw a monkey wrench into things.
A sensitive kid in New York was dangerous business. Especially

when it came to critics. Eddie used to tell his players, "If you want to read the papers, that's your business, but you've got to take the good with the bad if you're going to be a daily reader—and you can't take anything personally." Imhoff never heeded that advice—or, more likely, he didn't have the constitution that allowed him to run it through his bloodstream. Criticism backed up in his arteries until it formed an emotional embolism, and then, *ka-boooooom!* Imhoff self-destructed.

Warren Pack, a columnist for the old *New York Tribune,* had been on Imhoff's case for some time, blaming poor Darrall for the team's usual losing ways, when the Knicks faced the Philadelphia Warriors in an important game. Imhoff played the best game he ever had—or *could* play against Wilt Chamberlain. In the last couple of minutes, Wilt could have put Imhoff himself in the basket if he'd wanted to. Still, Darrall was pleased with his performance. The next day, however, when he picked up the *Tribune,* he discovered Pack had ripped into him again. Imhoff was crushed. Eddie could see it in his eyes—the kid had blown a gasket. Mentally, he'd gone somewhere else. So Donovan called his boss, Freddy Podesta, and said, "It's impossible for this kid to play here. We can hold onto him, but it'd be best to move him while we can get something for him." And in a few days, Imhoff was gone.

New York City could do that to the best and biggest of men. Eddie warned Willis Reed, as they rode through Bramley, that playing pro basketball was one thing—playing in New York was another. Willis had to be sure he was up to it.

Reed wasn't anyone's idea of a city kid to begin with. He was born in 1942, in a town—no, it wasn't even a town, it was a village, a *hamlet*—called Hico, Louisiana, and he grew up a few miles down the road in Bernice, a *settlement* in Union Parish, on National Highway 167. Reed called them Nowhere and Almost Nowhere, respectively, and to say more about them would be an exaggeration. He was an only child, whose religious upbringing was based on the dogma of hard work. His parents' sole commandment was "If we got to work, you got to work," so Willis cut the grass, weeded flower beds, and hauled cotton and watermelons for Ed Hollis, a white man for whom his mother worked as a domestic. The Reeds were laborers by trade, but they weren't uneducated people. His father's brothers and sisters had graduated from college, his mother's brother was a doctor, and there were teachers in the family. So Willis was expected to do it all—and he *did,* too; he worked like a dog and he got good grades.

And he grew.

He was already six-two the day he graduated eighth grade and by the time school started again he was six-five and wearing size thirteen shoes. My God! He'd grown three inches in three months! The boy needed a dose of weed killer. He felt like a freak, living in a small town like that. Everybody stared at him. Christ, that hurt. He'd walk to school all hunched up, hoping people wouldn't notice. Well, the only thing he could do was . . . play basketball.

Back then, there wasn't any playground ball in Bernice. So Willis nailed a basket to the side of the house. The damn thing was so limber that if you hit the front of the rim—hell, if you even came close—the ball would bounce up and drop through the hoop. And he had to play by himself. There was no other choice. He never got the chance to go three on three or play in pickup games or dunk over some playground legend, and ultimately that's what made him such a great shooter. He could take his time setting up shots, hitting from—well, anywhere. From under the basket, the top of the key, in the corners—from thirty feet out. He developed accuracy. It wasn't until later, in high school, that he began putting the rest of the game together. His coach, a tough-talking disciplinarian named Lendon Stone, subscribed to scholastic coaching magazines, and after school Reed would camp out in Stone's office studying the diagrams and photographs of guys making moves. Stone gave him a key to the gym, and Reed would take the magazines in there with him, walking through the moves with the pages opened in front of him until he could execute the plays on his own. It was basketball by the numbers—*yes!*

When he got to Grambling, the game finally opened up for Reed. One night during his freshman year he watched Jim Dandy, a six-eleven senior, perform a feat that ultimately changed his life. The big guy got a rebound, threw the ball out on the fast break—and wound up getting the dunk at the other end! Well, Reed almost fell out of his seat. He'd never seen a big guy operate at both ends of the court like that. Then, on the next play, Dandy blocked a shot, got the ball, and went the other way with it—he actually ran the lane and got the dunk going the other way. Mother of Christ! Is that what it took to play this game at the next level? Reed wondered. Obviously, the answer was yes. That just blew his mind. He had a lot of work to do! So he learned how to run the floor with the little guys, he built up his stamina. Ran five miles—twenty laps around the track— each day, did wind sprints, ran the stairs, jumped rope. Endured three-a-day practices. It practically killed him. Played morning, noon, and night, all summer long. It was fucking torture. But he worked himself into condition. He'd never heard the word used in such a way before—"conditioning." He taught his body to do things that it had never done before—he made his body respond—and in doing so, in conditioning himself, he learned how to play a fast-paced game of basketball.

And that, he told Eddie Donovan, was why he could play ball anywhere—even in New York. He was all toughened out. His body was ready for the pros. As for his mind—well, hell, you couldn't find a better mind in a big man in all of Louisiana. Still, Reed never for a moment believed he'd be drafted by the Knicks. At least he hoped not. New York was a horrible team, with a reputation to match. At the time, their most famous player was Johnny Green, which just about said it all. And anyway, he'd been scouted fiercely by the Detroit Pistons, who were in desperate need of a big man. Earl Lloyd, a former Piston player and Detroit scout, had seen him play often during his college career, including the night he scored forty-one and picked off twenty-six rebounds against Southern University, with big ol' Butterbean Love breathing down his neck. The way he figured it, Detroit would take him early in the first round of the draft.

When the day came, Reed was doing student teaching at Webster High School in Mendon, Louisiana, teaching phys ed to junior high school kids. In the middle of practice he was called to the principal's office. Eddie Donovan was on the phone.

What the . . . !

"I got some good news for you," Donovan told him. "We've just completed the draft. We took Jim 'Bad News' Barnes in the first round, and we were also very fortunate to get you as the first player taken in the second round."

What the . . . !

That wasn't good news, man. He didn't say that to Donovan, but he was thinking it, all right. The Knicks . . . in the second round. That meant he was taken tenth (there were only nine teams in the league then). Tenth! Well, shit! He'd like to hear the names of the nine players who were considered better than he was. He didn't ask Donovan, but he was thinking it, all right. Man, he was steamed. What happened to Detroit? He asked Donovan that one. Who had the Pistons taken? And he nearly fainted when he got the reply: Joe Caldwell. Caldwell! That chump? Honest to God! This was some league he was joining. It wasn't like those scouts didn't get a good look at him. Earl Lloyd, Marty Blake, George Lee, Vince Miller, Jerry Colangelo—Red Holzman—they'd all seen him. He'd been in enough national competition, he'd played in the Pan-American Games, the Olympic trials. His coach had sent them plenty of film. What were the scouts doing when he was on the floor—playing tiddledywinks? The New York Knicks!

What the . . . !

He eventually concluded that the pros went for guys out of Division I colleges, thinking they were better or more mature players. And what it boiled down to was: Reed had played small-college basketball. So, sure, they'd take guys like Jim Barnes (Texas—El Paso), Mel Counts (Oregon State), Gary Bradds (Ohio State), Walt Hazzard (UCLA), Jeff Mullins (Duke), Barry Kramer (NYU), and Joe Caldwell (Arizona State) ahead of him. Anyway, Reed had been sick during the Olympic trials at St. John's, which had worked against him. And calling himself six-ten—that must have been a mistake, too. Well, no one had ever dreamed that another Louisiana lefty named Bill Russell would play in the pros either, so he'd show those suckers.

What it all came down to, of course, was money. Reed knew that a second-round pick had no bargaining power. This was long before agents got into the picture, so Reed negotiated his own contract with the Garden's Freddy Podesta. Well, he didn't quite negotiate. Podesta told him what the Knicks were offering: $3,000 to sign and an $11,000 contract if he made the team. That was it—take it or leave it.

"I really think I'm a better player than that," Reed replied, in a quiet and respectful manner. "I deserve more money."

That caught Podesta on the chin. More money—the nerve of this kid! "I've had All-Americans sit there in that same chair and tell me how great they were going to be," Podesta barked. "And they never did anything for this team, never helped us win anything. *Never!*"

Reed nodded. "Maybe. But I'm not going to be one of those players," he said.

What's wrong with this fuckin' kid? He won't give up.

"So, since I know I'm going to have a great year, how about another twenty-five hundred when it's over if I live up to your expectations?"

Well, Podesta nearly had a coronary. A counteroffer—can you imagine that? This Reed was an operator. But—well, it was a hell of a concept. An incentive clause. The way Podesta read it, he couldn't lose. If the kid fizzled—fuck him! It wouldn't cost him a thing. But if he was great . . . well . . . what's another two and a half grand in exchange for greatness? Either way, it'd be an incentive for the kid. So he said *deal*. When the season was over, they'd leave it up to Eddie Donovan to decide if he was worth more.

Reed was determined that he'd embarrass the Knicks for taking Jim Barnes ahead of him. He played every game that year "as if it were a war." Come the end of the season, son of a bitch if Reed didn't make Rookie of the Year. When the time came to pony up, the Knicks practically threw the $2,500 at him. My God! They were so happy to pay him that money, it was a wonder he hadn't asked for more. $2,500!—the kid was a fuckin' steal!

Jim Barnes didn't quite fit into the equation. He was a talented power forward, certainly, but he never really learned what to do with all that talent, he never seemed able to get it onto the floor when the team needed it. A month into the second half of the next season, the Knicks went on the road and Barnes was perfectly awful. When the team landed back at JFK, Eddie Donovan was waiting inside the TWA terminal. He had news for the team: Barnes, Johnny Green, and Johnny Egan had been traded to the Baltimore Bullets for . . . Walter Bellamy.

What the . . . !

Reed felt his heart slip out and slide across the terminal floor. Bellamy was a *center!* His position. What did a guy have to do to get some respect in this league? Did he have to kill someone? Was that it? Reed couldn't figure it out.

Donovan offered a limp explanation. He said they wanted Reed to play power forward, a position where he could be more productive offensively. *Say what!* Willis was averaging nineteen

points a night, not to mention a bonus of fourteen rebounds.
What did they expect him to do, hit fifty? Was that the only way
you earned an extra $2,500? He should have said, "Get your hand
off my dick, Eddie—you're bringing Bellamy in because he's two
inches taller than me. You want to make sure there's a guy in
the middle who can measure up to Chamberlain and Thurmond."
That's what he should have said, but he didn't. He nodded and
said of course he'd do it, he'd do whatever they asked of him. So
Reed moved to the forward position and learned how to defend
against smaller men with quicker, more deceptive moves. And
he ceded the spotlight to Walter "Board Hands" Bellamy.

For two and a half years the Knicks floundered with Bellamy
in the middle. Calling him "Board Hands" was a compliment,
the way he played, which was when he felt like it. Reed could
have played circles around him at center. He could have shot out
the lights! As it was, Willis averaged 20.9 points in 1966 and
21.3 in 1967. As a goddamned forward! That was hardly *bool-
shit*. What it came down to was respect.

The first few weeks of the 1968–69 season, Bellamy was at
the top of his game. He played Chamberlain even, he played Bill
Russell even, he played Nate Thurmond even, too. He held his
own against those mastodon legends. Bill Hosket, then new to
the club, was blown away by Bellamy's tenacity. By the time the
Knicks rolled into Cincinnati, Hosket had talked all his Columbus
and Dayton friends into coming to the game, telling them, "Keep
your eye on Walt Bellamy—this guy's something special!" Hosket
was reasonably sure of his boast because Bellamy was going
against Connie Dierking, who wasn't even to be mentioned in
the same breath as Chamberlain, Russell, or Thurmond. Guys
like Dierking, however, proved to be Bellamy's undoing. Bells
couldn't get up for games against the lightweights. He simply
zoned out for the night. Hosket remembers watching in horror
as Dierking picked his teeth with Bellamy, scoring thirty-four

points to Walt's pathetic seven. Even worse, after the game Bellamy slumped on the bench and said, "Gee, Connie's hook was amazing tonight."

Somewhere along the line, the Knicks' management woke up and realized they'd never win anything with Bellamy steering the ship. They already had the answer to their problem at center—only he was playing at the power-forward position. They owed it to Reed to move him back to the middle.

They owed him *respect.*

Now, here it was almost two years later, with the Knicks solidly holding first place, and they were still yapping about Reed's ability. *Playing over his head!* If that didn't beat all. Didn't they read the damn newspapers? Hadn't they seen him on TV? Reed couldn't figure it out. What did it take to get some respect in this league?

The papers were already speculating about an MVP. For Chrissake—it was only December, they hadn't even reached the All-Star break, and already the rumormongers were rustling. The New York dailies were campaigning for Reed, they were flaunting him like a savior. The man who saved the Knicks! What boolshit! In other corners of the country, another name was circulating in the breeze—Jerry West.

What the . . . !

When the Knicks got back to New York, Willis checked the standings. Well, sure, there were the Knicks, in first place, with an .825 winning percentage. And the Lakers . . . hmmmmm . . . oh, there they were, in fourth place, behind Atlanta, San Francisco, and Chicago, with a .459 percentage. That meant, let's see, now . . . Jerry West had led his team to fourth place with less than a 50 percent winning average. Sure, no contest—he was MVP material. Were they out of their fucking minds?

Reed wasn't a vain man, but he certainly coveted respect. He'd worked his ass off getting to this point—a puny six-eight center who'd risen from out of the segregated South to become the best center in the league. A long-shot stallion. He'd come a long way, baby! Here, as the year 1969 was drawing to a close, he'd guided the New York Knickerbockers to the top of the heap. And while the team was on a steady course with destiny, Reed felt he still had a lot to prove.

9 | THE
HOME
STRETCH

January–February 1970

F OR MOST OF the country, the year 1969 had proved to be a prosperous one, despite the almost insane pitch of circumstances that had threatened to spin it out of control. The Nixon presidency was driving a wedge through the inharmonious population, a result of the Administration's position on escalating American involvement in Southeast Asia. By year's end, there were more than a half million American men in South Vietnam, with troops spilling secretly into Cambodia and Laos. At home, Judge Julius Hoffman had begun hearing testimony in a conspiracy case against the "Chicago Seven." The Concorde supersonic jet made its first flight. Ted Kennedy drove off the Chappaquiddick Bridge, killing his young campaign worker, Mary Jo Kopechne. Neil Armstrong and Buzz Aldrin became the first men to walk on the moon. Charles Manson and his disciples went on a murderous rampage in southern California. Woodstock rocked the counterculture . . . then Altamont killed it. Chevrolet introduced the Camaro (retailing at $2,800). And the New York Mets, those perennial deadbeats, had won the World Series.

All in all, it had been a year to remember—and to forget.

The New York Knicks were happy to leave 1969 behind, because they were heading toward an even more harmonious and productive year—1970. This was going to be their year—they could feel it. Everyone was healthy. Their position in the standings looked invincible. They were 33 and 7—*unbelievable!* Their closest competitors in the Eastern Division, the Milwaukee Bucks, were 26 and 14 and still developing as a team. The Knicks felt they could handle them. Right behind the Bucks were the Bullets, at 24 and 15, and if the Knicks had anyone's number it was the Bullets'. Since last year's play-off sweep, the Bullets hadn't been able to beat the Knicks, and now it was more than simply a matter of competition—now it was fear. Against the Knicks, the Bullets had begun to doubt themselves as a team. All in all, it appeared too late for any Eastern Division team to make a run at New York.

In the West, the division title was still up for grabs. The Atlanta Hawks were the only team with a winning margin, at 25 and 14. Behind them, San Francisco, Chicago, Los Angeles, and Phoenix were gridlocked for second, but they were all playing below .500 ball. That would never do if they expected to mount a serious challenge, especially if they squeaked into postseason play. At that level, you had to play consistent percentage ball, otherwise you'd get taken out early in the running. No, the Knicks felt they could beat any Western team, as well, in a long series.

By January, they'd seen every team at least twice. They knew what was out there and what they had to do each night—the little adjustments they were required to make—to increase their chances of a victory. There were very few surprises left. Nothing they hadn't seen before.

Then, right after New Year's, Milwaukee caught fire. Lew

Alcindor had settled into the professional game and began offering opponents a preview of the Abdul-Jabbar he would become. With him in the middle, the Bucks had won ten of their last eleven games. He was playing brilliantly, after some initial growing pains. It had taken him some time to acclimate himself, to get his bearings. People forgot that this diehard city boy was now stuck in a factory town called Milwaukee. The godforsaken place was famous for beer and reindeer. Well, maybe not reindeer, but it seemed like those sled dogs would be right at home there. Why, there were days—routinely—that the thermometer dropped to ten below zero. And that slag heap they called an arena was practically uninhabitable. All those white faces in the stands—Jesus! It was enough to give anybody the heebie-jeebies.

The Milwaukee team had undergone a drastic makeover. Any time you introduce an element as strong as Alcindor into the equation there is combustion. There are fireworks. All the old plays the guys are used to running no longer work the same way. The big guy has to get a piece of everything, to be figured into every move. So, for the first few months of the season, the Bucks were erratic. And at times Alcindor himself was a freaking disaster. He'd be out on the floor looking, as one paper put it, "bewildered."

He never imagined the pros would be so rough. In college he was simply the best player in the nation, but in the NBA he was only another big kid with potential. Those first few months in the league, the other big men ate his lunch. They outmuscled him, threw him off his game. As a result, Alcindor rushed his shots. He made rookie mistakes. Bobby Dandridge, too, seemed physically and emotionally adrift. Bobby D. was completely intimidated playing in the pros. He showed none of the poise he'd exhibited at Norfolk State. And together, Alcindor and Dandridge were clumsy. They were two fish out of water.

By January, those rookies had swum upstream. They'd spawned. Dandridge was running and stealing the ball with impunity, and Alcindor was . . . well, he was incredible. He'd learned how to bang heads with the best of them and had stood his ground against some of the thugs who'd assaulted him earlier in the season. What's more, he was starting to look for his shot. It was a lot for him to work out all at once—not just to play in the league, but to lead the team—but he'd managed it. He'd even brought the rest of the team to the game. Flynn Robinson, who ran the Bucks' backcourt, was operating in overdrive. Jon McGlocklin, their other crack shooter, was on fire. The Bucks were comers, and the Knicks were sitting up and taking heed.

So far, the Knicks had beaten the Bucks all four times this season. Their last meeting, on December 10, had ended in a one-point victory for New York when Bradley hit on a jumper with eleven seconds left. So everyone figured the next game would be a dogfight.

On January 2, the Knicks flew into Milwaukee for the first game of the new year. The Bucks were seven out and they were desperate to win this one. It would put them back by six, but, more important, it would put a crack in the Knicks' near-perfect mastery of them; it would give the Knicks something to think about.

It was apparent from the opening tip that Alcindor had stepped up to another level of play. Until now, he'd allowed Reed to push him around the floor. Willis had taken advantage of Lew's long, skinny frame and his rank inexperience, in their first four meetings, and had leaned hard on the young colt. He kept Alcindor occupied so that it was impossible for Alcindor to go to his wide array of shots. Even today, Reed waves a hand aside when Alcindor's name comes up and says, "He wasn't gonna bother me, he was a lightweight." That might have been so, but Alcindor had apparently had enough. Someone must have reminded him that he had a good six inches on Willis, because this time he shot over Reed whenever he got the chance.

The other Bucks spent the night clearing out the lane for

Alcindor. They opened it up so that no one could drop off and help Reed, allowing Lew to get loose inside, under the boards. Once that happened, nothing could stop him—not even Willis Reed. Alcindor hit for twenty-four points in the first half and another seventeen after the intermission, ultimately sinking the Knicks, 118–105.

The Knicks had been beaten by thirteen points, the widest margin of the season. But the determining stat was Reed's. He got only sixteen points against Alcindor. Well, that said a mouthful. Alcindor's size had always thrown a scare into opposing teams, but he was never considered a serious threat, at least not on the scale of guys like Chamberlain or Thurmond. For whatever reason, the dominant centers wrote him off as a freak of nature. Now, however, they were learning that his brain matched his physical stature, enabling him not only to compete in a game, but to dominate it as well. Down the line, that'd spell a good deal of trouble for a team, and nowhere did that make as much of an impression as it did on the Knicks. Come play-off time, no doubt they'd be at each other's throats, and by that time Alcindor would be more than ready for them.

The Knicks were stung by their loss to Milwaukee, but it was nothing compared to how they felt when Boston beat them the following night. The Celtics were downright pitiful, a team that couldn't beat a rug. In fact, the joke was that they were so bad they went and beat themselves every night. They were completely dispirited. The retirement of Bill Russell had been more devastating than anyone had anticipated; it had disrupted the whole flow of the team. None of their centers could do the job. The veterans—Bailey Howell, Satch Sanders, Don Nelson, Em Bryant, and Larry Siegfried—seemed bored. Perhaps they were depressed. (What a way to end a career!) It didn't help matters when Red Auerbach, the gnarly GM, decided to fine his men for incompetence and announce it to the press. (Today, the Players Association would have prevented Auerbach from doing something so thoughtless and humiliating; it would have stepped in and muzzled him, but in 1970 management still exercised a whip hand over the players' fortunes and cracked it whenever it suited its purposes. All of which is why the Knicks expected to breeze past Boston on January 3. That should have been the scenario, except that they ran out of steam down the stretch and fell, 111–104.

The Knicks were a tired team, and they were also ailing. Reed had developed a stomach problem in Milwaukee. The team doctor wrote it off to nerves—"hyperacidity," he called it, "just cramps"—but the condition only seemed to worsen. Mylanta cocktails didn't improve matters, either. A few nights later, in San Francisco, Willis scored a measly six points against the Warriors, despite the Knicks' notching a win. Clearly his game was off; he was playing in pain. The next week, when he was voted the MVP in the All-Star game, his teammates voiced skepticism. "What you got there, Cap—sympathy pains?" they chided him. He took a lot of shit for that! But he was hurting, nonetheless. Then DeBusschere pulled a muscle in the lumbar region of his back and was sidelined for three games.

Those injuries, coming down the stretch as they did, alarmed the New York Knicks. They paled in magnitude, however, to the one that struck on January 27, during a rematch against Boston. Toward the end of the game, one in which the Knicks took their revenge on the lowly Celtics, beating them 133–100, Bradley twisted his left ankle and limped solemnly to the bench. No one made a fuss over it, but after the game Dollar hid out in the New York Rangers' dressing room, soaking his bum foot in ice. By the next afternoon, it was swollen and discolored.

Despite Bradley's denials, the Knicks knew it was serious. Ankles are fragile equipment under the best conditions. But put them on a basketball court supporting two hundred-plus pounds of human machinery, run them at varying speeds for forty-eight minutes at a clip, night after night, for seven months of the year, with all the cyclic pounding, stress, and impact of a pneumatic press—well, you're going to experience viscosity breakdown. And when that happens, it's hard to restore them to their peak operating level. Ankles, as a rule, take longer to heal than most other body parts. They require plenty of rest and loving attention. Everybody, including Danny Whelan, knew that. Bradley knew it, too, but he was ultrasensitive about his role on the team. He was concerned that he would be perceived as soft or thin-skinned, that he couldn't stand up under adverse playing conditions. So he taped the ankle and remained in the lineup. With all that education, it showed very poor judgment.

The next night, against Detroit, Bradley managed only a half minute of play. Two nights later, in Chicago, he went the stretch, scoring nineteen points in an all-out attack, but the damage was done. Everyone could see the ankle was causing problems. Bradley was favoring it. He was damaged goods, and it wouldn't take long before other teams picked up on the disability and turned it to their advantage. On February 10, Bradley finally took himself out of the lineup for a long rest.

Two nights later, Frazier went down with the flu. Damn luck! His timing couldn't have been any worse. One starter sidelined presented some strategic problems for a team, but having two starters on the bench was a plague. The same day, in practice, Donnie May caught an elbow in the mouth that nearly took off his tongue. That put three men in street clothes as the team sought to regroup. Dr. Yana had his hands full.

With a little over a month left to play in the regular season, the Knicks were determined not to give up any ground to the Milwaukee Bucks. The Bucks continued to come on fast, but in the face of New York's solid play, they were still six games out of first. A comfortable cushion for the Knicks. No matter, they scrambled to keep the team well in front. They stepped up their offense and on February 13, they beat the 76ers, 151–106, in a game described as a "laugher." It was the worst defeat ever suffered by the 76ers' franchise and one point shy of the Knicks scoring record (152, against the Syracuse Nationals in 1959).

On the bus back to New York, the Knicks were jubilant. They'd won, sure, but they'd also succeeded in sending a message to the league's other thirteen teams, notifying them that they remained in top form. It had been great to play focused like that. It felt meaningful. Cazzie Russell was especially charged. Starting in place of Bradley, he'd scored thirty-five points. Russell's shooting was sensational. Naturally, he attributed it to his diet. Really! He owed it to the way he took care of himself, he said. Now, most of the guys knew more than they wanted to when it came to Russell's devotion to exercise and health food. He was in incredible shape, just a beautiful specimen of a man, with museum-quality muscles, silky smooth skin, a gorgeous complexion—and he was the first to let you know it. He had a little gizmo called the Wonder Wheel, a rubber disk with handles on either side, on which he rolled out his trim six-eight frame and then pulled himself back, almost like doing a push-up, but harder. Barnett, his roommate, would wake up at two in the morning and find Cazzie on the floor with that damn wheel, grunting and wheezing as he hit ten or twelve sets. He was always lugging it around with him. And his damn teapot. After a game, Cazzie would go to his locker, get out a teapot, and . . . *brew a pot of tea.* Reporters would gape at this screwy ritual, always conducted with great form and ceremony, and Cazzie would offer them a cup, like a *prah-puh* gentleman from "Upstairs, Downstairs."

"Excuse me, but would you care for some tea?" he'd inquire in a genteel manner.

The journalist, sensing a terrific personal-interest story, usually took the bait. "Oh, gee—you drink . . . *tea?*" They could hardly get the word out of their mouths.

"Why, yes," Cazzie'd explain, pulling out a plastic bear filled with honey. Oh, my God! "Here—try this. It's very good for you." He'd go on like that, extolling the virtues of chamomile, eucalyptus, ginseng, verbena, hibiscus, rose hips—every fucking herb in the firmament—until the reporter had heard enough and fled to DeBusschere's locker, where he could always depend on getting an ice-cold beer.

In Philadelphia, Cazzie had made a big production about carrot juice. He and Barnett had spent half an hour searching for a special organic voodoo brand, then served up frothy orange-colored cocktails in the locker room before the game. "You never saw a rabbit wearing glasses," Russell lectured one New York reporter who seemed revolted by the drink.

Carrot juice. Cazzie took a lot of shit from the guys over that lame-ass drink. He acted shocked, hurt. "You guys'll see, when I'm seventy and playing basketball. You'll be watching from the wheelchair section!" They gave him the royal business as the bus pulled away from the Spectrum and headed back to Manhattan. Even when they stopped at a local delicatessen, where Danny Whelan was getting them all sandwiches, they continued to pour it on. Cazzie the health nut, Cazzie the nutritionist. When it was his turn to give Danny his order, however, Cazzie the famished checked to see if anyone was within earshot and then confided to Danny: he wanted baloney, cheese, and liverwurst.

You had to hand it to the guys—they were having the time of their lives. The team was winning, they were operating on cruise control—coasting—and the prize was looming steadily closer.

Elsewhere around the league, however, the landscape was changing. In San Francisco, Nate Thurmond broke his leg, which virtually jettisoned the Warriors from the pennant race. Thurmond had been the backbone of a seriously disjointed team. His replacement, a skinny guy named Dale Schlueter, was a man of whom Dick Barnett had once said, "He's got two moves—backwards and forwards." It was a fair assessment, and within a week of the Thurmond shakeout the Warriors were languishing in fourth place. Considering what the team might have been with a healthy Thurmond, Al Attles (broken hand), and Jerry Lucas (broken hand), plus Rick Barry (sitting out, in a dispute with the ABA), it was an ignominious descent.

Even so, they were a world above the Pistons. The Detroit franchise was an unsightly mess. Butch Van Breda Kolff wasn't happy with his players, the players weren't happy with Van Breda Kolff, and the chaos from both corners was coming to a head. Dave Bing, the supertalented guard, had been benched in a dispute. Jimmy Walker couldn't find his shot. Steve Mix, whom they'd drafted to play up front, had been drafted; Uncle Sam nailed him for military service. For most Pistons, they were a team going nowhere. Fortunately for Happy Hairston, he had escaped to Los Angeles, and in early February two more Pistons got long-awaited lube jobs. Eddie Miles was shipped to Baltimore, and Walt Bellamy flew south, this time to Atlanta. Both deals practically assured Detroit of finishing in or near the cellar—again—and gave the Bullets and Hawks a sharper edge.

The Hawks were grasping for reinforcements down the stretch. They were in first place in the Western Division, but just barely hanging on. Los Angeles was creeping up their asses, and if Chamberlain managed to come back—well, no one in Atlanta even wanted to think about that. Wilt—God forbid! But if . . . if he did come back, Bellamy would give Atlanta some insurance. Bells had been known to handle Chamberlain in the past. Historically, he also played well against teams that had traded him, so in the event that the Knicks stayed their course—and it looked as though they were going to do exactly that—there was some hope from Hawks management that Bellamy would seek his revenge.

The Knicks prepared to take a good hard look at all the competition during the last week and a half of February. As luck would have it, they were meeting each contender in a span of six days. Los Angeles was up first on the schedule, but by the time they arrived at Madison Square Garden the Lakers were barely a shadow of a team. Wilt, back in L.A., was still non-committal about his prospects of returning, Keith Erickson was out nursing two swollen ankles, guard Willie McCarter was finished for the season with a foot that was jammed off the leg bone, Happy Hairston was sidelined with a bruised right shoulder, Rick Roberson had a groin injury, Elgin Baylor was day-to-day with sore knees, Jerry West was bruised and battered. Los Angeles had a total of eight men in uniform, and only a few were legitimate pro specimens. Joe Mullaney might have done better using ringers.

Early in the game, Reed and DeBusschere put a lid on the Lakers' prospects of pulling off an upset. The Knicks' big men were fierce off the boards, pulling down any ball that came within twenty feet of the basket. This is an exaggeration, of course, but that night it seemed as if they had that kind of extraordinary range. Reed and DeBusschere had thirty-four rebounds between them. Someone from the Pentagon must have caught the game, because their performance was certainly a model for the Strategic Defense Initiative of a decade later. Even Nate Bowman, to whom defense was anathema, came on and scooped up another thirteen rebounds. The Lakers were that impotent against the Knicks.

Not even the tag team of Baylor and West could rescue the pitiful Lakers. Elgin shot a horrendous five for fifteen from the field, thanks to DeBusschere's tremendous muscle, and Jerry suffered exponentially, with fourteen points in the first half— and only three foul shots the rest of the way. The Knicks, who weren't dazzling offensively, won with a late push, 114–93. Mullaney made excuses for his all-star marksman, but West paid the proper respects.

"The Knicks are too tough," he admitted after the game. "You never get a chance to breathe with them."

That may have been so for the Lakers, but the Hawks and Bullets uttered sweet sighs of relief following their trial runs.

On February 21, Atlanta handed the Knicks their worst loss of the season, 122–106. It was the third time in a row that they'd beaten the Knicks, and in New York it was cause for mild alarm. A landslide loss was unthinkable at this point in the season. The guys should have been better prepared. Especially against the Hawks, who weren't anything to crow about. Well, the Knicks had slipped, they'd proved themselves mortal. Bradley was still out; they missed his integral contribution. The defense got sloppy. It was an off night. Everyone vowed it wouldn't happen again. No way! They couldn't afford it at this point in the season. It was a foregone conclusion that the Knicks and Hawks would meet up at some point in the play-offs. Atlanta held a two-game edge over the Lakers, and the addition of Bellamy made them that much stronger. The Knicks had to step up to the challenge.

A lesson like that one was good for character, the Knicks decided. It served as a wake-up call, a reminder that a wannabe could shatter the dream. Just like that! The guys swore they'd take it to heart. Then, two days later, the unthinkable happened. In a supposedly routine skirmish with the Baltimore Bullets, a team they'd beaten ten times in a row, the Knicks got drilled, 110–104.

First Atlanta, now Baltimore. You'd have to say there were a few problems that needed ironing out. But, no, the Knicks weren't overly concerned. It wasn't posturing; they really weren't concerned. The team's confidence was extraordinarily high. They were satisfied with their overall performance and recognized that from time to time they would be outplayed by the top teams. That's the way things evolved over an eighty-two-game season. Over the course of the year, you occasionally dropped a few.

Often, the losses came in bunches. In a long play-off series, however, every player was certain the Knicks would prevail. It was that simple. No one panicked. Management didn't try to interfere with a successful formula or threaten players. Red Holzman was especially supportive. In an interview with the *New York Times,* he admitted that the Knicks had to work on some things in practice, "but nothing in particular."

This may seem like an extraordinary position for a professional sports organization to take, but in essence there was no reason for them to get nutty. The Knicks seemed destined to win their first division title since 1954. What's more, they were on course to become the winningest team in the franchise's history, with fifty-five victories. Not to be overlooked in this scenario—the financial picture looked especially bright. The bottom line—yes! The Knicks had become the first pro basketball team to attract more than a million spectators in a single season. That little biscuit alone made Ned Irish's heart swell. Irish was a businessman first, a sports fan second. As such, his primary concern was filling seats and stuffing the Garden's coffers. The 1970 Knicks had done that to perfection a total of twenty-two times so far. Twenty-two sellouts! It was extraordinary box office for a team that only two years earlier had drawn less than half that figure. The organization's fortunes looked rosy. Rosy, hell—they looked positively golden.

Basketball in general was blooming beyond imagination. It still languished far behind baseball and football in the pantheon of sporting syndicates, but it was coming on strong. The emergence of personalities certainly helped attract new fans. Chamberlain had been a gift from God; Bradley was a cultural phenomenon. But Alcindor was the Messiah. He attracted a new coalition to the emerging game, first as a curiosity, and later as a bona fide superstar. A seven-footer who could *play.* Now, that was a sight to see. Sure, Chamberlain could do the job, but

Alcindor did it all. He inspired college players to elevate their game, to imitate his style of play. And that ultimately made basketball more exciting to watch.

Someone was taking notice. The first week in February, the NBA negotiated a new three-year contract with ABC-TV that exceeded $17 million. To put that into perspective, it is important to note that the previous deal between the league and the network had been for . . . $1.5 million per year. Pocket change! ABC wasn't being particularly charitable. They'd experienced a 13 percent ratings jump, thanks in large part to the Knicks playing in the country's biggest advertising market. But the relationship was symbiotic. In announcing the deal, NBA Commissioner Walter Kennedy acknowledged that fact by saying: "The great growth of the NBA has been directly related to our games being carried by ABC the last five years."

Now the league was prepared to grow in more substantive ways. That same week, the owners approved an expansion that would add new teams in Buffalo, Cleveland, Houston, and Portland. Each city, strategically chosen for its location and size, would stretch the basketball audience across America. Why, before long, the whole country might tune in. Basketball, a prime-time spectacle—imagine that! Of course, in retrospect, we know how that situation unfolded. Within twenty years basketball would challenge baseball and football as the leading spectator sport in the country. But in 1970 few owners foresaw the tremendous impact that their four-city expansion would eventually have on the game.

The players appreciated the new status. Their salaries were exploding. A rookie taken in the first round of the draft could now expect to negotiate a contract for something in the vicinity of $100,000 a year. That was a tremendous sum in those days. It made young men rich. And there was no ceiling in sight. Spencer Haywood, a nineteen-year-old ABA star, was in the process of hammering out a deal that would bring him a whopping

$1.9 million over three years. College sensation Pete Maravich, who would be in the next draft, had been making noises about wanting $3 million for a six-year deal. So, naturally, the players' eyes were bugging out of their heads.

In New York, though, money wasn't the subject that elicited the most heated discussion. No, the main beef among many of the Knicks was playing time. There wasn't a lot of it to go around; in fact, playing time was rooted on the endangered-species list, with no hope of any recovery. The Knicks' rotation was pretty well set in stone: Reed, Frazier, Barnett, DeBusschere, and Bradley went most of every game. With Bradley out, Russell got the call. Mike Riordan got his minutes, Stallworth gave DeBusschere a blow. But the rest of the guys made only the briefest of appearances down the stretch.

The team liked its winning ways, but no one was satisfied with his role on the bench. Donnie May was clearly frustrated. He'd been one of Dayton's most prominent hoop stars—he was a legend in Ohio—and his New York experience bespoke a true waste of talent. May wanted to play. Nate Bowman was another dissatisfied scrub. Now, the Snake was truly lucky to be allowed anywhere near a basketball. His "talents," as he called them, could make a grown man cringe. Part of his problem was that New York prided itself on being a defensive team, and in that department Bowman didn't have a clue. But Nate, who was never one to see the whole picture, felt truly underappreciated. "I'm looking forward to expansion," he told a teammate following the game in Baltimore, referring to a mandate that directed established franchises to help stock the new clubs. "No way the Knicks'll protect me. So hopefully I'll wind up somewhere I can play."

But for the time being, the supporting players had to keep themselves in shape, physically and emotionally. They had to be prepared to come off the bench at a moment's notice and perform at the same level as a man who'd been in there from the beginning of the game. That was an incredible challenge for most players. For three quarters, they were rooted to the bench like mannequins. With nothing else to do, they watched the game and chatted with each other: "What you got going later tonight?" "I dunno. A few of the guys are heading up to Mikel's to catch some jazz. Want to check it out?" "Sure. Hey, did you see *Easy Rider* yet?" They'd scan the crowd for hot babes. "Hey, check this out. Section 142, three or four rows up, the chick in the blue sweater." "Hold me back!" Then, suddenly, Holzman might point a finger in your direction, and there you were, thrust into the fray. Well, brother, that was a chore of the tallest order.

Keeping yourself hot was a bench player's primary function. On most teams it was a nightmare; the scrubs weren't remotely interested in the game. But on the Knicks, the bench subscribed to the Boy Scout oath: "Be prepared." Riordan, May, Hosket, and Warren were diligent in that respect. They played hardest during practices; on off days they'd find a place to shoot and get in some running. Otherwise, they played two-on-two pickup games whenever they got the chance. The night of a road game, they'd check in early at the local arena, then hit the floor for a scrimmage.

Warm-up for the Knicks' bench was a game called three-o'-cat. The rules were simple: three guys went one on one against each other. If you scored, you stayed in. The defensive player— the man responsible for letting the score get through—had to step off and be replaced by a reserve player, whose job it was to guard the last scorer. If the same man scored again, you switched the defensive player, so that the defender was a fresh face every time a basket was made. Riordan was the Knicks' unofficial three-o'-cat champ. Hosket, Warren, and May were better shooters, but Riordan had a wicked first step that eluded the bigger men and sent him spinning toward the basket.

Riordan, Warren, Hosket, and May made up the bench's

eastern contingent. Stallworth and Bowman were the "Wichita linemen," so named by Barnett because they had both played for Wichita State. Dave and Nate weren't nearly as concerned about being ready to play; nevertheless, they seemed eager to get the nod. Both were fun-loving, easygoing guys despite outward appearances. Bowman loved to mix it up with the fans, enjoyed sneering at them and sharpening his self-image as a tough guy, but for the most part it was all bluff. He'd fight if he had to— and when he had to, he was a mean motherfucker—but Nate preferred a different kind of action. He used to brag that he had a woman in every city in the league, and the way he operated, perhaps that was true. Once, in Detroit, Danny Whelan found in the hotel elevator a black address book that contained the names and phone numbers of over two hundred women. Later that night, he encountered Nate in the lobby and the poor guy looked positively frantic.

"What's going on, Snake?" Danny asked matter-of-factly.

"Trouble." Nate could barely talk. "Lost something . . ."

Danny let him look for five minutes, turning the hotel lobby upside down, before producing the book from his jacket pocket. "Is this the little culprit?"

Well, Nate just about snapped an intestine. He snatched the book and thumbed through the pages, determining if anything had been removed.

"Jeez, that thing must contain top-secret information," Danny said, "the way it's organized." If only Nate could transfer that kind of discipline to the court, he thought.

One night not long before, Bowman had taken a shot and the ball squirted out of his hands, before he batted at it, forcing it out of bounds. Dick Barnett cruised by, and in that dry, arch voice said, "Oh for two!" That was the type of game Bowman played, but the guys got on his case as the season wound down. They reminded him how important he was to the equation. The way things were going, Nate would be a necessary evil in the clutch.

Toward the beginning of March, word began circulating that Chamberlain was set to return, and the Knicks realized that could mean extra duty for their big reserves. The rumor seemed improbable, considering the nature of the injury Wilt had sustained, but in the back of everyone's mind was the awareness that the big guy was capable of pulling off such a magnificent stunt. Los Angeles was being cagey about the whole business. The team physician, Bob Kerlan, had gone on record as saying that Wilt was through for the year. Even when the Lakers began making noises, announcing that Chamberlain would probably practice with the team, Kerlan expressed surprise. It was unlikely, he said, that Wilt's leg could have healed so quickly.

Willis Reed wasn't nearly as skeptical. He'd suspected all along that Chamberlain would resurface, especially if Los Angeles figured in the play-offs. There was no way ol' Wilt was going to miss a shot at the play-offs, *no way*. He'd play with a prosthesis and a pair of crutches if need be. On the one hand, Reed welcomed a chance to battle his old nemesis in a long series. It was the ultimate challenge for a center, a test of muscle and finesse. Besides, Reed had a lot of old scores to settle, not the least of which was a night in 1961 (before Willis's time) when Wilt had scored a hundred points against the Knicks in a single game. But the news also troubled Reed, who worried about the physical cost to him of such fierce play.

Unbeknownst to his teammates, Reed had been battling his own leg injury throughout most of the season. He'd first felt a twinge of pain in his kneecap back in November but had ignored it. It was acutely localized, "like a little toothache," on the top of his kneecap. It gave off so little pain that, most nights, he wouldn't even notice it during the first quarter, but by the time the game was over he could barely jump. His discomfort must

have been apparent. So often, after a strenuous match, a teammate would stop by his locker and ask, "What's the matter,
Willie?" Reed's response was always the same: he simply shook
his head, insisting everything was fine. But the pain had increased lately, and the specter of Chamberlain didn't help.

His worry was compounded by the loss of Bill Bradley's defensive contribution on the floor. By the second week in March,
Bradley had missed thirteen straight games, and his ankle showed
little sign of improvement. It was still painfully sore and swollen.
Much of the problem, of course, had been of Bradley's own
making. In his effort to ensure a speedy return, he had taped his
leg, which complicated the injury by cinching the bandage. It
was a bad move. The ankle became infected; it looked like an
eggplant. That game against Chicago hadn't helped, either—
clomping around the Garden floor for twenty-four minutes. The
injury had left Bradley in sorry shape, physically and emotionally.
He was frustrated; he wanted to play. What's more, he worried
about what the other guys thought of him. Finally, on March 14,
in San Diego, Bradley decided to test his leg in a game against
the Rockets.

The game was significant for two reasons. The first, of course,
was to see how Bradley fared going full throttle. The Knicks
desperately needed his presence on the court, but they needed
him healthy. They were 45–11 when he played, a woeful 5–6
without him. Cazzie Russell, who was filling the hole at small
forward, could shoot out the lights, but he was a defensive nightmare. His man usually eluded him without too much effort. And
under the basket—forget about it. He'd go up for a rebound with
one hand. Holzman would constantly jump off the bench screaming at Russell, "Get 'em up! Put your fucking hands up." But
nothing doing. The guy was too busy looking for his shot. Bradley,
at least, followed the Knicks' game plan, providing a cagey defensive shield and looking for the open man.

As Clyde wrote later in his book, *Walt Frazier: One Magical*

Season and a Basketball Life, "[Russell] was the type of player who scored a lot of points, more than Bill, but he didn't make the players around him better. Bradley made us all better because of the continuity he gave us." Bradley's absence was making it obvious to every New York player how much he contributed. Once and for all, it answered the question about which man rightfully deserved to start at the small-forward position.

"Bradley gives us more movement out there," Holzman allowed, after the Knicks dropped a close one to Seattle on March 12. "[His] loss takes away from our depth."

Bradley wanted to be on the court when the Knicks clinched the division title. They had expected to seal it against Seattle. The game was being televised back to New York especially for the occasion. Danny Whelan had ordered champagne. Even Phil Jackson, out for the season, flew out to be part of the postgame celebration. "This is clinching day," Russell predicted before the opening tip. But the Sonics, who'd been informed about the planned high jinks by their coach, Lenny Wilkens, converted their indignation into baskets and spoiled the party by beating the Knicks, 115–103. It was just as well. The Knicks had been behind most of the game, and Holzman rejected using Bradley in a come-from-behind situation. It would have been too strenuous for him.

As it was, there had been enough tension of another sort on the court. This was one game the Knicks had been determined to win. They'd worked hard all year, and with the title on the line, each of the players was feeling extra pressure to end it there and then. Midway through the third quarter, it was clear that wasn't going to happen. The energy wasn't right, shooting was off, defense had gone south, and the guys were too damn edgy. At one point, after Stallworth had replaced Russell and blew a shot, Clyde's frustration boiled over. He'd been open, dammit! Stalls should have seen him, instead of showboating, going one on one, and Clyde wasted no time reminding Dave the Rave what his job was out there. DeBusschere sped over and shut Frazier up. He reminded Clyde that he had no business yelling at a teammate. Frazier, however, thought otherwise. He was steamed. It was a touchy moment for everyone, with the TV cameras sending the whole scene back home.

Well, it wasn't all going to be "Ozzie and Harriet," for Chrissake! There were bound to be times when the fur flew. Hell, you play ball with the same group of guys for six months straight, it gets a little close. A play doesn't go your way, someone's dander goes up. You have words. Perhaps you play him tight in practice. Maybe you even carry a grudge for a week or two. Eventually everything gets worked out and is forgotten. Still, everyone had wanted this win badly. Expectations had run high. After the game Russell stormed into the locker room and lobbed a Coke bottle against the shower wall. The guys cracked up when they saw that. A Coke bottle? We must be off our fucking gourds.

The next night, against the Rockets, Holzman put Bradley into the game in the second quarter, when San Diego was threatening to nip the Knicks' sturdy lead. Reed and Bowman had their hands full containing Elvin Hayes, who wound up scoring thirty-two points, and Russell looked dazed in his assignment of guarding Jim Barnett. He just couldn't handle that kind of pressure. Bradley played almost four minutes, without scoring, but it was long enough for the Knicks to reestablish control. On the breakaway, he bounced a tricky pass to Clyde, who took it in for a lay-up, and everyone heaved a massive sigh of relief. Some stability had been returned to their game. A touch of finesse. It was that evident in a single play. Dollar Bill was their money man; he gave the team the most bang for its buck.

With the 119–103 win, the Knicks finally clinched the Eastern Division title. It was official: they owned first place. No matter what happened from here on, no one could take that away from them. Only two years earlier they'd been the team that couldn't shoot straight. They'd been the NBA *chumps*. Now they were on top of the heap.

They'd played so long and so hard for this moment that when it arrived it hardly seemed real. As they had done hundreds of times following the final buzzer, the five men who were on the court wearing New York jerseys glanced up at the score for validation. The score—a blush of beaded light. It didn't mean anything. *"Rockets, 119. Visitors, 103."* After a while all the nightly scores ran into one another. 111–104 . . . 113–116 . . . 117–99 . . . 115–103 . . . They defined a particular set of events, like bookends, but as far as meaning and interpretation went, they offered nothing substantial. 119–103. If it's Tuesday, it must be 119–103. It told them nothing specific about the grueling, hard-fought, sweaty, bruising battle that had been waged. It provided no breakdown of the three hundred-odd plays that went into the game, the pounds per square foot of tension exerted in grappling for the ball, the milligrams of anxiety spent as blood pressures throbbed relentlessly on those young hearts. Nothing about the incredible year. 119–103!

It had been a good game—another good game. They'd played well, done their jobs, *hit the open man*. The five Knicks on the floor shook hands in a businesslike manner, then greeted their teammates, who were waiting for them by the bench with outstretched arms. There was no jumping, no leaping, no high fives, no collapsing in a heap, no *We're number one, we're number one*. No attitude. A few handshakes and pats on the back. A smile from the coach, a couple of words—"Nice job, fellas." *Nice job!*

They'd been braced for this moment all year, waiting for the game in which they clinched the division title, proved they were best—better than the fucking Celtics—and could pop the corks and unwind. But it didn't happen that way. The Knicks moseyed back to their locker room, had a few beers, a few laughs, and waited for the bus to the hotel. That was the extent of their victory celebration in San Diego.

"Hey, man," Barnett deadpanned. "This is the wildest party since V-J Day in Tokyo!"

Well, of course! It was typical of this team.

If nothing else, the New York Knicks had character.

10 |BITING
THE
BULLETS

March 23–April 6, 1970

THE CITY OF Baltimore, Maryland, had a bug up its ass. For twelve months, the good folks who lived along the heavily indented shores of Chesapeake Bay had been whipped and taunted by a northern neighbor whose fulsome airs had become so noxious that it was no longer possible for them to take in the words "New York" without wanting to knock the Big Apple from its lofty limb. *Damn Yankees!* A year ago, the New York Knicks had marched south across the Mason-Dixon line and swept the Bullets in a four-game play-off that ended their championship dream. Then, in January, Broadway Joe Namath and the New York Jets upset their beloved Colts in the Super Bowl. And in October, those mongrel New York Mets—the *Mets,* for Chrissake—stole the World Series from the city's sainted Orioles. Now it was the end of March. The damp, raw chill that had enveloped the city for so many months had finally lifted, and the magnolias were in bloom along the dainty downtown streets. Handsome Baltimoreans, with sweaters knotted fashionably around their necks, sat outdoors at the cobblestoned wharfside cafés where a pungent highball of cappuccino and saltwater threw a faint giddyness into the early spring air. The clipper ships had returned to the harbor. The city had been lifted out of its wintry funk, and yet, all anyone could think about was *New York*. That infernal satellite of hell was knocking at their door again.

It was as if the city of Baltimore had been jinxed. Three championship events, three spectacular goose eggs. It didn't make any sense. People could have stood up to the disappointment of defeat much better if the spoilers each time hadn't been so annoyingly familiar. Consider the odds: in one year, the Baltimore sports franchises had played thirteen different basketball teams, fifteen different baseball teams, and eleven different football teams—thirty-nine possible combinations—and their postseason efforts had been upended by New York, New York, and New York. It was enough to give anybody a goddamn inferiority complex.

There wasn't a sports fan in Baltimore who felt any better about the Bullets' current chances against the Knicks. During five of their six regular-season meetings, New York had beaten the Bullets by an average of nineteen points and forced them into twenty more turnovers per game. Those spreads were daunting for Baltimore. To close such a gap—such a *gulf*—the Bullets would have to play miles over their heads. They'd have to forget the season that was, devise an entirely new, aggressive attack, and deter the surging Knicks' momentum. It wasn't going to be easy.

Injuries were already threatening a Baltimore comeback. Mike Davis, their high-strung, streak-scoring guard—called "Mini-Pearl" because of the way he imitated Earl Monroe—was out with a broken wrist. Davis was considered extremely proficient at putting ten or twelve quick points on the board. They'd often looked to him to come off the bench and change the pace of a game. Without Davis, the Bullets would have to get more from their starting guards, Monroe and Kevin Loughery. Monroe wasn't a problem. He was a sensational shooter, a human canister of compressed energy, who could go the distance every night of the week. Loughery, however, remained a question mark.

On February 25, in a game against the Bucks, he had run smack into Lew Alcindor and suffered injuries that nearly ended his playing career. It was an accident Loughery compared to surviving a plane crash. He'd suffered three cracked ribs, one fractured rib, and a punctured lung. Most guys sustaining injuries like those would have hung it up for the year. They'd have flown to Aruba, chartered a boat, and done a little deep-sea marlin fishing. Most guys, that is, but not Loughery. The balky wounded gladiator was not to be denied. He was a scrappy little rooster from Fordham Road in the Bronx, with a constitution of solid concrete, and he'd actually finished the season in uniform. That's right, he'd dragged his broken ass to the arena and played, on about half a tank of gas. Talk about determination. Nevertheless, Loughery expected to start the play-offs for Baltimore, at point guard. His trainer, a man who'd obviously had some experience mending chain mail in the Crusades, constructed an aluminum-and-foam rubber corset that covered his right rib cage and extended around his back, like armor. It would be impractical for releasing his patented one-handed push shot, but—hey!—he'd played under worse conditions. The year before, Loughery had nursed a painful groin injury and had gone the stretch on a diet of cortisone injections. That's the way things went down in the postseason. You played hurt. It was not a subject you dwelled upon. You just let it wash over you and hoped the rest of the fellows would pick up the slack.

Baltimore still had plenty of guys who could give the Knicks trouble. Monroe, of course, and Wes Unseld. Together, they were ready to mix things up. Gus Johnson, the stalky six-six forward with a deadly shot, had missed last year's play-offs with a knee injury. For Johnson, it was payback time. Jack Marin, the tireless small forward, was raring to go. Freddy "Mad Dog" Carter was already into his routine—parading bare chested in front of Johnson, flexing his muscles, and talking trash. Eddie Miles, just over from Detroit, and Leroy Ellis. This was a team that could inflict some damage. They could pull off an upset. The people of Baltimore were praying for it. They'd had enough humiliation for a lifetime.

"We've lived with this thing long enough," Loughery declared on the eve of the opening game. "Now we've got to do something about it."

The Knicks were confident they could keep the Bullets on a short leash. Hell, they'd done it all season. They'd had those Baltimore boys jumping through hoops since October. They'd simply overplayed them. The trump card, as most Knicks saw it, was in their sturdy defense. It had been a powerful deterrent to the blazing Bullets guns. In fact, it had throttled nearly every team who came at them. Frazier and DeBusschere had worked tirelessly on some last-minute strategy to tighten the screws. If they could smother Earl Monroe and Gus Johnson, play them so tight that it would be impossible for Baltimore to establish their running game, then the rest of the team could employ a methodical, structured attack. They could get down to business, play their own game. As always, the defense would generate the offense. If it became a shoot-out, however, the Knicks would have their hands full.

Always, through the season, the Bullets' trigger-happy marksmen would roam the floor saying, "Have one of *these*, sucker!" or "In yo' *face!*" or whatever—the remarks varied—and laughing as they shot. The Knicks would ignore them, but the comments had a residual effect. There was no question but that the verbal abuse worked to unsettle a team's concentration. Especially a team like New York. Before the trash talkers descended, the Knicks adhered to a diligent, meticulous game plan. See the ball, spread it around, hit the open man. *Click, click, click*—you could practically hear the tumblers fall into place. But a new breed of basketball, the game of the playground graduates, was becoming part of the new face of the 1970s: an individual, gutsy, one-on-one setup that was completely keyed to the gunner. And Baltimore's most loquacious motormouths, their most hyperactive hot hands, could take you right out of the game. The Knicks had to avoid that happening, at all costs. They had to bear down and deny the Bullets the ball.

A number of other intangibles continued to worry New York right up to the opening tip. There was Bradley's ankle, which still wasn't a hundred percent. Clyde's groin continued to bother him. And now Reed's knee—that had thrown a new monkey wrench in the mechanism. *Click, click, skronnnkkkk!* The Cap had continued to play hard, right up to the last minute of the last regular-season game. But during the final two nights—in Atlanta, the other in Boston—there was a marked difference in his vertical movement. It was evident to the guys that he couldn't get off the floor. His jumper had no spring to it. He wasn't crushing those rebounds. The game in Atlanta had proved especially debilitating. Reed hated that damn floor, it was rock hard, and by the end of the game with the Hawks, the muscles in his leg felt pulverized. Willis knew he had a major problem to contend with. A series of X rays provided no help—nothing turned up to which the doctor could minister with his magic amulets. There was no calcium buildup, which Reed had suspected and feared. The only thing left to do was for him to rest the knee and take cortisone injections to mask the pain.

If that wasn't bad enough, the Knicks were also up against a postal strike. Really! Two days before the play-offs, the nation's postal employees went out on the picket line, throttling businesses and home delivery from coast to coast, and the National Guard—fifteen thousand Rainbow Division troops—was called up to deliver the mail. That sounded harmless enough—except for the fact that Private First Class Cazzie L. Russell and Private Michael Riordan were activated and deployed to postal installations in the outer boroughs of New York City. You can imagine how that little tidbit affected Knick management. Ned Irish nearly had a stroke. The first shot his modern-day team had ever had at a championship, and their first two men off the bench were *mailmen*. Irish pounced on the phones, calling in every political favor that was ever owed to him, but the situation looked bleak. Both men missed some critical team workouts, and the way things stood, there was no guarantee they'd be available for the play-offs at all. The day before the first game, against Baltimore, Riordan was driving a truck for the 274th Mobile Command Squadron in Roslyn, New York, and Russell was working at the Kingsbridge Armory in the Bronx.

You could almost hear the chatter on the court tomorrow night: "Yo, man—you wanna lick my stamp?" That'd get it rolling. "I'm gonna cancel you, suck-ah!" And following a slam dunk. "Postage—overdue!" The Bullets, like Karl Malone in the early 90s, planned to deliver the mail.

In the midst of all of this chaos, the Knicks were strangely serene. They remained intensely confident, despite the added pressure. During two extended practices, at a school for the deaf in Queens, they exhibited the poise that had carried them victoriously through the season. They worked on presses, practiced shooting. Holzman even put in a new play meant to draw Unseld into a guard and free Willis for a possible breakaway. A new play, at this stage of the game! That took considerable courage. It also said that the coach had a lot of confidence in his team. By this point in the season, most basketball players just wanted to run their standard game. They wanted to continue doing the things that had gotten them to the play-offs and concentrate on their money game. But not the Knicks. They were eager to throw anything into the strategic stew that might give them an edge. They were still willing to evolve.

A new play like this one stimulated their interest, and there were other signs from which they could draw a measure of strength. For one, Bradley seemed fine. He ran hard in the workouts, setting difficult picks that required intricate, labor-intensive footwork, and took his shot from deep in both corners with enviable success. He also appeared loose, which wasn't a word that was normally used to describe his style of play. Bradley was serious, definitely intense, attentive, composed, preoccupied, fixated—uptight. But loose? Not Dollar Bill. Too many factors threatened his concentration. Yet as practice wound down, he was yapping and clapping his hands like a goddamn cheerleader. It was a sight to behold. Meanwhile, Reed had returned to the fold, ran surprisingly well during scrimmages, and assured everyone that he was ready to go.

"Hey—bring on the Bullets!" Clyde roared as Nate Bowman sank one from the top of the circle. "We're ready for 'em. Let's go!"

Actually, no one was quite ready for the spectacle that descended on Madison Square Garden for the opening game of the 1970 play-offs. The arena had been the scene of some twenty-five Knicks sellouts, had hosted its share of freaky rock concerts, historic prizefights, a brilliant circus, and the usual political set-tos, but the mob that showed up there on March 26 was something of a completely different order. This crowd *was* New York. They were people from the five boroughs who had to be inside the building because it was The Place To Be. Something was *happening* there. It didn't matter what was going on inside those cinder-block walls. Basketball? Okay, if you insist. But what's everybody wearing?

These weren't the usual pack of brown-baggers who rode in on trains and subways to root like banshees for their beloved Knicks. This crowd arrived in taxis, they pulled up in Town Cars and limos. They parked their Oldsmobile 98s in neighborhood garages, for Chrissake! That should have been a dead give-away. No true New York basketball fan paid $6.95 to put his car in a garage. A true basketball fan drove around the block forty-seven times, screaming and blowing his horn at Afghani cabdrivers, pushing his blood pressure into the ozone while he stopped to ask every Macy's shopper, "You pullin' out? You pullin' out?" until he invented a parking space that left him the legal six feet from a fire hydrant. Or maybe it was four and a half feet. Well, fuck it!—he'd rather risk a $50 ticket than let one of those thieving maf garage joints palm his $6.95. But this crowd—ho boy!—they spent money on air. They carried Ther-moses of takeout iced tea, they tipped the ushers, they bought Knick souvenir programs in order to identify the players. They perused copies of the *New York Times*. They paid a criminal $12.95 for a courtside seat—nearly twice the usual ticket price. And . . . they . . . brought . . . their . . . goddamn . . . kids!

You had to hand it to Ned Irish. He was a fuckin' genius showman, like P. T. Barnum or Sol Hurok. He'd invented a new form of entertainment never before seen in New York City. It wasn't basketball, at least not the way the Garden regulars knew it. Not by any stretch of the imagination. It was—"A Night Out with the Knicks." Bring the whole family. Bring the cat and dog. And while you're at it, park your shiny Olds 98 in our $6.95 lot.

Play-off fever! Jesus, it was ruining their beautiful city game. The Garden regulars were beside themselves as they scrunched low in the rainbow-colored seats, seething, especially when the generic frisky little suburban housewife in her shag haircut tapped them on the shoulder to ask, "Would you mind putting that cigar in the other hand, thanks?" The other hand! The other hand was holding his beer, his bookie's receipt, and enough le-verage to flip the ref the finger when a call went the other way. "Who d'ya think you're gonna see here tonight, lady—Liberace?" The other hand! These poor slobs who'd been to every game since Fuzzy Levane, an early Knicks coach, worked the bench didn't know what the hell was happening. All the years they'd put into those miserable teams, screaming their hearts out— And now—*this!* Some twelve-year-old in khakis, with a voice like Tiny Tim, was shrieking, "Yay, Knicks! Let's go, Knicks!" What had they done to deserve this?

Something quite extraordinary was building up. It was a wave and a half. It was the beginning of the end for old-guard Knicks fans. Basketball for the masses. A prime-time sport. But there was precious little time to brood. When the lights dimmed, at 7:35, and the Knicks inched toward their bench, the wave of adoration became so big it simply carried everyone along with it. There, for everyone to see, under a frosted beam of light, were the newest princes of New York City, the newest superheroes. You didn't need a scorecard. Willis Reed was right up there at the end of the bench, talking to Red Holzman. And Private Russell standing alongside Private Riordan. They'd finally been discharged that afternoon, with assurances they'd be available for the rest of the games. Dick Barnett was right beside them, stretching a thirty-three-year-old tendon like it was Silly Putty. Then Dave DeBusschere, and Bill Bradley—wait until Madison Avenue got ahold of those faces. They were positively gorgeous. And Nate Bowman, another gorgeous puss, shadowboxing with Dave the Rave Stallworth. Then two more white guys—who were they? Oh, yeah, Bill Hosket and Donnie May, a couple of innocent bystanders. And whatsisname—you know, the rookie kid from St. John's. Warren, Johnny Warren. Well, the building shook with intangible joy when the New York Knicks took their bows. The reception was so long and so loud that it almost drowned out the announcement that Willis Reed had been chosen the NBA's Most Valuable Player for 1970. *The league MVP!* Well, that did it. That brought the crowd to their feet. No, they were already on their feet. It brought them another silly millimeter closer to levitation. They were screaming and clapping and trying to juggle their beers all at the same time. It was a sight to behold.

Basketball seemed almost secondary. And then, suddenly, without any great fanfare, the game was under way. The ball was tossed up by referee Mendy Rudolph. Wes Unseld and Willis Reed lifted vertically into the air like twin Atlas rockets, and the eight large men surrounding them dispersed in a rippling circle as if they'd been scattered by a cue ball.

At the start, the Bullets took complete command of the game. Earl Monroe, who set the tone, came out blazing like a brilliant shooting star, hitting a quick jumper, picking off a Knick outlet pass that he took in for a lay-up, and scoring on a drive around two defenders. Jack Marin head-faked Bradley off the ball, then hit an outside jump shot and after only two minutes the Bullets were up by 12–2.

Needless to say, it wasn't supposed to happen that way. The Knicks' starting five seemed stunned, confused. Every time they got their hands on the ball, one of the Bullets was on top of it, right in their face . . . creeping up their ass. What was going on here? Barnett finally managed to fade into a corner, where he took a pass from Clyde for an open jumper. It was 12–4, and the Knicks called for time.

"These cats are on fire!" Frazier exclaimed as the team converged on Holzman.

"Don't worry, we'll catch 'em," the coach said. Holzman waved everyone in closer in order to talk over the crowd noise. Red never worked with a chalkboard; he never diagrammed plays or moved magnets around like alien invaders. His huddles were usually flash analyses in which he pointed out obvious mistakes and pumped up confidence. "You're forcing your shots out there. You're calculating every move." He took his hands out of his jacket pockets and pointed a finger at Frazier. "Clyde—play your own game, dammit, look for your shot. You're too tight, you're not relying on your instincts. Okay?" Frazier nodded, but he was wary. "Now go out there and play your game."

Well, it wasn't much to go on. But the breather had given

the Knicks time to regroup. After a quick Bullets turnover, Barnett brought the ball upcourt, working against the propeller hands of Fred Carter, who had started in place of Kevin Loughery at the point-guard position. Somehow, Rich drew him seriously off stride with a nimble head fake toward the corner, then drove up the middle for an easy lay-up. Okay, that was a start. Quickly the Knicks picked off a Baltimore pass, DeBusschere scored, Frazier followed with a jumper from fifteen feet, and before long New York had regained their composure to take a 14–13 advantage.

The score went back and forth like that for most of the first quarter. The Knicks staged several surges, but they couldn't shake free of the combative Bullets, they couldn't pull away. It was perplexing to them. Here they were playing in front of a home crowd at Madison Square Garden, which in itself was an intimidating factor for visiting teams, against a squad that was mediocre at best, and they couldn't make a decent run. Nobody said anything, but it was clear that something was amiss. Baltimore had been playing more like the Knicks. That was it! As a team, the Bullets had survived much of the season on the strength of good individual shooting, but here they were playing *defense*. Aggressive defense. They were overplaying the ball, double-teaming. They were spreading the ball around the perimeter and hitting the open man. Those little peckers! Besides, the Knicks had been scouted by Baltimore's assistant coach, Bob Ferry, who had cued Unseld to various New York set plays. The Bullets had stolen several pages out of the Knicks' playbook and were using them to their own advantage.

In the second period the Bullets continued to attack the Knicks in the open court, playing a pressing defense. Freddie Carter shadowed Barnett as if his life depended on it, and Monroe played Frazier chest to chest; they refused to cut the Knicks guards an inch of slack. Gus Johnson and DeBusschere harassed one another in an area just beyond the circle. DeBusschere had been leaning on Johnson in order to force him farther outside, and for the moment his strategy was working; Gus couldn't get inside for a good percentage shot, and he missed all three of his long-range attempts. DeBusschere was wearing him down, frustrating him, but it had sliced into his own offensive output. Well, the hell with points, DeBusschere decided. He'd worry about that after intermission.

Bradley had done practically the same thing with Jack Marin. Both men had good outside shots and fought a fierce battle for bragging rights to the corners, where they felt comfortable from long range. Marin had a fabulous left-handed jumper, and he was nothing if not smart and crafty. He could decoy Bradley as well as any forward in the league. It wasn't just his selection of shots, it was his motion as well. He could show the jumper and at the last second cut to the basket for a lay-up. Unlike Bradley, however, Marin could be rattled. He had a hot temper, and nobody knew better than Bradley how to fire it up.

Marin hated to be bumped. In fact, the only thing that bothered him more than being bumped was being bumped by Bill Bradley. Dollar had an annoying move he used time and again on Jack. He'd hook a shoulder into Marin's side or use his hip to knock his man off stride, and the refs never called it. Jesus, that burned Marin's ass. It wasn't so much the bump that got him, it was Bradley's getting away with it. He was the Teflon bumpster. Goddamn! Marin would become irate when the refs missed an obvious foul like that. He'd complain loudly, wave his hands to get their attention. His face turned a deep shade of crimson, his brow knit furrows into his skull, his mouth twitched—and he'd get flustered. He'd blow an easy shot or lose a ball out of bounds. Oh, how it burned that man's ass! Later in the game, when Bradley bumped him yet again and the refs missed it again, Dollar threw a little grin Marin's way, just a flicker that barely creased one side of his mouth, as if to say, "Chump!" After a while a grin like that could take Marin out of the game.

All these strategies worked in the Knicks' favor through the second quarter, but they couldn't close the gap. Earl Monroe put on a high-octane shooting exhibition, nailing six in the final two minutes of the half, and after twenty-four minutes the Bullets led, 52–46.

In the third quarter the Knicks finally managed to turn things around. New York's big guns came alive, with Reed and De-Busschere combining for twenty-five points and nearly as many rebounds while shutting down the Bullets' hot hands. It was as tight a twelve-minute stretch as the two teams had played all year. DeBusschere was magnificent on defense. He drove around Gus Johnson for key blocks and rebounds, and somehow doubled off to help Bradley contain Marin, swatting away several of the small forward's shots. Picking up the rhythm of the game, the Knicks began scrambling, harassing, forcing Baltimore to make costly mistakes and turnovers. And after having trailed by six at the half, they led by three going into the final quarter.

The fans got into the game even more than before. Chants of *"De-fense! De-fense!"* rocked the Garden rafters. Cheers and moans accompanied each move, each shot, each play—each heartbeat. *"De-fense! De-fense!"*

No one in that arena, however, was prepared for what came next. The fourth quarter was all Earl Monroe. The man who had more moves than Allied Van Lines put on a clinic that left the fans'—and the Knicks'—heads reeling. It was uncanny. The Bullets isolated Monroe on Frazier through most of the period, and the Pearl ate Clyde alive. He'd go up in the air, lean to the left, reach forward like a ballerina, then quickly shovel the ball under his legs and into the basket. Or he'd back in, soar ten feet off the ground, and, twisting blithely against all anatomical limitations, shoot cleanly over his shoulder. Or he'd disappear into a crowd of Knick jerseys, pop the ball through the traffic jam, appear out the other side, and drop a lay-up into the hoop.

Clyde normally defended against a player by watching his eyes. He'd wait for the errant glance or flicker that would give away the next move. But Monroe's eyes were glazed over, they were—*dead*. "I don't know what Earl's looking at out there," he'd told DeBusschere at halftime. "I know one thing—he's not looking at the rim. I have no way of telling when the guy's gonna shoot." Half the time, Monroe never even showed the ball when he released it; instead, he launched it from somewhere behind his right hip, like a Frisbee. Clyde tried everything. He shoved a hand in Earl's face, he pushed his body right up against the wiry man. But nothing doing. There was no way Frazier could stop him.

With three minutes to go in the game, Monroe ran off the Bullets' last eight points. His final basket was a twisting, fading one-hander from the sideline that put the Bullets ahead, 101–100, with a minute and a half left. When Baltimore got the ball back, with thirty-eight seconds to go, Holzman, playing the percentages, ordered Barnett to foul the Pearl. Monroe made one shot, raising the score to 102–100. Then Reed put the ball inbounds to Bradley, who surveyed the court, saw gridlock in the middle, and drove down the baseline for a shot that tied it at 102.

There were twenty-three seconds left—enough time to have dinner, catch a movie, and still make three or four buckets, especially if your name was Earl Monroe. Before he took the inbounds pass, however, Monroe asked Frazier what the score was.

"You're leading, man," Clyde deadpanned. "You guys are up."

Welllllllllll . . . c'mon! That's the oldest trick in the book. Nobody fell for that one anymore, especially not an old trouper like Monroe. But Earl was nearsighted, he couldn't see the damn clock, and he figured Frazier would be square with him with the game on the line.

The Pearl had the ball and took it down across the line, where he lingered around midcourt looking for the last shot— or was he just holding the ball to end the game? There were three seconds left on the clock. Without any sense of urgency, he took three or four steps and launched a lazy little jumper from the top of the key that ricocheted off the rim as the buzzer sounded.

Overtime!

"What's going on?" Monroe asked Frazier as they walked off the court. He glanced up at the scoreboard. "What's that five minutes doing up there?"

"Overtime, baby," Clyde said.

As it turned out—*Earl had actually thought it was the end of the* third *quarter.* He'd lost track of the game. That's why he had taken his time on that last play; he figured he had another twelve minutes in which to wrap things up.

The Knicks had gotten an incredible break. A gift.

But Baltimore jumped off to a quick lead in the overtime. The Knicks continued to have trouble scoring and made only one field goal in the first three minutes. Still, they closed a four-point lead, but fell behind again by three with 1:31 remaining. Time was running out. DeBusschere got fouled and hit the first of his two free throws, narrowing the gap to two, but Unseld swooped past Reed and grabbed the rebound, his thirty-first of the game. Now all the Bullets had to do was make one to put the game comfortably out of reach.

A few minutes earlier, Kevin Loughery had come off the bench, and now Unseld found him all alone, standing twenty feet out, with an unobstructed view of the basket. This was Loughery's money shot. He'd made it so often from that spot, he could probably do it with his eyes closed. Nothing to it. You just put your lips together—and shoot. This time, however, Loughery was racked with pain. That damn corset was climbing up his back, his ribs were clacking together like chopsticks—and the ball missed by half a mile. The Knicks drove the ball down to Reed, who popped a quick one and narrowed it to two.

Gene Shue, the Baltimore coach, called a time-out. "Clear it out for Earl and let him go clean against Frazier," he instructed his team.

Well, what else did anyone expect? That's the play anyone in his right mind would have called. The little woman with the shag haircut and an aversion to cigars could have called the damn play from her seat. Only this time, Clyde was ready. This time, he switched from watching Monroe's eyes to his waist. That's right—he kept his eyes on Earl's breadbox, the area between his abdomen and his knees, not to anticipate the Pearl's next move but to seize a moment when he could go for the ball. Clyde knew he had to attempt a steal. There was no time for him to see how the chips fell. Time was running out.

Monroe headed for the top of the key again, his old stomping ground. Frazier stayed on him every step of the way. He wanted Monroe to feel his breath, to know he was right there waiting. Then he saw Barnett closing in from the other side—who knows, maybe Earl saw him, too—and as Rich loomed into view, perhaps distracting Monroe, Clyde thrust his right hand out and batted the ball cleanly to Barnett. Carter promptly fouled Barnett, and he hit both of his free throws, tying the score, 110–110.

There were twenty-three seconds left, the game was on the line—as Yogi Berra said, It was *déjà vu* all over again. In came Earl Monroe—again—with the assignment of putting the game in the history books. He brought the ball up slowly, dribbling it cautiously with his left hand. There was plenty of time for him to set up a good shot. Without realizing it, however, he'd allowed Frazier to slip behind him. Clyde crept up softly, like a panther, enabling him to reach in undetected and slap the ball neatly to

Barnett. Rich grabbed it and headed straight to the basket for a lay-up. Fred Carter was hot on his trail, but, with two seconds showing on the clock, Rich got off a clean shot that hit the rim on the right side. The ball skidded across and was pulled down by Carter. *Goaltending!* Only no one called it.

That is, none of the officials called it. Willis Reed called it—he skidded to within an inch of Mendy Rudolph, arguing the Knicks' case. Red Holzman called it from the sidelines, where he alternately stomped around like Rumpelstiltskin and pleaded for a break. And 19,500 Knicks fans called it. But the buzzer sounded without an official call, and the game was still tied.

Double overtime!

This time the Knicks didn't monkey around. They scored five quick points on shots by Riordan, DeBusschere, and Frazier. Monroe and Carter barreled back to tie the game at 117, with fifty-two seconds remaining. Then Reed, who had played fifty-four of the fifty-eight minutes of the game, made a short under-handed shovel shot from beneath the basket to clinch the victory for the Knicks.

They'd done it, they'd won the opening game of the play-offs in *double overtime*. My God, it had been an incredible battle. *Double overtime!* No one had ever expected that to happen. Why, no one expected it to be close. The truth was, the 19,500 folks who filled the stands had anticipated a bloodbath. They'd expected to see the Garden floor littered with Bullet bodies instead of . . . Double overtime! Reed had scored thirty hard-fought points, Monroe connected for thirty-nine. Was it going to be this crazy every step of the way? The Knicks certainly hoped not. Their bodies couldn't take it. For that matter, their bodies couldn't take one more game like that if they were going to get through this thing alive.

The next night, in Baltimore, the Bullets came out cockier than roosters. Rock music thumped over the arena's souped-up

PA system, and during warm-ups the entire team staged a flashy slam-dunk exhibition—guys were flying through the air, holding the ball out like it was a platter of pasta being served by an Italian waiter, then slamming it through the net with *al buon gusto*. The Knicks watched this little morsel from the other end of the floor and wondered what the shameless Bullets thought they'd accomplish with this bit of posturing. After all, what did they think had happened last night? They didn't win. They only came *close*.

Whatever the Bullets intended, it worked. The Knicks started the game carrying a chip on their shoulders that interfered with their aggressive play. They couldn't seem to get anything going. Bradley was shut out for the entire twenty-four minutes of the first half, Barnett managed only one basket, Frazier had his hands full guarding Freddie Carter, and DeBusschere pulled down only a single rebound. Baltimore was up, 51–48, at the half and pulled ahead by 71–62 midway through the third period.

Part of the problem was Earl Monroe; he was at it again. He was burning the Knicks with those acrobatic jump shots, hitting from just about every point on the floor. *Swoosh . . . swoosh . . . swoosh!* What a performance that man gave the home crowd. In a desperate bid to shut him down, Holzman shifted Barnett to Monroe, hoping to free up Clyde to shoot and get to the ball. Barnett was a master at playing position defense, which is why he was usually assigned to guard the bomb throwers like Oscar Robertson and Jerry West. Even so, Monroe was too tough to hold. He ran rings around the thirty-three-year-old Barnett. He seemed unstoppable.

Mike Riordan, though, had been watching the battle from the bench and had spotted a chink in Monroe's armor. He noticed that whenever Earl went into his dance, he invariably pulled the ball up to his right ear. As Barnett cruised by the bench, Riordan yelled, "His right ear! Guard his right ear!" Monroe had one shot that made it seem as if he wasn't getting off the ground. He was an upright guard but could spin, twirl, and pirouette. And he was draining Barnett—not just draining him, he was hanging the net. Through it all, Riordan continued to cup his hands around his mouth and scream, "Right ear! Guard the right ear!"

Finally Holzman got good and frustrated. He looked down the bench at Riordan and said, "Mike—get Dick!"

Riordan tore off his sweats and bounded onto the floor. He was dying to see action, having missed those two days of workouts while driving a mail truck in Queens. And he was prepared for Monroe. Both nights, after National Guard duty was over, he'd practiced shooting with a friend, instructing the guy to back into him the way Earl did. Now the genuine cultured Pearl was taking him into the boards, waggling his fanny at him, thrusting that big black can of his into Mike's Irish face. Well, Riordan was ready for him. Not only was he ready, Mike had that big paw of his up beside his head so that when Monroe turned he'd be right on Earl's ear.

The first attempt to silence Monroe worked like a charm; Riordan forced him to pass the ball instead of firing at will. Still, the play came back to Earl with seven seconds left on the shot clock. He began backing into Mike, trying to get to his spot. Riordan was bulldogging him all the way. Now Earl had to fire from downtown. They were deep, practically in front of the Knicks' bench, when Earl brought the ball up to his right ear again. Mike's hand was there again, with a second on the clock. So Monroe just brought the ball down, switched it to the left side of his head, and launched a bomb that got nothing but the bottom of the net. He sank that baby!

Riordan glanced over at his buddies sitting on the bench, then at Dick Barnett, who said, "Yeah, baby. Way to check that right ear."

Holzman jumped up in disgust, pointed at Barnett, and said, "Dick—get Mike!"

It was a hot old time through the third quarter, but as the clock ran down it was clear that Barnett had run out of steam.

The Bullets led, 75–66, when Riordan came off the bench again to alter the rhythm of the game. He'd decided to forget about Monroe. Let the Pearl get his points, he figured. There was nothing anyone could do to stop him. What the Knicks needed was an injection of offense, they needed points. So Riordan went to work, grabbing eight rebounds and canning thirteen points that ultimately put the Knicks ahead for good. In addition, he muzzled Monroe, allowing him only a single free throw for the entire fourth quarter. The Knicks won it, 106–99, and were up two games to zip for the series.

The Knicks had any number of superheroes whose brilliance shone in dark moments. Probably the least conspicuous, measured against the Covenant of Holy Stallions, was Mike Riordan. A hard-nosed kid from a Queens working-class family, Riordan had been a twelfth-round draft choice in 1967—an afterthought, really, tossed in to complete the Knicks' pool of college talent. No one ever expected him to make the pros, least of all his college coach, Joe Mullaney. Riordan had gone to Providence in the same class as Jimmy Walker. But while Riordan may have been in Walker's class, he wasn't in Walker's class—as far as basketball went. He was small, he was raw, and he was overly eager to prove himself in every game.

"Mike loved basketball to the point that forty minutes was too short a game for him," Mullaney recalled recently. "He was so hyped up, so energetic and aggressive, that it often interfered with his play." He'd overplay the ball and make emotional mistakes, which is what coaches call playing from your dick instead of from your head. As a result, Riordan had fouled out of twenty of the eighty games he played in college.

Mike's only hope was to develop into a pure shooter, but in college he was looking for Walker all the time, and so he never found his range. The main reason the Knicks even bothered to look at him was to provide another body for Bradley to work with when he returned from Oxford. It was late May of 1967, and

Riordan was working for the fire department in Queens, when Eddie Donovan invited him to join a scrimmage at Madison Square Garden. "Bradley's coming back," Donovan explained. "We're having a few boys in to work out with him, so we thought we'd take a look at what you've got."

Riordan accepted the invitation—but he didn't have any illusions. "I'm about to become a practice dummy," he thought, riding the Long Island Railroad into the city. "No way it turns into a legitimate tryout."

Mike had played against Bradley once, in the semifinals of the Eastern Regional NCAA competition in 1965. Mullaney had given him the suicide assignment of guarding the great Princeton stallion, and Riordan had known after only three or four calls that he couldn't play with him anymore. Bradley was magnificent and he'd buried Riordan.

This time, at the Garden, Riordan had some professional help guarding Bradley. Emmette Bryant was there, so were Freddie Crawford, the Van Arsdales—Tom and Dick—and the Knicks' young stud, Walt Frazier. The scrimmage didn't last long, maybe a half hour or so, but Riordan performed like a beast. He played way over his head. He hustled and ball-hawked, hit jumpers and picked off passes, and he went to the boards like the fucking wild man of Borneo. The other guys shuffled glances his way as if to say, "Take it easy, brother, it's only a scrimmage."

Not quite. For Riordan, it was the only chance he'd ever get to prove he could play. And it threw the Knicks an uneasy curve. Eddie Donovan remembers thinking, "What do we do with this guy? He's fantastic. If we pass him up, he'll wind up on some other team and come back to haunt us." Well, it was a nifty little predicament for both parties. The Knicks had a useful player practically fall into their laps—and Riordan got an unexpected shot at the pros. At Donovan's suggestion, he played Eastern League ball in Allentown, Pennsylvania, in order to develop his game, and a year later New York signed Riordan to a long-term Knicks contract.

It had been a fantasy come true for "Iron Mike." First the Knicks, now the play-offs—it was a moment of supreme personal achievement. On the team plane back to New York, he was flying high, with adrenaline.

"Hey, Bill," he said, interrupting Bradley, whose head was buried in a book. "Remember that game we played in college?"

"Um-hmmm." Dollar's face remained blank. This was an old routine, like Abbott and Costello's *"Who's on first?"* and he knew where it was headed.

"What did you wind up getting that night? Forty? Fifty?"

"Yeah." Bradley relented. "Something like that."

Riordan refused to quit. "The guy you were guarding— Walker. He got that, too, didn't he?"

"Perhaps, but I don't think I was guarding him that night."

Riordan threw his head back and cackled.

Finally Bradley pointed at him and said, "I believe we went to the Final Four, didn't we?"

Oh, baby! Riordan *loved* this life. He loved playing ball, he loved the guys, and he loved carrying on. He was a relentless ball buster, known affectionately as "Bags," in honor of the nightly award he handed out. The scumbag ball had been a Knicks team custom for most of the year. Early in October, Mike had decided that since pro football awarded game balls, the Knicks should do it too—only theirs would go to the guy who made the worst shot of the night. To the honorary *scumbag!* After a game, in the locker room, Riordan would grab the dirtiest, most lopsided ball out of the trainer's bag, hold it up, and present it with great fanfare. Occasionally guys refused to take it. "What chew talkin' about—scumbag ball! I didn't get it, suckah. So-and-so had a worse shot. Talk to that chump."

Normally, the worst offenders were guys right off the bench, who were cold and tried to seize an opportunity—and had no idea where the ball was going. Guys who launched bricks and air balls were other prime candidates. If you hit the corner of the backboard, you were definitely in the running. But the hands-down winner was usually the guy who shot an air ball from the free-throw line. No contest. He was it! The hardest thing was for the culprit not to break out in a smile. He'd be so embarrassed, so humiliated, and so pissed off at himself! The guys standing on the line with him would be looking at each other, biting their cheeks. He'd glance over at the bench to see if the scrubs had caught it, and there they'd be—Riordan, May, Warren, Hosket, and Russell—rocking back and forth and slapping each other.

The scumbag ball was an inspired piece of silliness, but it was awarded only on nights when the Knicks won. No one wanted to hurt a teammate's feelings for costing them a game. Accordingly, the ball remained out of sight the next day, when the Bullets beat New York, at the Garden, by a score of 127–113. It was Easter Sunday, and Wes Unseld must have gone to church that morning, because he pulled down a miraculous thirty-four rebounds, four more than the entire Knicks team. Kevin Loughery, too, experienced a personal resurrection by removing his metal corset and adding a neat seventeen points to the final score. "I couldn't do a thing with that damned brace on," Loughery complained after the victory. "I couldn't shoot, and you get so damned sick and tired of the Knicks beating you. If we didn't win this one, there wouldn't be much breath left in us." New York was ice cold. They suffered from excessive turnovers. Reed picked up three quick fouls and hugged the bench through most of the second half. It was a game the Knicks decided to forget.

When you're a team like the New York Knicks, and you have an off night, it's fairly easy to shrug it off. You know you can come back the next game and regain the momentum. But in play-offs, when you blow one—and lose the next one as well—it doesn't matter who you are, the sweat starts to sluice. In fact, that was what happened to the Knicks in the game following their Easter Sunday fiasco. The series swung back to Baltimore, and drawing an immense lift from the previous game, Wes Unseld completely dominated the boards, grabbing twenty-four rebounds and outletting the ball for a Bullets fast break. The Bullets won, 102–92.

"They're beating us at our own game," Frazier complained. "They're playing a more aggressive defense. They're overplaying our forwards."

That was it in a nutshell. Gus Johnson and Jack Marin had played superbly; they'd limited DeBusschere, Bradley, Russell, and Stallworth to a miserable thirteen-for-forty-three performance. Earl Monroe had been sensational, holding the ball until the shot clock wound down to four seconds, then almost casually bagging a basket before the buzzer sounded. Damage control was left to Frazier and Reed, who'd scored half of all the Knicks' points, but there was a mounting concern that Reed could not continue at that pace because his knee had flared up again.

The pain had been building slowly over the last two games, but during the fourth quarter of Game Four Reed could barely move. He couldn't get off the floor. Unseld took complete advantage of the moment to walk him around inside the paint. He leaned hard against Willis, pushed him right up under the basket, and destroyed his inside game. That little maneuver took its toll on Reed's knee. He iced it after the game, but the soreness remained. Unfortunately, there was a well-known cure for his ailment, called "cortisone." Most guys took the shot willingly; it enabled them to play under the worst physical conditions and without encountering too much pain. But Reed had balked at the suggestion of another cortisone shot. The fellows teased him about it. They thought he was afraid of the needle. He let them think that, too. When the doctor pulled out one of his fifteen-foot syringes, Willis practically went white. He'd wince and mince and go into his scaredy-cat act. In truth, he'd read up on the effects of cortisone and discovered that if you kept taking those shots, it would soften the tissue around the knee until it eventually turned to sponge. He couldn't come out and actually say that, because there were guys on the Knicks who'd taken cortisone throughout their entire careers, and he didn't want to alarm them. So he pretended it was the needle, routinely refusing further treatment.

Trouble was, there was too much riding on the next game. If he didn't take the shot, chances were he wouldn't be effective against Unseld and the team would lose. That'd put the Knicks in too big of a hole. Besides, he was sick of Wes pushing him around the floor like that. Sick of seeing him get position at both ends of the floor. This wasn't Chamberlain, for Chrissake. Unseld was the only center in the league who was smaller than Reed. Every time he played Wes, Willis felt like he was back in college playing a little guy again, and it gave him that extra jolt of encouragement he needed to bust out.

"If the unity and closeness of this club is ever going to pay off, it's now," Reed told his teammates in a closed-door meeting. "This is our moment of truth."

Well, that worked both ways. Two hours before game five, Reed headed into the trainer's room and took the damn shot.

After the game, someone suggested that there had been something other than cortisone in the injection—like rocket fuel. Playing nearly forty-six minutes without so much as a wince, Reed grabbed thirty-six rebounds, scored thirty-six points, and took Wes Unseld completely out of the game. Game five, in Madison Square Garden, was a one-man show. Reed completely dominated the "little guy," playing Unseld like a frisky guard. Every time Wes got good position, Willis was on him; if Wes went up for a rebound, Willis was on him; if Wes moved out for a shot, Willis was on him. He was on him . . . he was on him . . . He boxed out Unseld all night long.

Taking the Bullets' big man out gave the rest of the Knicks a chance to play their game—solid defense. DeBusschere finally stopped Gus Johnson, limiting him to only one basket in fourteen tries. Barnett smothered Freddie Carter, and after twenty-three minutes, when the rookie was finally benched for the rest of the game, he hadn't scored a single point. Even Earl Monroe was held to a tepid nineteen points by Walt Frazier. The Bullets shot limply, sinking only seven for fifty in the second half (three for thirty in the last quarter) for a .269 shooting percentage. The Knicks, for their part, never quite shot out the lights, but Bradley had a decent offensive night, and Cazzie Russell fired in twenty-one off the bench to give the Knicks a 101–80 rout of the Bullets.

With the series tilted at 3–2, the Knicks were determined to finish it in Baltimore on April 5. Nice idea—lousy execution. Bradley and DeBusschere got into early foul trouble and spent long shifts on the bench, which allowed Carter and Johnson to run wild. Monroe was merely excellent, with twenty-nine points. And Unseld got revenge on Reed for his previous humiliation, limiting Willis to two baskets. The Bullets had achieved the unthinkable. They'd beaten the Knicks 96–87 for the third time in six games and sent the play-offs to a seventh-game, sudden-death finish.

No one could have predicted it would come to this. A play-off series against the Baltimore Bullets, a team that the Knicks had beaten in nine of their last ten regular-season meetings, a team that hadn't won a single play-off game in five years, a team that seemed frustrated and demoralized, a team that was racked by injuries, a team that most basketball fans dismissed as a group of selfish dilettantes—you had to figure it would end in five games, tops. And that was being kind. Truthfully, every New Yorker had been thinking sweep but wouldn't admit it for fear of jinxing the Knicks' prospects. The fans had expected their team to blow Baltimore out of the box. Now it all came down to a single deciding game that, as Bradley said, had a life all its own.

"How bad do you want it?"

Before the game, Dick Barnett had stolen into the locker room and scrawled that peppy phrase across the green chalkboard on the wall. It was an ironic piece of graffito, implying: "the $20,000 winner's share" that went with the victory. Dick had even told a reporter that he wouldn't feel like a winner until he saw his paycheck. Have some decency, man! All year, he'd been chattering, "You gotta *want* it! You gotta *want* it!" and now he plotted to burn the message into the team psyche. One by one, the guys glanced at it as they checked in with the trainer, but nobody said a word.

Dick McGuire strode decisively to the board and erased the idiotic slogan. "They are high enough as it is," he said to Danny Whelan. "Why get them any higher?"

There was no room for that rah-rah crap in the pros. For the most part, messages meant to pump up the guys were kept to a minimum. Maybe Reed would mention how important a particular game was, or Mr. Irish might stop by to wish them luck, but that was about it. You never heard Red Holzman give one of those hokey inspirational pregame speeches. Nobody ever exhorted the guys to go out and win one for the Redhead. No self-appointed team chaplain ever ordered his teammates to drop down on a knee and pray. In the NBA there was a nice piece of built-in professionalism. Most players respected each other's need to be businesslike in the workplace and refrained from rolling out the ol' college spirit. It was enough trouble to play with the same pack of bubbleheads every day and put a public face on it.

Everyone in the locker room was nervous enough. There was some good-natured chatter as the guys suited up, but you could tell they were already tuned into thinking about the Bullets. Holzman was unusually quiet. "There's nothing I can say, fellas," he said before leading the team out to the court. "Just run your plays, play good defense." The guys nodded. A few shrugged. They couldn't argue with Red's logic. No one had any better ideas. It had all come down to this: one game. They had to win it to stay alive.

For all the unspoken tension, the game was almost matter-of-fact. The Knicks came out and played just like—the Knicks. They demonstrated a team ethic of near-perfect balance and concentration. They forced the Bullets and got them into foul trouble, without trying to shoot over them all night. They protected their interests by playing defense and rebounding. And they put on a shooting clinic that saw six New York men score in double figures. Dick Barnett must have really wanted it, because the old man ran off twenty-eight points, to lead the team in scoring. He also gave Monroe a dose of his own playground tonic, going one on one against the Pearl—and burning him. Reed took care of the team's other nemesis by limiting Unseld to two measly points. By the time Wes fouled out, with less than a minute left, he appeared bruised and broken. The Knicks beat their Bullets tormentors decisively, 127–114, and sent them packing to an early vacation.

As the teams departed, news drifted back that the Milwaukee Bucks had vanquished the Philadelphia 76ers in their play-off series and would next meet the Knicks at the Garden on April 11. Earl Monroe, the first Baltimore player to leave the Bullet dressing room, was asked who he liked in the next round.

"Good luck to both of them," the Pearl responded, heading toward the exit. "I'm not a basketball fan. I hate to watch the game. I just play it."

11 |SHOOT
OUT THE
LIGHTS

April 11, 1970

B Y THE TIME the Knicks were ready to square off against the Milwaukee Bucks on April 11, Wilt Chamberlain had regained his footing as a celestial force. The Big Dipper had returned almost meekly to the Lakers' front line—no longer the wrathful, snarling beast that breathed fire on puny challengers. But in a closely watched contest with the Phoenix Suns, he'd showed that he still had plenty of the imperial moxie necessary to intimidate a lesser team into submission. Chamberlain, at thirty-three, had the same trim muscular build as always. He'd spent two months playing competitive volleyball on the beach near his home, four months rebuilding his tortured legs. And so he'd returned to the fold in pretty much the same tip-top physical condition, but without all the collateral bluster.

Phoenix loomed as Chamberlain's Chinatown, that unseen neverland of plague and pestilence that would torment Jack Nicholson's shamus psyche. Phoenix was where Chamberlain had damaged his knee, back in early November, and no doubt there were gremlins in his cerebral cobwebs warning him of the consequences of playing there again so soon. It was as if a voice from the past whispered, "Wilt, don't. It's . . . *Phoenix.*"

When Chamberlain had gone down in Phoenix, the Suns were barely breathing. They weren't competition back then—hell, they weren't even much of a scrimmage. They had too many loose nuts and bolts. But Connie Hawkins had become everything they'd promised—even more. And the guards, Goodrich and Van Arsdale—those plucky white boys could shoot out the lights. Paul Silas, too, had come on like gangbusters. With Atlanta, he'd been flat and pokey, all muscle and no punch. The trip west must have invigorated his spirit, because by the time he arrived in the desert there was a sting in his stroke. He'd also dropped twenty pounds for the play-offs, so he could stop Elgin Baylor from turning the corner on him.

That much Chamberlain had expected; those were the developments he could anticipate and keep track of in the newspapers. The Suns had shone brightly through the last few months of the regular season. They'd earned a place in the great aurora that preceded the NBA championship series. But when the Lakers found themselves down by three games to zero in the best-of-seven series—well, Wilt got good and angry. And when Wilt got angry, he got good, and he took his frustrations out on the human rubble.

But Wilt. It's . . . *Phoenix.*

To tell you the truth, Chamberlain had had just about all he could take of that voodoo monkey business about Phoenix. Fuckin' little cactus-eating tank town! You could see the anxiety drain from his consciousness as he fired up the jets. Up to this point, Wilt had been rebounding, playing the gentleman's game, like one of those pantywaists in a league instructional film. "Here, brother, you take the ball while I clear things out for you! Here's one for Elgin . . . one for Jerry . . ." He must have fallen on his head, the way he'd been playing.

Slowly, effectively, Chamberlain regained his scoring strength. He began looking for, *demanding* the ball. The Lakers climbed back from the bowels of hell. Next thing you knew, they were 3–1, then 3–2. After they tied the series at three games, the outcome became a foregone conclusion. He threw in thirty points and picked up twenty-seven rebounds in the finale. The Suns couldn't stand the heat and just collapsed, just melted under Chamberlain's torrid intensity.

"I have a strong suspicion we'll be meeting up with the big guy," Willis Reed acknowledged, as the Lakers flew off to Atlanta for the second test of their stamina.

Willis could feel it, even now—even before he tested the *truly* biggest guy he'd ever seen.

Wilt, Willis, and their fellow giants had watched from the sidelines as Lew Alcindor was plucked from the collegiate ranks and installed as the Messiah who would lead basketball into the Promised Land. That, if anything, was what the past year had signaled. The future of basketball was height—men who would serve as lightning rods to attract more fans. The strategy had certainly worked in Milwaukee. Before Alcindor, the prospect of a team's survival in that dismal, freezing factory town was about as favorable as a return to Prohibition. No one there knew from the Bucks, except that some jerk had shelled out a million of them on a black kid fresh out of UCLA. But Lew's arrival on the scene validated the investment. Almost single-handed, he was responsible for more than doubling the team's gate receipts, not to mention the transformation of rank losers into a dynasty in waiting. And miraculously, overnight, Milwaukee was one of America's basketball boom towns.

You had to hand it to the Big Guy. He'd done his job, playing up in that frozen tundra in front of a Schlitzed-out crowd, night after night. He'd finished the season second only to Jerry West among the league's leading scorers. And he'd taken the Bucks through the first round of the play-offs, disposing of Philadelphia in a snappy five-game transaction. He was making his presence felt in a very big way.

The New York newspapers were playing up the Return of Lew Alcindor as if it were an earthshaking development. His picture was on every sports page every day for weeks. Lew this, Lew that . . . turning it into *his* play-offs—"The Battle of the Big Men," they'd dubbed it. Lew vs. Willis, in the tradition of Ali vs. Frazier. The whole thing made Reed laugh. Lew Alcindor—who were they kidding? That twig? Sure, he was tall—Reed guessed that Alcindor had about half a foot on him—but he was supple and delicate, like Play-Doh. He'd give when Willis gave. And, sure, he could shoot. But he'd have his hands full with Reed on his back; there wouldn't be time for him to set up. Come to think of it, there was that interesting little item in one of the morning columns. Supposedly, following the 76ers series, Billy Cunningham had praised Alcindor but said he'd have to get more physical if he expected to handle the tougher centers. Reed read that and thought, "Exactly!"

Willis scoffed at the reporters when they quizzed him about muscling Lew Alcindor. "I don't muscle him," Reed said, laughing derisively. "I just keep him from moving in. This isn't going to be a duel. It's going to be a dalliance."

As always, Reed turned out to be a man of his word. He played Alcindor as if the big guy was a marionette, pulling his strings whenever it suited Willis's purposes. He took Lew on a walking tour of the Garden floor, showing him places Lew had never seen when he'd played there in high school and college. Alcindor shot out the lights, but he couldn't do it all by himself—not against the Knicks, anyway. The rest of New York's defensive regiment shut down the Bucks and made them work overtime for every scrap and point. The Knicks knew after the first game that they could embarrass these wannabes. And they did—vanquishing them in five games, the last one, at the Garden, a bona fide screamer.

The Knicks had been watching the scoreboard and knew that the Lakers had swept the Atlanta Hawks. "I ain't going back to Milwaukee!" Frazier complained in the locker room before the fifth game started. "Let's get this thing over with and move on."

"Damn straight!" Barnett agreed.

Russell shook his head. "We're ending it tonight, and then we'll take out the Lakers."

"Damn straight!"

The Knicks charged onto the court with a full head of steam and went to work taking apart the wounded Bucks. After one quarter New York was up by thirteen, and by twenty-four at the half.

"Don't let up!" Barnett pressed the guys during intermission. "Let's get these chumps—right now!"

Damn straight!

When the Knicks went up by forty points, the Milwaukee coach, Larry Costello, lifted Alcindor, and the Garden gallery exploded.

"Good-bye Lewie . . . good-bye Lewie, good-bye Lewie, we hate to see you go!"

The voices careened through the arena, resonating in beautiful two-part harmony as Alcindor stalked glumly off the floor. Oh, it was a low, low moment for the Alcindor highlight film, courtesy of the righteous New York fans, but Lew was inured to it. After all, he'd grown up in Manhattan, he knew the city's highs as well as its lows. He'd be back.

"Good-bye Lewwwwwwiiieeeeee . . . we hate to see . . ."

Red Holzman had heard enough of that tune. Taking his cue from Costello, he lifted his team of stallions—first Reed, then Barnett, and fast on their heels DeBusschere, Frazier, and Bradley—and the ridicule segued into applause.

The wave of cheers and exultation continued as the crowd broke into another topical hit: *"Califorrrrrrrrnia here we come . . ."*

Okay, we'll give them something to sing about tonight, Holzman thought, we'll let them get it out of their systems, because they might have to whistle a different tune when the Lakers take the court.

Since the Dipper proved to be fully operable, officially, and the Suns and the Hawks were eliminated convincingly from the play-offs, the Lakers were the only team left to beat. Their rookie coach, Joe Mullaney, was ecstatic. "We expect to do away with the Knicks in seven games," he boasted. That was the idea. Neither the Lakers' win over Phoenix nor their deliberate series with Atlanta measured up to the dream season the Knicks had enjoyed, but the very fact that Los Angeles had chalked up two winning play-off series suggested that they were battling back successfully in their quest for another NBA championship.

On the face of it, Mullaney couldn't have been happier with his team's progress. He had Chamberlain back in the fold. Elgin Baylor was as healthy as he'd ever be again. Jerry West was his normal remarkable self. The team was coalescing as a unit, they were winning games, spinning ever forward toward that great golden door prize. That's how it looked to the Laker public. At the team's core, however, there was nuclear fission.

Just thirteen days before the end of the season—which is to say, on March 10—Chamberlain rejoined a team that had altered their style of play to suit another center. It was comparable to visiting your ex-wife and her new husband. When Wilt played center, every play went to him; he was Options Number One, Two, and Three. The team set a lot of two-on-twos, a healthy cross-section of screens—everything designed to accommodate the Lord Chamberlain. With Rick Roberson in the low post, however, everything changed. The "young" Laker squad that took over in Wilt's absence initiated a UCLA style of help-out defense to assist their inexperienced center. They turned everything to-ward the baseline, with the aim of trapping the ball. If a guy was on the foul line, they'd jump out on him and invite him to go baseline. If he had a quick-release jumper, he was turned. They did this the whole season with Roberson, with considerable success. They'd written off Chamberlain; no one expected him to return this season, if ever. Now, with five games remaining in the regular season, Wilt shows up rarin' to go, and the team had to get him ready for the play-offs.

The trouble was, many of the guys didn't even know him. Happy Hairston and John Tresvant (whom the Lakers acquired mid-season from Seattle) had never played with the man. Rob-erson, Garrett, and McCarter had been in uniform with him for a total of eight—count 'em, eight—games. Then all of a sudden, there's a new face in the middle—and not just your ordinary new face, but one of the fiercest mugs on one of the fiercest trunks that had ever roamed a maple court. And from Mullaney's point of view, a perfectly good system was rent asunder. "With Wilt back, nothing meshed," he said. "We were completely out of sync."

No question about it. The Lakers were a team in transition. This late in the year! It burned some of their quintessential role players. Just imagine how Roberson felt. All year, in difficult situations, he had been their go-to guy; now suddenly he's on the bench. And not just on the bench, but anchored there, with chains wrapped around his ankles and no chance of parole. With Chamberlain back, he'd never play—not a minute, not a milli-second. Understandably, Roberson was grumbling. And that set off a chain reaction of colliding superegos.

In Phoenix, in the sixth, make-it-or-break-it game, it was clear that the Lakers didn't have it. They were behind from the start and falling fast. Mullaney could see how tired Elgin Baylor was; they weren't getting much from him. So he called time and sent in Keith Erickson to give Elg a blow. Slowly the Lakers began knifing into the Suns' lead. They tightened up their play, made their shots, came from behind, and won. Game Seven would tell the whole story. Mullaney was so keyed up that he got to the Forum at four in the afternoon to prepare—and encountered a grim-faced receptionist.

"Mr. Baylor is in your office," she said.

Mr. Baylor. Uh-oh, Mullaney thought, here's trouble.

Baylor was sitting on the couch, and he looked positively incendiary. "I just wanted you to know," he said, seething with anger, "that lifting me in Phoenix was the worst thing that's ever happened to me in my career as a basketball player. I was humiliated." The way Baylor explained it, his son had had a bunch of friends over to watch the game on television, and here was his dad, one of the greatest players in the history of the sport, getting yanked before the half. "When I got home the next day, he was still crying. No one—*no one*—has ever done anything to embarrass me the way you did."

Well, holy gee, Mullaney thought. I've got the seventh game of a play-off starting in a couple of hours, and Elgin Baylor, perhaps my greatest player—a guy I depend on in tight situations every night of the year—has condemned me to hell.

Wilt, too, was on the warpath. Mullaney had taken him aside one afternoon and, in a soothing, fatherly fashion, had tried to explain how his sudden reappearance might affect the team. Adversely. He didn't use that word, but he implied it. "There are *possibly* going to be times when, *if* we're down and the new system isn't working with you, I *might* take you out and give it a shot with the other guy," Mullaney said. Wilt had nodded soberly throughout the conference, then said, "You do what you have to do. But I can tell you right now, I'm never going to be the problem. *Never!*"

But Chamberlain was plainly suspicious of Mullaney's strategy, Baylor was furious with his coach, Roberson was outraged by his banishment, and everyone was prickly over the midseason

appearance of Happy Hairston, a backbiter whose negative attitude consistently wore the guys down. This was the team Mullaney was bringing into New York to face the Knicks, the same
Lakers team whose public face belied little of the festering chaos
that was biting into their former unity.

The Knicks were eager to see what Los Angeles had. A Laker
team with Chamberlain healthy was one thing, but if Wilt was
showing signs of wear and tear, the Knicks were prepared to take
him apart. Individually, each Knick had immense respect for the
Dipper. Why, the week before the opening game, Bradley's parents had sent him a scrapbook they'd found that he had kept on
Wilt during grade school. And Reed—you had to know how much
he loved the big guy. Nevertheless, the Knicks secretly hoped
he'd blow out both knees on the plane into JFK or would suffer
a ruptured appendix. Nothing lethal, just something serious
enough to keep him out of, oh, say, seven games.

A notorious motormouth, Wilt had already spouted off to the
press about New York's obvious weaknesses. Their weaknesses!
The guy had played a single, meaningless game against them back
in October, and he had it all figured out. Talk about cheek.

No, if Wilt showed up in one piece, the Knicks decided to
test him early. And hard.

Willis Reed had his own strategy worked out when it came
to his famous dance partner. For a while he'd contemplated using
the method that had supposedly stopped Wilt in five previous
play-off series. The Celtics' Bill Russell had contained him by
keeping a hand posted low in Wilt's back. The Dipper had hated
to feel that fucking hand there. It pestered the hell out of him,
threw his concentration off. Well, Willis thought, that was one
possible answer. But there was more than one reason to try
something out of the ordinary. As everyone knew, Chamberlain's
game was stuffing the ball. He played like a wrecking crane. So

if you were touching his back, he might eat up the distance to the basket by taking a step backward and dribbling. Or if you were belly-up to him, he could pivot. But if you were behind him—if you leaned on him and pushed him—he might have to force a fallaway jumper, and that wasn't necessarily his best shot. In fact, along with foul shooting, it was his worst shot. The guys who muscled and leaned and pushed were the centers who gave Chamberlain problems. And Willis had the equipment to do exactly that.

Oddly, he chose none of those options for the first game, on April 24, 1970. He'd decided to run on Chamberlain and make him come out to play the ball. The plan surprised some of Reed's teammates—and it especially surprised Wilt. The Knicks knew that Reed's knees were deteriorating. In practice, he'd been limping and favoring the good leg. There were plays when he'd backed off completely in order to limit the contact. But "You okay, Cap?" usually drew no response—a precarious omen, especially coming from the diplomatic Reed.

Chamberlain had apparently heard the rumors and parked his ponderous frame beneath the Knicks' basket, in the type of come-and-get-me challenge that had served him well for more than a decade. Reed took one look at the Dipper and uttered a silent laugh. See you later, chump! In a cyclone of motion, Reed proceeded to give a virtuoso shooting performance the likes of which his Garden fan club had never before witnessed. He hit from deep in both corners, shooting over and slipping around Chamberlain, then came at him down the middle, pulling up at the foul line for a soft bucket. For some strange reason, Wilt refused to challenge Reed. He stayed his ground, clogging the lane, while the Knicks hit jumpers from all angles. Then Reed moved in closer, as if to say, "Here I am, big fella, come out and play." Still—nothing. So Reed continued to shoot. From around the world. By the time Reed took a breather, a few minutes before the half, he'd racked up twenty-five points and put the Knicks up by a mammoth seventeen-point margin.

But the Lakers made them work down the stretch. Frazier had picked up three quick fouls guarding Jerry West, and following the intermission Los Angeles resorted to their trusty weapon. Mullaney instructed Chamberlain, Baylor, Garrett, and Hairston to "overload the offense," to draw their men to one side of the court, leaving Jerry West all alone across the floor so he could perform. In effect, it enabled him to go one on one against a hapless Knicks defender. Jerry worked it like a charm while he put up sixteen points in the third period, running through Frazier, Riordan, and Barnett as if they were invisible. Baylor and Johnny Egan also had hot hands, giving the Lakers an 86–84 lead. But Cazzie Russell came off the bench, and he was on fire. In the first half, Russell had been dismally ineffective, just ice cold, missing all his shots. At the time, Stallworth had suggested to him that he was hesitating, holding back on his jumper. Now, grabbing a loose ball, Russell drove the length of the court for a decisive bucket that put the Knicks ahead, and then he added six more points—sealing the win at 124–112.

The Knicks had played terrific defense, but they won the game as a result of their shooting. Reed finished with thirty-seven points, DeBusschere and Riordan had nineteen each, and Barnett and Bradley added thirty-three between them, in a good all-around effort that put New York over the top.

The good news was that the Knicks had won the first game. The bad news was Reed's admission that he'd jammed his left shoulder. Halfway through the second period, he'd collided with Happy Hairston while slamming home a dunk over the cranky Laker's stalky frame. By the third quarter the shoulder had tightened. But afterward Reed was reluctant to give the injury much play. The story was Chamberlain, he insisted.

"I think he's hampered by his knee," Reed said, as friends

and reporters shoved in around his locker. "I don't know how much less mobile he is, but he can't move as fast on a drive. I don't think he reacts as quick, and I don't think he can go up as high."

Frazier, sitting nearby, overheard the conversation and agreed. "He's lost a lot of his movement," Clyde said. "I saw a couple of times when his knee gave out and they called Wilt for traveling when he had to take an extra step."

The Knicks were buoyed by Chamberlain's timid performance. But three days later, when the teams took the Garden floor for Game Two, Wilt played like a monster reborn. On the Knicks' first drive, he came out to challenge Reed's jumper from the foul line, giving Willis a clean facial, and from that point on he completely controlled the game. Reed's shoulder seemed fine; at least, it was no factor in the constant push-and-pull that paced almost forty-five solid minutes of breakneck play. In the game's final minutes, however, it was Chamberlain who pushed hardest.

With less than a minute left, the Lakers led, 105–103. Reed got the ball and worked for a shot from just beyond the foul line, which drew Wilt out on defense. It'd be too difficult, Reed determined, with that beast in his face. Giving up the long shot, Willis passed to Frazier, then ducked in close, but Wilt stayed with him, he was right there, when Reed launched his shot— and Wilt blocked it cleanly. The Lakers had won.

"That'll give him something to think about," Wilt chuckled after the game. "Everybody thinks I'm crippled, but I guess I'm not. Man, I came to play! Do you think I worked four months on my knee so I could come here and jive?"

The man was beautiful!

Playing offense at every juncture.

Five minutes after running mercilessly on a leg that had recently had two holes bored through the bone below the knee, a pair of ligaments fastened through the holes and reattached through two holes bored in his lower shin, and he remained:

The Big Dipper!

The series had temporarily run its course in New York and now shifted to Los Angeles, where Games Three and Four were to be played in the Fabulous Forum. *The fabulous Forum!* You could tell right away that it wasn't Madison Square Garden. This was years before Pat Riley, Magic Johnson, and Showtime moved into the space, but even so, there was enough razzmatazz in the spectacular building to entertain any fan. First of all, it was bright. The lighting was such that Warner Bros. could have shot a segment of "Starsky and Hutch" there and not added a single light bulb. They could even have landed a few extras on the cheap, because the Forum's employees, as everyone knew, were gorgeous. In New York, you were showed to your seat by one of the hawk-nosed ganders who might have moonlighted at the Stage Delicatessen. A real sourpuss. In L.A., where wild starlets roamed the streets in herds, a luscious young thing in a brief toga accompanied you to your seat and then bent over, generously, in fact, to dust off the seat cushion. That's right, in a hermetically sealed building comparable to Biosphere II, where giant ducts pumped in and recycled purified air faster than anyone could suck it into their lungs, she tipped those firm little buns at a ninety-degree angle and . . . *dusted the cushions.* You just had to love a place that provided that kind of service.

The Knicks enjoyed playing there, too. The locker rooms were spacious and plushly carpeted. The equipment was state of the art—a vast assortment of weight-training apparatus, a whirlpool, a sauna, a screening room. Food was plentiful and was served by a courteous staff. Even the floor was in A-1 condition; there were no dead spots or black holes like in the Garden, where the ball might ricochet off a pipe that was part of the icing system for the hockey team. No, instead of fighting nerves and anxiety, the Knicks were lulled into a tranquillity induced by the Forum's copious amenities.

As Game Three got under way, it seemed as though the Knicks would prefer to snuggle into one of those deep-cushioned seats, order a tangy fruit-juice cocktail—that's right, they served fruit-juice cocktails—and watch the action along with the rest of the friendly spectators. They were that laid back! The Lakers got off quickly, and Chamberlain looked to be in the game again, contesting Reed's every shot. Offensively, the Knicks seemed spent, but their lack of scoring was easy to misconstrue by anyone who wasn't on the floor with them. Yes, Dick Barnett missed his first nine shots and was completely shut out in the first half. But he was preoccupied with a little peccadillo called Jerry West.

Barnett drove West crazy all night, hand-checking him up and down the Forum floor. Rich got the angle on West and kept his paw thrust into Jerry's side, right up under his rib cage, where he kept jabbing away at the Lakers star. Every time Jerry brought the ball up the floor, there was Dick's hand—jabbing, jabbing, jabbing. He was unrelenting. As a result, West got into early foul trouble by slapping Barnett's hand away from his side. Joe Mullaney went nuts, complaining to the refs about it every two minutes. He was furious with Barnett, incensed that the tactic was taking a toll on West's game. "What is this shit? If you knock a guy's hand away, it's a foul," he shouted at Mendy Rudolph. "But if you jab him in the side, it's okay!" Rudolph just stared blankly back at the Lakers coach, he looked right through him, which only seemed to make it worse.

Once, before a game, Mullaney had been standing in the tunnel with one of the officials and began jabbing him in the side. The guy wheeled on Joe and knocked his hand away.

"What did you do that for?" Mullaney asked innocently.

"You're bothering me."

Mullaney smiled. "That's exactly right," he said.

Still, it was permitted, according to the rules of the game.

And Barnett continued to hound West, uncontested, throughout the first half of the game.

At intermission, the Knicks were down by fourteen points. It soon became apparent, however, that they had saved their aggressiveness for the second half. New York went on a tear down the stretch, shooting out the lights and catching the Lakers at 96 all with 1:18 left in the game.

Barnett, who scored thirteen emergency points in the final period, made a critical basket that gave New York a 100–99 lead with eighteen seconds on the clock. Five seconds later, however, he fouled Chamberlain, who hit one of his foul shots to tie the game again. The Knicks worked furiously for a final shot, and finally DeBusschere took it, sinking a seventeen-foot jumper with three seconds to go—and that seemed to ice it for New York. The Knicks would win, 102–100. The Lakers had no time-outs left, they were out of tricks. Chamberlain inbounded to West from under the Knicks' basket and then ran off the court to avoid an angry crowd. Everyone else just went through the motions— except West and Willis Reed, who came out to press Jerry, but only halfheartedly, as a formality. With two seconds left, West took three steps, dribbling straight up the middle. Reed forced him to the left, and as the buzzer sounded Jerry launched a sixty-foot shot . . .

Frazier was looking into West's eyes as the ball sailed through the air, and he thought, "That motherfucker's crazy. He really thinks it's going in!"

Indeed, West felt confident all the way. His body was behind the shot, and he was up in the air. Shit, he'd made these shots before—at Madison Square Garden, of all places. He knew the moment the ball left his hand he had a shot . . .

Are you ready for this?

. . . that went right into the basket to tie the game.

Well!

There was a moment—just a moment, nothing more—when

everything stopped, nothing moved, no one breathed, when time stood still, so that the exact nature of the incident they'd witnessed could travel the distance from everyone's eyes to their brain, to be registered there in utter disbelief.

"The Lakers tie it! The Lakers tie it! Oh my God!" Chick Hearn, the team's broadcast commentator, was having a fucking seizure in the press box. *"The Lakers tie the game! Oh . . . my . . . God!"*

There was pandemonium in the Fabulous Forum. Spectators lost complete control of themselves, jumping in their seats, holding their heads between the palms of their hands, and swaying back and forth in utter disbelief and jubilation.

The Lakers tie it! They tie the game.

DeBusschere, who was holding the ball, sank to the floor. He just sat down at midcourt to contemplate this nasty little miracle. Finally Bradley walked over and helped him to his feet. Someone ran into the Lakers' locker room to get Chamberlain, who had missed the buzzer-beater and was unaware of the situation. Now there were five more minutes to play. They were going to overtime.

Well, nothing—not even an overtime between two mighty teams—could compare with that spectacular finish. Even to spell it out play by play would be anticlimactic. Suffice it to say, the Knicks battled back from the shock of West's desperation shot and had to win it all over again, 111–108.

New York had accomplished what they had set out to do in Los Angeles—to win at least one from the Lakers on their home turf—even if it had to go fifty-three minutes. Reed scored thirty-eight points in the effort, a total made even more astonishing when you consider that, in the third quarter, Wilt Chamberlain had accidentally kicked him above the left knee, reaggravating the old wound.

Reed wasn't concerned. He'd come too far to let a bum leg keep him out of action, especially with the title a game closer within his grasp. He'd play Game Four if they had to wheel him out on a hospital gurney. The prospects were grimmer, it seemed, for Jerry West. He'd performed magnificently, he'd made a shot that many players would consider to be the most exciting experience of their careers, but he'd also jammed his left thumb, during the second quarter, and although X rays revealed no fracture, he'd lost a great deal of muscular control over his left hand. That threw a new tidbit into the stew. Throughout the day off between games, there was much overheated activity in the Lakers' medical complex. Bob Kerlan, the team doctor, concluded that if the game had been scheduled for that night, there was no question that West couldn't participate. If the injury had happened during the regular season, he'd insist that Jerry sit out three or four games. But with the title at stake, he listed West as day to day and kept much of the free world gripped in edgy suspense.

By evening, West's thumb had swollen up to twice its normal size, he couldn't make a fist, and Kerlan listed him as doubtful. Doubtful, hah! His teammates considered the diagnosis to be a joke. Certainly West was in pain, and certainly no man in his right mind would attempt to play basketball in his condition— against the New York Knicks, no less. But there wasn't a moment when any of them believed anything other than that West would be on the floor with them for Game Four. He'd be there, they knew. He'd play.

Doubtful!

The only thing doubtful about Game Four was how many points West would rack up. The Knicks knew it, too. He wasn't fooling anybody with that swollen-thumb routine. A little disability like that never stopped Superman. A cartoon in the *New York Daily News* offered a few blithe suggestions for dealing with this "doubtful" Lakers stallion. "Nail Jerry West's sneakers to the floor with spikes," they said. "Clamp a steel lid on top of the basket. Tie a blindfold on him. Put him in chains, like Houdini."

Doubtful!

West showed them who was doubtful. He came out like an octopus with all eight tentacles flinging passes to openhanded Lakers, whose men had deserted them to assist Barnett on defense. Baylor got thirty points, Erickson and Chamberlain were the beneficiaries of fourteen West-assisted points each, and Jerry West—*Mr. Doubtful*—scored thirty-seven, as the Lakers beat the Knicks in another tense overtime game, 121–115.

Doubtful!

The series was tied at two apiece. The only thing doubtful about the Knicks' future was how much damage West would inflict on them in the throes of Game Five.

Despite the loss to the Lakers and the extremely tight series, the Knicks were supremely confident as they prepared to play back at home again. They felt close to the Lakers now, felt they had turned the corner on them. It was almost as if, in the first four games, they had cracked the mystery of the Lakers' spell. It sounded like a Hardy Boys adventure—*The Mystery of the Lakers' Spell*. Frank and Joe Hardy, along with their buddies Willy, Bill, Rich, Walt, and Dave, had stumbled across a key morsel of information: the Lakers were beatable. And hurt. West's thumb was as sore as ever, Elgin Baylor had pulled a muscle in his abdomen and was listed as—right—doubtful, Keith Erickson's ankle was sprained. And the Knicks felt they had the necessary artillery to handle what was left of those brats.

One of the luxuries of playing at home was protection from well-wishers. Wives and girlfriends kept friends and autograph seekers securely at a distance so the players could relax before games. The Garden management protected them from the 19,500 half-crazed fans in the stands. And the beat reporters who had followed the team throughout the season protected them from the outside world. The evening of the fifth game, especially, not one columnist asked them to comment on a story that had been circulating at their city desks since late that afternoon: four students at Kent State University, in Ohio, had been gunned down by National Guardsmen following an anti-Vietnam rally on the school commons. The whole country was stunned that such an atrocity could occur on a midwestern college campus whose most serious previous demonstration had been a 1958 panty raid on a women's dormitory, and a photo—*that* photo—of a young coed hunched angrily over a dead student lying facedown on a campus path had brought the incident into every home in America. Today, "Hard Copy" would probably have had a correspondent stationed outside the Knicks' locker room to get a comment from PFC Russell and Private Riordan. No doubt they would have hounded the two guardsmen as they strode from their lockers, through the hallway, into the tunnel, and onto the court. "Why are you afraid to talk with us, Cazzie? What about you, Mike—would you have shot those kids? What do you guys have to hide?"

But the Knicks were oblivious to the tragedy as they took the court and played a game that had its own fateful repercussions. Eight minutes into the first quarter, with the Lakers leading, 25–15, Reed drove toward the basket for what appeared to be an easy score. Suddenly Chamberlain stepped out of the shadows to block the path, forcing Willis to the left, which was his normal direction to the hoop. This time, however, Reed's right foot got tangled with Wilt's pretzel legs and down Willis went, landing heavily on top of the ball. Play continued as Reed rolled around writhing in pain. Finally a foul stopped play, and Willis got up slowly. He seemed to be all right, but after about eight seconds more, he limped off the court and, with Danny Whelan's help, disappeared into the locker room.

For the remainder of the half, the Knicks tried helplessly to contain Chamberlain. First Nate Bowman went against him, then Bill Hosket, and even DeBusschere was switched to the center spot, with comical results. The Lakers maintained a steady ten-point lead throughout the half and went off at intermission leading by 53–40.

The scene in the Knicks' locker room was one of shocked disbelief. Reed was stretched out on a training table while the team doctor and Danny worked furiously to massage some feeling into his side. As near as anyone could determine, Reed had landed on his hip, and the muscles in his side weren't responding. He had several cortisone shots, but they did little to relieve the pain. He was finished for the game.

Holzman nodded soberly. He'd expected as much when Reed limped off the court. A guy didn't fall the way Willis had, then come back and play twenty-four minutes of unrelenting ball. Not even Willy. Reed was gone for the night; Red would have to figure out another way to win the damn game.

"How about a one-three-one offense?" Bradley suggested.

Holzman gazed thoughtfully at his brainy star forward and nodded. "We could try that," he said.

The one-three-one was a college type of offense designed to draw out a big, imposing center so that the rest of the team could get off their shots. The idea, in this case, would be to put Bradley in the center, spread Russell and Barnett out on the wings, about fifteen feet from the basket, while Stallworth and DeBusschere manned the baseline. It was like having five shooters on the floor at the same time; the Lakers wouldn't be able to double off on any of them. If the Knicks' shots began dropping, Wilt would have to come out to challenge one of them, allowing the others to go to the hoop. It was risky, inasmuch as it was illegal to play a zone—in this case, a zone *offense*—but the Knicks had practiced it on several occasions and felt they could pull it off without getting caught.

As luck would have it, the Knicks came out in the third quarter and played a picture-perfect one-three-one offense that went right over the refs' heads. For some reason, Mendy Rudolph and Ed Rush refused to call the zone, despite wild protests from

West and Mullaney. It completely flummoxed the Lakers, so much so that they switched from a determinedly aggressive style of play to one that could only be characterized as overcautious. To illustrate exactly how overcautious the Lakers were, Jerry West took only two shots in the entire final half. And Chamberlain, with all that height advantage, could score only four more points.

The Lakers blew a certain victory because of a mismatch and a tricky zone. On defense, Frazier sparkled. He swarmed all over the baffled Lakers guards, especially Dick Garrett, with whom he had played for a year at Southern Illinois. At one point, the Knicks went ahead, 95–93, when Frazier picked off a ball from his former teammate. Clyde turned on the speed, and Garrett fouled him from behind as the shot went up and into the basket. While Clyde was on the foul line, Garrett skulked toward the Lakers bench with his head down.

"What's the matter?" Mullaney asked.

Garrett shrugged. "I can't get the ball up the floor against this guy."

Mullaney stared at his rookie. *What the . . . ! He can't get the ball up the floor against this guy!* "For God's sake, Garrett, it's the middle of the damn play-offs! Now, get out there and do your job!"

That's the kind of game it was for the Lakers. They knew that with Game Six back at the Forum and the Knicks up by three games to two, their backs were up against the wall.

The Knicks could have flown to Los Angeles without a plane, they were so high from that win. No one ever thought they could come back without Reed. No one, not even Holzman, felt they could stop the onslaught of Chamberlain.

"These guys can do *anything!*" he kept repeating after the game, the way a drunk babbles incoherently. "There's *nothing* they can't do."

Well, he should have waited until after the next game to make such a grandiose statement. Reed didn't play; he could barely walk without help. X rays of his hip had proved inconclusive, but the doctor had found a strain in two muscles—the tensor and the rectus femoris, which is the muscle that runs from the pelvis across the hip to the knee. He'd put Willis on a diet of Prednisone and was continuing to shoot him with cortisone, but the hip wasn't responding. Willis needed rest.

It was immediately obvious that not Bowman, Hosket, DeBusschere, or Stallworth could replace Reed. With Willis watching from the bench, the Lakers came out blasting, as they'd done before after suffering embarrassing defeats. Chamberlain was a beast, he was uncontrollable. West was annoyingly accurate. And little Dickie Garrett, the rookie who couldn't bring the ball up the floor against Walt Frazier, hit his first eight shots in a row. Well, when Chamberlain and West were on, it signaled danger, but when Garrett ran the floor and played like an all-star, it was time to throw your hands up in surrender.

The Knicks did exactly that as the Lakers buttered their fannies, 135–113. Wilt Chamberlain tallied forty-five points. It was an amazing feat of marksmanship, even for the Dipper. In regular-season play, he might score forty-five against a team like San Diego or the Pistons. But in a championship series, dragging a surgically repaired knee against the Knicks—you can bet the oddsmakers had a tough time explaining that one to their miserly bosses. Chamberlain proved once again that he functioned on something more than "D" batteries. He operated on some otherworldly current. Whatever it was, it defined brute force. It was frightening. By comparison, West, who scored a mere thirty-three points and had thirteen assists, went practically unnoticed by the fans. He operated from somewhere just below the surface of the action, but what he did and how he did it were the life force of the Laker team.

Somehow, some way, the Knicks needed to get Reed into

uniform for the seventh game in New York. It was hard to chart the locus of Reed's spirit at that juncture. Never in the history of pro basketball, it seemed, had a man suffered as much pain as this. Naturally, every player expects a few days here and there when aches—even breaks—conspire to keep him out of action. But Reed hadn't bargained for anything like this. The pain was excruciating. His knee was shredded like coleslaw, and his hip— Well, you could chalk that one up to his stupidity. He knew now that if he'd taken a cortisone treatment earlier in the series he wouldn't have had all the pain in the left knee, and therefore wouldn't have put all that pressure onto the right side of his hip. That was what had done him in, not Wilt. He'd begun favoring his right side and had thrown his whole body off stride. Wilt had only been the catalyst. If he hadn't gotten in the way, somebody else would have. Sooner or later Reed would have gone down, with the same result.

The doctors were more than skeptical about his getting back, but they were willing to try anything toward that goal. The afternoon following Game Six, in fact, they'd accompanied Reed and Danny Whelan to the International Hotel, on the perimeter of LAX, where, at a spa frequented by boxers, he took an experimental thermal cure designed to stimulate muscle response. In a step-by-step procedure designed, most likely, by the Tontons Macoute, Reed limped into a 104-degree hot room, then spun directly into a 140-degree moist-heat room, and finally entered a 180-degree dry-heat room, before being dropped rudely into a Swedish ice plunge.

"Hey, Willy—this is a good way to know if you got a good heart," Whelan chirped, at a safe distance from Reed's swing. "You jump in there, and if you die, you know you had a bad heart."

Fucking Danny! The guy couldn't let it rest. There was a time and a place for his jokey crap—and this was neither of them. The entire Knicks' year, the championship included, was in serious—no, horrendous—trouble. They had a scant forty-eight hours to get something going. Otherwise, the whole year would be a joke.

Later the same day, instead of Reed's returning to the hotel, the doctors had Danny bundle him up and take him back to New York on TWA's red-eye flight, in order for him to have two full days of additional treatment. Two full days. The way things were going, anything could happen in that time.

May 8, 1970

All of New York was in an uproar. The dream of a championship—the coveted first championship in the history of their heroic Knick franchise—rode on the scorched excrescence of one man's hip socket. That was some kind of funky luck, all right. What else could anyone do except sit and hope, finger those holy glass prayer beads, and mumble a prayer? The whole thing was in His hands now.

Even so, news bulletins flashed hourly providing updates on the breaking headline story: Would Willis Reed play? The doctor had given him a fifty-fifty chance. Well, you couldn't do much with those odds. *Fifty-fifty!* What kind of a worthless chance was that? Reed himself remained merely optimistic. What did that mean—optimistic? It meant that he could move, barely. He could raise his right leg, barely. He could bend the knee, barely.

"I'm much improved," he had said the night before the game. "But if they said right now, 'Come on, Willis, play,' I couldn't do it. I'm just hoping when they get done with me that the soreness will not be there."

When they get done with me . . .

That afternoon, Reed stole into Madison Square Garden around one o'clock and headed straight for the trainer's office. Stripping down, he took an hour of ultrasound, then sat in the whirlpool massaging his weary side. Afterward, he hobbled around the room trying to get the hip to respond. Nothing happened. He popped a hot pack on his side and gave it twenty minutes. Still no luck. Pain shot through his right side whenever he put pressure on his leg. He grimaced. There wasn't enough time, he thought. He'd never be ready to play tonight. They were going to have to do something else for him if he was going to play, something drastic. Eventually he'd have to take a few shots. He knew that. But there had to be something else they could do.

Around three-thirty, the rest of the guys started coming in, but Reed didn't want to talk. He slipped out of the locker room and took the elevator upstairs to the arena restaurant, where he sat with Danny Whelan over a tired-looking steak. This was it, he thought dolefully. It all comes down to one game. The whole fantastic year, the dream, the once-in-a-lifetime opportunity to do it all. One goddamn game. And I have to feel like this!

Reed devoured the steak without tasting it. Back in the locker room, he took a phone call. It was Lendon Stone, his high-school basketball coach, and Stone wasn't particularly cordial. What, he wanted to know, was this business about Willis *not* playing against the Lakers? Answer me, boy! Willis grinned, thinking about the solid old disciplinarian who had taught him everything he knew about the game. *Everything!* That gentleman never let up. Never. Willis's smile widened. Tonics come in many forms, he thought. Who said you couldn't squeeze blood from a Stone?

He wondered how the guys would fare against Wilt tonight. Even if he went out there, he couldn't go the whole game. That was for certain. And no matter how much time he was on the court, he doubted he'd be effective. He was weak, crippled. He'd need all the help he could get.

Little did Reed know that Chamberlain, in his own inimitable style, had already thrown some emergency assistance his way.

A day earlier, the Lakers had flown into New York on a commercial 707 flight, along with practically the entire Los Angeles front office, a few local celebrities, and several bubbly team boosters. The team was in high spirits. Their win in Game Six, coupled with the knowledge that Reed was suffering and might not play, gave the Lakers enormous hope that the time had come for them to win the championship that had seemed so elusive. The guys were jacked up and ready to go. They were still on the runway in Los Angeles, whooping and hollering, when the flight attendants came around with an assortment of newspapers. It was a story in the *Herald Examiner* that ultimately did in the Los Angeles Lakers. Above columnist Doug Kerkorian's byline was a headline that said, "WILT BLASTS EMPHASIS ON WINNING." The previous evening, Philosopher Wilt had entertained a few of the local scribes with his boundless pith and wisdom—and had blabbered like a magpie. The gist of the story was: when you come this far, too much credit goes to the team that wins and not enough is said about the team that doesn't make it. And so forth and so on.

Well, hold it right there, brother. *The team that doesn't make it?* You could see the guys throwing glances at each other, as if to say, "What the fuck is he talking about?" Dick Garrett was hunkered down in his seat, with the article open on his lap, and his expression provided a visual summary of the whole story. His face was wrinkled in disbelief. It was as if he had just looked out the little window of the airplane and discovered half a wing was missing. *Not enough credit goes to*—the guys were pointing out the article to each other and analyzing its hidden meaning—*the team that doesn't make it.* The atmosphere in the cabin underwent a sudden change. It seemed as if they'd experienced a pressure drop—and they hadn't even gotten off the ground yet. Can you imagine? That stupid son of a bitch spends the whole season on the beach—playing *volleyball*—and he gives this pathetic little interview about the glory of losing. Two nights earlier, before the sixth game, Wilt had sat in the Lakers' dressing room and said, "Gee, I hope we don't lose it." What was it with this guy? Couldn't he keep his yap buttoned for a minute? Did he always have to be such a pompous asshole? By the time the plane landed in New York, several of the guys were thinking mutiny.

Across town, the Knicks gathered stoically at four-thirty for the usual taping and wrapping ceremony. Nobody appeared to be down, nor were any of the guys especially tense. Through it all, they had remained the Imperturbable Knicks. They were ready, with or without the Cap. That's the way it had to be. They were on their own.

Willis remained on the training table through the pregame rituals, getting yet another therapeutic rubdown from Danny Whelan. Around six o'clock he slipped out again, to call his daughter, Veronica, who had turned five that same day, in Mansura, Louisiana. Reed and his wife were separated, so he was relieved when Veronica's grandmother answered the phone. When Veronica came on the line, she wanted an answer to the same question that was tormenting every basketball fan from New York to Inglewood, California: was he still hurt?

"Yeah, babe," he answered. "I'm still hurting. But I'm gonna play."

Reed said it, but even then he didn't believe it.

"Good luck, Daddy," his daughter said.

A little after six, Dr. James Parkes, a young sports-medicine specialist who'd been treating Reed, gave Willis a cursory examination. Parkes was optimistic that Reed would be mobile enough to take the court, but he wanted to wait as long as possible to give him the cortisone injections, so their effectiveness would last throughout the game. "We'll start around seven o'clock," he said. "It shouldn't take us more than a few minutes."

Red Holzman waited until Parkes had gone and the rest of the guys were occupied. Then he walked over to Reed.

"How's it feel, Willy?" he asked.

Reed grimaced. "Not so good."

Holzman nodded. "Look, I want you to hear this from me. We could use you out there, but you don't have to play. I'm not going to force you to play, not in this condition. We can win it without you."

We can win it without you, he said. The old man was lying through his teeth. He knew they didn't have a prayer in hell without Reed; nevertheless he had to say it. He had to let the guy off the hook in case he was completely immobile.

"Thanks, but I'm gonna try, Red. I'm gonna go."

Holzman just nodded and walked away. He had a well-known passion for playing the ponies and happily dropped an occasional C-note on a race that everyone else knew was fixed, but Holzman wouldn't have bet a cent on seeing Reed play against the Lakers that night. Not even as a twenty-to-one long shot. A little later, the coach and Dr. Parkes went into the arena to watch Willis attempt a few shots. Well, the odds on his playing just sloughed right off the chart. Reed could shoot, he could dribble, but he couldn't get off the ground. If he tried that against Chamberlain, there would be a massacre.

The team held a brief meeting at six-thirty, a few minutes before they officially took the floor for the warm-up session. Holzman allowed Reed to skip his pregame talk, but he desperately wanted him to go out on the floor with the team. Not for appearances, but for the guys, for moral support. Reed's teammates had each let him know that if he could give it twenty minutes or one half, they'd win the damn game. If he could get up and go out with them now, maybe that would be enough.

Reed, however, never made it. At seven o'clock, he was inside the trainer's room with Dr. Parkes and Danny Whelan, waiting for them to decide how to administer the various painkillers needed to embalm the rogue hip.

Whelan hopped around annoyingly, with one eye trained on

the clock. The game was scheduled for a 7:30 start, and at a quarter past seven there was still some indecision, some confusion.

"C'mon, doc, you gotta do something," Whelan pleaded. "If you're gonna shoot him, you better get to it, because the game's starting."

Parkes glanced at Whelan without responding. He'd expected the procedure to last no longer than ten minutes, fifteen tops, but it now appeared that he had miscalculated. Reed wasn't your normal patient. He was six-nine, for chrissake, with thighs like the trunk of a two-hundred-year-old oak. A beast like that required special equipment. Parkes was forced to use a scary six-inch spinal needle, because of Reed's gargantuan muscles, and yet he couldn't seem to hit his mark. He needed to give Willis a series of injections—cortisone first, with a Carbocaine chaser—but the shots had to be randomly inserted in order to avoid tearing any muscle tissue.

"Is it gonna be worth it to do all this for one game?" Whelan asked, trying to distract Reed.

"I told you all year that if we ever got to this point, I'd be there," Reed said, growing a bit testy. "I'm gonna crawl onto that floor if I have to."

Phil Jackson peeked in at 7:25 to see how things were going. Jackson, wearing a press pass, was on assignment to photograph the play-offs for the *New York Post*. Willis was on the table, lying on his side, his head thrown back in agony, and when Jackson got a look at that needle he nearly needed Whelan to administer smelling salts to him.

The doctor went at it for nearly twenty minutes, poking around in Reed's hip and thigh area, until he was satisfied with his shot selection.

"How does it feel?" he asked Reed.

Willis eased himself off the table. He could still feel the pain shooting through his side. "There are a few ways I can move," he answered. He knew that if he could keep the leg stiff and drag it, then he wouldn't have a problem. It was only when he flexed that it hurt.

"Move around on it a few minutes," Parkes instructed him. "See if it responds."

Outside, in the arena, the players were starting to lose their patience. It was 7:35; the start of the game was five minutes overdue. Warm-ups were still in progress, and it didn't seem as though anyone was doing anything to get the game going.

Bill Bradley kept glancing at the tunnel, looking for any sign that suggested Reed's emergence. He's not coming out, he's not coming out, Bradley thought. He turned to Stallworth, beside him, and said, "He *is* coming out, isn't he?"

The Rave flashed him a wide, toothy grin. "I'll bet the fans pull down the roof when Willis comes out."

Pull down the roof. It was going to take that for the Knicks to win this one, Bradley thought. Something had to give—Willis, the roof, something.

Joe Mullaney had waited long enough. He left his post at the Lakers' bench and bounded over to the scorer's table scratching his head. "Does anyone have a time on this game?" he demanded. "When are we going to start?"

The timekeeper threw up his hands and shrugged. "Relax, Joe—this is New York."

This is New York! What a guy.

"Don't think I don't know what's going on here," Mullaney said. "I got to tell you, it's really cheap. If you had a World Series game scheduled to start at two, and I told you that so-and-so's got ten more minutes of treatment so we're not going to start until he's ready, you'd say, 'Too bad. The game starts now.' " He shook his head and instructed the Lakers' P.R. man to find Walter Kennedy, the NBA commissioner, and lodge a protest.

Everyone was standing around now. Waiting . . . waiting . . . The Lakers remained under their basket taking a few shots, and the Knicks did the same at the opposite end of the floor. Guys were shaking their heads, getting edgy. It was T plus fourteen minutes and counting past the official starting time. Enough already! The tension was getting under everyone's skin.

No one was aware that, at that very moment, Willis Reed had left the locker room and was dragging his bum leg, like Frankenstein's monster, through the tunnel on his way to the court. It was tough sledding, hobbling through the hard arena halls like that. Each stride, each random motion, sent new needles of pain shooting through his aching side. Midway through the tunnel, Reed spotted a familiar figure standing with his back turned—Sam Goldaper, the *Times* sports columnist, whom Reed had nicknamed "Poison Pen," was watching the crowd, unaware of Reed's approach. This is my chance, he thought. As he passed Goldaper, he feigned a sudden twinge of pain—the first time he had ever misrepresented his injury—stumbled, and bumped the journalist hard. That'll teach the little bastard, Reed thought, allowing himself a tiny smile.

At first no one saw him coming—then everyone saw him all at once, and a roar went up that shook every seat in the house, not to mention the steel-reinforced backboards. Section after section of the crowd, in waves, joined the standing ovation. Then the ushers and the soda jerks and the security guards and the maintenance men and the cops stopped whatever they were doing and began cheering, too. It was that contagious. Even the dispirited Lakers, stricken by the mystical vision, felt like applauding. For them, there was no getting around Reed anymore. At this point, fifteen minutes past the game's scheduled start, Reed had ascended to the status of a prophet. He had become the uniformed emissary of God, with the divine mission to lead the chosen people—those twelve New York warriors—out of oppression and into the record book. From ancient times, the prophets had been studied for revelations of the future, and now Willis Reed, basking in this celestial aura, was being scrutinized by the righteous throng for signs that he could pivot without pain. For what it was worth, he seemed to be walking well enough, he was mobile. He took a few warm-ups and sank two shots.

Thank you, Lord.

The crowd applauded each shot, they applauded when he went to the bench, they applauded when he removed his warm-up suit. They applauded and applauded and applauded, so hard that their hands hurt.

While the uproar continued, Holzman corralled Danny Whelan and asked him for an update on Reed's condition.

"Parkes gave him the shot and says he can play," Whelan said. "But personally I don't think so. He was limping all the way out."

Holzman nodded somberly. That was what he had figured. Still, maybe once Reed got out there he'd be okay. Maybe he'd get so caught up in the game that the pain would be secondary. Maybe . . .

Somehow, Reed schlepped himself onto the floor for the start of the game. When the ball went up, however, he didn't even bother jumping against Wilt—he couldn't—as Chamberlain won the uncontested tap. Willis didn't have to worry, though. Bradley stole the first Lakers pass and whipped it demonstratively to Frazier. Clyde fed it to Willis, who had dragged himself underneath the basket—and he scored. Well, the cheers began all over again. It was bedlam in the Garden, and the referees had to wait until the commotion subsided a bit to start the action up again. Seconds later, Reed scored again, and the crowd went insane.

Madison Square Garden was deafening in its approval of Willis Reed's effort. Everyone was caught up in the emotional wave now. It had taken on a life of its own. And that was just the start. Soon it was 9–2, Knicks; then 38–24. Joe Mullaney had planned to stress a pivotal offense to get the ball inside to Chamberlain every time the Lakers went down the floor. With Reed barely showing signs of life, Wilt ought to be able to wheel around him without so much as a finger being raised to obstruct his drive. Reed couldn't run, or jump an inch, but somehow, during his twenty-seven minutes of play, he blocked Chamberlain's route to the hoop; he just stopped the big guy cold—and that was all the Knicks really needed from him.

With the Knicks out in front, they switched to a sagging defense on Chamberlain, conceding West and Baylor the outside shot in order to double up on Wilt. It was a risky strategy, with bomb throwers like those two on the wings. West and Baylor— they were the very models of outside shooters. They could *shoot out the lights*. They could—but they didn't. West had been given injections in both hands before the game, and his shot was seriously off the mark. Of course, he hit the random jumper, he tossed in a few from downtown, but he wasn't deadly. And the Knicks left Baylor in the dust. Age caught up with the fearless Laker as the Knicks accelerated the tempo of the game beyond what he felt comfortable with.

By halftime the score was 69–42. The Lakers had already committed fifteen turnovers. Bradley and Barnett were scoring from outside; Frazier was laying them in from the left side. DeBusschere was muscling inside to assume Reed's share of the rebounding, helping Nate Bowman rise to the occasion. The game was never close. The Lakers mounted a last-ditch effort in the fourth quarter, but the Knicks pulled away and won it by a score of 113–99. They were the NBA champs—finally.

Afterward, there was a party at the Four Seasons restaurant, and several all-night champagne bashes at the livelier East Side sports bars. It seemed like the Knicks showed up at each one of them, celebrating the fact that they were warriors and could shoot out the lights. Even Jerry West, who had wept in the Lakers' locker room and talked about quitting the game, turned up at Phil Linz's joint and hoisted a few in honor of the new champs. Only one man was missing. Willis Reed went home early to his duplex in Rego Park. He checked in with his answering service, and took a few calls of congratulations, before finally taking the phone off the hook. All in all, it had been a hell of a night.

It had been a hell of a year!

At two-thirty, he turned off the light and went to bed. In the morning, if it hadn't all been a dream, he'd still be the MVP—and the Knicks would still be the NBA champs.

BIBLIOGRAPHY

Abdul-Jabbar, Kareem, and Mignon McCarthy. *Kareem*. New York: Random House, 1990.

Albert, Marv, and Jim Benagh. *Krazy about the Knicks*. New York: Hawthorn Books, 1971.

Anderson, Dave. *The Story of Basketball*. New York: Morrow, 1988.

Auerbach, Red, with Joe Fitzgerald. *On and Off the Court*. New York: Macmillan, 1985.

———. *Red Auerbach: An autobiography*. New York: Putnam's, 1977.

Axthelm, Pete. *The City Game*. New York: Penguin, 1970.

Barry, Rick, and Bill Libby. *Confessions of a Basketball Gypsy*. Englewood Cliffs, NJ: Prentice-Hall, 1972.

Beckham, Barry. *Double Dunk*. Los Angeles: Holloway, 1980.

Berger, Phil. *Heroes of Pro Basketball*. New York: Random House, 1968.

———. *Miracle on 33rd Street*. New York: Simon & Schuster, 1970.

Bradley, Bill. *Life on the Run*. New York: Times, 1976.

Chamberlain, Wilt, and David Shaw. *Wilt*. New York: Macmillan, 1973.

Cole, Lewis. *Dream Team*. New York: Morrow, 1981.

Cousy, Bob, and Al Hirshberg. *Basketball Is My Life*. Englewood Cliffs, NJ: Prentice-Hall, 1957.

DeBusschere, Dave. *The Open Man*. New York: Random House, 1970.

Feinstein, Jon. *Dream Team*. New York: Villard, 1990.

Frazier, Walt, and Ira Berkow. *Rockin' Steady*. Englewood Cliffs, NJ: Prentice-Hall, 1974.

Frazier, Walt, and Joe Jares. *Clyde: The Walt Frazier Story*. New York: Holt, 1970.

Frazier, Walt, and Neil Offen. *Walt Frazier: One Magical Season and a Basketball Life*. New York: Times, 1988.

George, Nelson. *Elevating the Game*. New York: HarperCollins, 1992.

Goldaper, Sam, and Arthur Pincus. *How to Talk Basketball*. New York: Dembner, 1983.

Gutman, Bill. *The Pictorial History of Basketball*. New York: Gallery, 1988.

Halberstam, David. *The Breaks of the Game*. New York: Knopf, 1981.

Halter, Jon. *Bill Bradley*. New York: Putnam's, 1975.

Harris, Merv. *On the Court with the Superstars of the NBA*. New York: Viking, 1973.

Haywood, Spencer. *The Spencer Haywood Story*. New York: Tempo, 1972.

Heeren, Dave. *The Basketball Abstract*. Englewood Cliffs, NJ: Prentice-Hall, 1990.

Heinsohn, Tommy, and Joe Fitzgerald. *Give 'em the Hook*. Englewood Cliffs, NJ: Prentice-Hall, 1988.

Holzman, Red, and Harvey Frommer. *Holzman on Hoops*. Dallas, TX: Taylor, 1991.

———. *Red on Red*. New York: Bantam, 1987.

Holzman, Red, and Leonard Lewin. *Holzman's Basketball: Winning Strategy and Tactics.* New York: Macmillan, 1973.

———. *The Knicks.* New York: Dodd-Mead, 1971.

———. *My Unforgettable Season: 1970.* New York: Tor, 1993.

Koppett, Leonard. *The Essence of the Game Is Deception.* Boston: Little, Brown, 1973.

———. *24 Seconds to Shoot.* New York: Macmillan, 1968.

Lazenby, Roland. *Championship Basketball.* New York: Contemporary, 1987.

———. *The NBA Finals.* Dallas, TX: Taylor, 1990.

Levine, David. *Life on the Rim.* New York: Macmillan, 1989.

Lipsyte, Robert. *Sportsworld: An American Dreamland.* New York: Morrow, 1975.

Nadel, Eric. *The Night Wilt Scored 100.* Dallas, TX: Taylor, 1990.

Naismith, James. *Basketball: Its Origin and Development.* New York: Association, 1941.

Neft, David, and Richard Cohen. *Pro Basketball,* 3rd ed. New York: St. Martin's, 1990.

Pepe, Phil. *The Incredible Knicks.* New York: Popular Library, 1970.

Peterson, Robert. *Cage to Jump Shots: Pro Basketball's Early Years.* New York: Oxford, 1990.

Pitino, Rick. *Born to Coach: A Season with the N.Y. Knicks.* New York: NAL, 1988.

Powers, Richie, with Mark Mulvoy. *Overtime.* New York: McKay, 1975.

Reed, Willis, and Phil Pepe. *A View from the Rim.* Philadelphia: Lippincott, 1971.

Russell, Bill, and Taylor Branch. *Second Wind.* New York: Random House, 1979.

Russell, Bill, and William McSweeny. *Go Up for Glory.* New York: Coward-McCann, 1966.

Ryan, Bob, and Terry Pluto. *Forty-eight Minutes.* New York: Macmillan, 1987.

Salzberg, Charles. *From Set Shot to Slam Dunk*. New York: Dell, 1987.

Schron, Bob. *So You Think You're a Basketball Fan?* Beverly, MA: Quinlan, 1988.

Seymour, Harold. *Basketball: The Early Years*. New York: Oxford, 1960.

Shaughnessy, Dan. *Ever Green*. New York: St. Martin's, 1990.

Strom, Earl. *Calling the Shots*. New York: Simon & Schuster, 1990.

Wolf, David. *Foul! Connie Hawkins*. New York: Holt, 1972.

The author wishes to express special gratitude to the beat reporters whose stories, columns, and play-by-play in the New York area dailies provided vivid descriptions of the 1969–70 season. The author is especially indebted to the *New York Times,* the *New York Daily News,* the *New York Post, New York Newsday,* and the *Newark Star Ledger,* as well as to the various colleges that supported the writing of this manuscript with clippings about the players' varsity experiences: Grambling, Princeton, Southern Illinois, Tennessee State, Michigan, Detroit, St. John's, Providence, Ohio State, Witchita State, and Dayton.

SEASON STATISTICS

INDIVIDUAL RECORDS
1969–70 New York Knickerbockers

PLAYER	GAMES	POINTS	REBOUNDS	AVERAGE
Barnett, Dick	82	1,220	221	14.9
Bowman, Nate	81	237	257	2.9
Bradley, Bill	67	971	239	14.5
DeBusschere, Dave	79	1,152	790	14.6
Frazier, Walt	77	1,609	465	20.9
Hosket, Bill	36	118	63	3.3
May, Don	37	96	52	2.6
Reed, Willis	81	1,755	1,126	21.7
Riordan, Mike	81	624	194	7.7
Russell, Cazzie	78	894	236	11.5
Stallworth, Dave	82	639	323	7.8
Warren, John	44	112	40	2.5

PLAY-OFF RECORDS
March 26–May 8, 1970   19 Games

Barnett	19 games, 321 points
Bowman	18 games, 43 points
Bradley	19 games, 235 points
DeBusschere	19 games, 305 points
Frazier	19 games, 304 points
Hosket	5 games, 11 points
May	2 games, 4 points
Reed	18 games, 426 points
Riordan	19 games, 131 points
Russell	19 games, 178 points
Stallworth	19 games, 137 points
Warren	10 games, 4 points

1970 PLAY-OFF HIGHLIGHTS

Eastern Division Semifinals
(vs. Baltimore Bullets)

March 26	Knicks 120	Bullets 117 (two overtimes)
March 27	Knicks 106	Bullets 99
March 29	Bullets 127	Knicks 113
March 31	Bullets 102	Knicks 92
April 2	Knicks 101	Bullets 80
April 5	Bullets 96	Knicks 87
April 6	Knicks 127	Bullets 114

Eastern Division Finals
(vs. Milwaukee Bucks)

April 11	Knicks 110	Bucks 102
April 13	Knicks 112	Bucks 111
April 17	Bucks 101	Knicks 96
April 19	Knicks 117	Bucks 105
April 20	Knicks 132	Bucks 96

NBA Championship Series
(vs. Los Angeles Lakers)

April 24	Knicks 124	Lakers 112
April 27	Lakers 105	Knicks 103
April 29	Knicks 111	Lakers 108 (overtime)
May 1	Lakers 121	Knicks 115
May 4	Knicks 107	Lakers 100
May 6	Lakers 135	Knicks 113
May 8	Knicks 113	Lakers 99